Investigating
*Veronica Mars*

C000134177

# Investigating
## *Veronica Mars*
### *Essays on the Teen Detective Series*

*Edited by* RHONDA V. WILCOX
*and* SUE TURNBULL

McFarland & Company, Inc., Publishers
*Jefferson, North Carolina, and London*

This work is not approved or endorsed by Warner Bros.
Entertainment Inc.

LIBRARY OF CONGRESS CATALOGUING-IN-PUBLICATION DATA

Investigating Veronica Mars : essays on the teen detective series /
edited by Rhonda V. Wilcox and Sue Turnbull.
    p.    cm.
Includes bibliographical references and index.

ISBN 978-0-7864-4534-9
softcover : 50# alkaline paper ∞

1. Veronica Mars (Television program)
I. Wilcox, Rhonda.   II. Turnbull, Sue, 1950–
PN1992.77.V47I58   2011
791.45'72 — dc22                              2010047903

BRITISH LIBRARY CATALOGUING DATA ARE AVAILABLE

Kristen Bell as the title character in a 2005 episode of the television
series *Veronica Mars* (UPN/Photofest). Front cover by TG Design.

Manufactured in the United States of America

*McFarland & Company, Inc., Publishers*
  *Box 611, Jefferson, North Carolina 28640*
  *www.mcfarlandpub.com*

# Acknowledgments

We wish to thank our excellent contributors, without whom this volume would not have been possible. We have been cheered by their thoughtfulness, hard work, and patience. We thank Jason Mittell and Jennifer Gillan for their professionalism and courtesy. We thank Gianna Martella for her research advice. We thank Dawn Heinecken for her comments on Rhonda Wilcox's chapter. We thank Heather Porter for providing information on how to contact Warner Bros. (though the result was not what we expected). We acknowledge that this book and its contents are not approved or endorsed by Warner Bros. Nonetheless, we thank Rob Thomas and all those associated with the creation of *Veronica Mars* for the art they have given the world.

Rhonda V. Wilcox also wishes to thank her family, in particular husband Richard Gess and son Jeff Gess, for their constant support in a myriad of ways — including the interchange of ideas — and she thanks Richard for his ever-helpful reading of her work. Sue Turnbull would like to thank Rick and Will for the incentive and the encouragement to keep watching the screen.

# Table of Contents

# Introduction.
# Canonical Veronica:
# *Veronica Mars* and
# Vintage Television

RHONDA V. WILCOX *and*
SUE TURNBULL

Who did you sit with at lunch in high school? If you were an American high school student, you know that this question means much more than it might seem; and we phrase it colloquially in hopes that we might cast your mind back to those times. Did you sit with the jocks and the other popular kids? Did you sit with the eggheads, the nerds? The normal-but-not-first-rank? The outsiders? A high school lunch table is a little fiefdom, and moving from one table to another can be more difficult than crossing a national border. When we see Veronica Mars in the pilot of the series, she is sitting at lunch alone. Rob Thomas, former high school teacher, former "young adult" novelist, and creator of *Veronica Mars*, is very well aware of the implications of her lunchtime solitude. It introduces us to her lonely heroism and at the same time makes very apparent (through those she observes) the implications for the web of social interaction in which we are all caught. *Veronica Mars* manages a remarkable balance between the focus on the individual and the recognition of larger social patterns — at least for the first two seasons, the vintage seasons of the series.

*Veronica Mars* began life as Untitled Rob Thomas Teen Detective Novel (Thomas, "The Origins"). It was planned as his sixth young adult novel for Simon & Schuster, for whom his most notable book had been *Rats Saw God*, published in 1996. Over years of tinkering, the original boy detective became

1

a teenage girl, and the novel became a spec script. On September 22, 2004, *Veronica Mars* premiered on UPN. It immediately, and throughout the first two seasons, received critical praise — from the *New York Times* to the *Village Voice*, from *TV Guide* to *Time* to *Variety* to *Salon.com* (Stanley; Press; Roush; Poniewozik; Gallo; Havrilesky). Intense fans, including ones as famous as Stephen King and Joss Whedon, were unable, however, to keep the series from struggling in the ratings, and after a season on the CW (once UPN went out of business), the series was cancelled, its last episode airing May 22, 2007. Despite its cancellation, people have not stopped thinking and talking about *Veronica Mars*, and this book sets out to make the case that it is canonical television, television that should live on the video library shelves of the future.

The series from the start was vivid, witty, harsh, compassionate, complex. The titular character is an attractive blonde teenage girl whose after-school job is helping her father in his work as a detective. Keith Mars was the sheriff of Neptune County until voters ousted him for supposedly botching the investigation of the murder of Lilly Kane, Veronica's best friend. Keith had accused Lilly's father, the generous and popular software billionaire Jake Kane, of the murder, and Jake Kane was indeed hiding the truth. When the Kane family produced a man who confessed to the killing, the voters — many of whom earned their livelihood directly or indirectly through the Kane business empire — kicked Keith Mars out of office. And when Veronica stood by him (though her mother did not), her schoolmates ostracized her. The upper class "09ers" (so called for their zip code) in particular despised her. Indeed, her boyfriend, Kane scion Duncan, had already broken up with her without explanation. In an attempt to show herself undefeated ("just to show everyone that their whispers and backstabbing didn't affect me"), Veronica had attended a big party given by the wealthy Shelly Pomeroy — only to find herself drink-drugged and date-raped, the ultimate ejection from her former socially-protected status. In many senses, she lost her virginity that night. Though she had a close relationship with her father, she never shared this violation with him. She did try to report the rape to his successor Sheriff Lamb, but was not taken seriously. All this we learn from a flashback in the pilot episode, during which we see Veronica use her wits and connections to protect another teenager who has been mocked and endangered. Wallace Fennell is a black student new to the school who, in a small version of what Veronica has gone through, has unsuccessfully attempted to report a crime and has been humiliated by being taped, naked, to the school flagpole by members of a local biker gang. In both their cases, local law enforcement was less than useless; and Wallace's nakedness faintly echoes Veronica's rape. Perhaps it is not surprising that Veronica and Wallace become best friends. Before the end of the pilot, Wallace is sitting at Veronica's lunch table.

This summary may sound complicated, but it is an extreme oversimplification of the fictional world we are presented with in *Veronica Mars'* pilot. Friendship, family, loyalty — and rape, murder, corrupt law officials, and gangs, whether bikers or 09ers — all are part of the mixture of honor and darkness, heroism and social cynicism, that is *Veronica Mars*. There are those who will argue that the written word of necessity invokes a more complex intellectual response than a televised story; however, more and more television series — from *The Sopranos* to *Buffy the Vampire Slayer*, from *The X-Files* to *The Wire*— seem to suggest otherwise; and the scholars who study them seem to make that argument more and more often. This is the age of the maturation of the medium of television, and *Veronica Mars* is one of those mature series. To compare the virtues of different media forms, one should not, for example, examine a great novel in contrast to a weak television series or vice versa. *Veronica Mars* offers a particularly interesting opportunity for comparison because of the fact that its creator, Rob Thomas, was first a novelist. Granted, he wrote young adult novels, but *Veronica Mars* is supposedly teen television. One might certainly argue that neither Thomas's best-known novel, *Rats Saw God*, nor his best known television series, *Veronica Mars*, should be age-limited; both are worth adult attention. But it is hard to imagine anyone seeing *Veronica Mars* as less sophisticated than *Rats Saw God*. Both *Rats Saw God* and *Veronica Mars* focus on a teen protagonist who tells the story — Steve York as first person narrator, and Veronica Mars as voiceover commentator. Both are brilliant but socially disaffected high school students. Both deal with their parents' break-up by bottling up pain; each one is living with the father and misses the mother. Each one also misjudges that mother by overlooking some of her flaws, and moves toward adulthood in part by recognizing those flaws. We see both of them repeatedly being advised by a high school counselor. Steve York and Veronica Mars both suffer sexual betrayal and confront issues of social class and status. Veronica's status as the daughter of a sheriff and Steve's as the son of a famous astronaut give them some protection — protection that Veronica loses when her father loses his job, and that Steve sometimes chooses not to use: when he finds he has been accepted at Harvard while an impoverished female friend with a better academic and activities record was not, he throws away the acceptance letter (158). The diary chapters of Steve's self-told tale switch back and forth between his senior year and his sophomore year, just as Veronica's tale often falls into flashback. Many of the same subjects and, though in a different medium, some of the same narrative strategies appear in both of these Rob Thomas works.

But the 219 pages of *Rats Saw God* cannot compete in terms of depth and complexity with the sixty-four episodes of *Veronica Mars*; it would take a Victorian triple-decker novel to come close. Television allows for both longer and subtler development of characters and themes, by those artists who know how to use the medium. Certainly the work does not happen in a vacuum, and the business side of the television world can make for serious aesthetic inhibitions or damage, as the mixed quality of work in Joss Whedon's *Dollhouse* can show us: Whedon's original pilot (included on the DVD) is superior to the revision he was forced into by the Fox network. The third season of *Veronica Mars* may also be seen in that light (as will be discussed later). The essays in this collection, however, demonstrate the variety of qualities, developed through its many episodes, that make *Veronica Mars* worth re-viewing. *Veronica Mars* is visually interesting; it makes good use of music and sound; but, like *Buffy the Vampire Slayer* before it (to which it has often been compared), its greatest strengths lie in character, story, and dialogue, all of which work together to make meaning on both the psychological and sociological level.

While sophisticated social observations are embedded as part of the series' bedrock, perhaps the first connection for any audience comes through the strength of the central character. Television studies long ago noted the importance of the audience's ability to re-connect, week after week, with the small-screen protagonist, to a series' success. In recent years the connection has become more complex. Networks still prefer virtuous, likable characters, but the world of television fiction now incorporates such protagonists as Tony Soprano, with viewers who may wonder about their own complicity. Veronica Mars is no Tony Soprano, but she is no Nancy Drew, either. She appeals to many viewers as a strong, smart female character; she quotes eighteenth-century poet Alexander Pope in the opening episode, but is just as street smart as she is book smart: in fact, we see her on a stake-out with a calculus book beside her (Pilot).[1] Veronica Mars can be seen as a Campbellian or Proppian hero: she has been to hell and back, "there and back again," as Tolkien put it first for Bilbo, then Frodo. She starts as a virginal, naïve young girl — dressed in white in her first flashback — but her rape takes her to a different place. The indifference of the authorities might have crushed a weaker spirit, but Veronica returns from that dark place a hero — a bitter, angry hero, but a hero nonetheless. In case after case, she helps others with not only her intelligence but every tool at her disposal — her father's old friends at the police station, her computer skills, the threat of the biker gang she's helped, her friend Wallace's position as school records office aide — whatever it takes. Information is her greatest asset, but she shows physical courage as well. She carries a taser and often takes Back-up, her emphatically loyal pit bull, along on investigations. Part of the believability of the character comes from the fact that she is not physically invulnerable; seeing Veronica attacked by the Fitzpatricks (a drug-dealing Irish gang) or bundled into the trunk of her car by the Tritons (a secret society of high school A-listers) makes all the clearer the reality of her courage. That she is sometimes quite willing to accept help from others is one more strength, not a weakness.

From her father, she accepts help in many ways — his intelligent advice, his access to databases of information open to detectives, even his participation in scamming evil-doers. The relationship between Veronica and her father has often been acknowledged as one of the greatest strengths of the series. The playfulness and caring between the two characters brings joy to what otherwise might have been a very grim world. Meals in the Mars household, time and again, convey the flavor of the relationship — whether it's Veronica announcing that it's "dessert for supper" night, or Keith proudly offering steak after getting a fee: "Tonight we eat like the lower middle class to which we aspire!" (Pilot; see Leavitt and Leavitt in this volume). Perhaps for any family, meals represent in small the whole relationship; as for Veronica and Keith, they cook for each other. The relationship is all the more believable because, though they're often honest with each other, Veronica hides things from her father, and he hides things from her. But when he tries to defend the woman who abandoned them both, Veronica says to him, "The hero is the one who stays" ("Meet John Smith," 1.3). Time and again, Keith is her hero — the hero's hero. The quality of his character reflects on hers, and makes Veronica more admirable: after all, she too is the one who stays, never turning against her father in spite of public abuse. That same loyalty is the core of the friendships that she makes, all of them based on the ability to see past the surface to the character within, whether it is with the head of the local biker gang, a computer geek, or a picked-on new kid with a job in a convenience store who later becomes a basketball star.

The series is also propelled by its romance plot; Veronica manages the feat of being both a hard-boiled detective and a romance heroine. She is the spirited, independent young woman who enters into a relationship with a bad boy, a rich boy — a relationship fraught with passion and misunderstanding. Rob Thomas had originally planned Duncan Kane to be the "femme fatale" equivalent ("Notes"), but was smart enough (like the best of television producers) to pick up on the chemistry between Kristen Bell's Veronica and Jason Dohring's Logan — a combination of the actors' skills and the characters' connections,[2] with both suffering the loss of their mothers and the death of Lilly, Logan's girlfriend and Veronica's best friend. The relationship brings a very adult sexual component to her character, even before it is consummated. And Logan's many failings, amidst too often hidden virtues, test Veronica's heroism.

But the hard-boiled detective elements — the *noir* elements — of *Veronica Mars* are those which may have received most comment in the press, and Veronica resonates as a *noir* detective.[3] In the twenty-first century, we somehow have no problem conceiving of a teenage girl having to face the darkness; one other element of her heroism, of course, is that she truly does so. The *noir* detective elements of the series are never far out of sight, from the moment Veronica asks, "You want to know how I lost my virginity? So do I." The dry, ironic voiceovers which begin most episodes recall classic *noir* films. Veronica is both the voice and the eye: time and again we see her using her camera to shoot someone who is the object of an investigation. But the *noir* detective is drawn into the darkness, never just an observer: in the fifth episode, we see photos taken of Veronica through the crosshairs of a gun sight, photos whose implicit threat apparently helped to frighten her mother out of town. Veronica's voiceover and her camera work are both ways of controlling the world; being the camera's object shows a loss of control. Like any good detective, she does not let the danger stop her search for the truth. But like any *noir* detective, she finds not just light but darkness. The iconic cheap hotel she often observes (ironically named The Camelot) turns out to be the location of trysts between her mother and Jake Kane — who, she discovers, had been together long ago as well. When Veronica realizes that she may be the daughter of Jake Kane and thus the half sister of her former boyfriend Duncan, she is walking the streets of *Chinatown*, with incest in the miasmal air.[4] The reason Duncan has broken up with her becomes clear. The camera motif recurs in her relationship with Logan: just as they are about to make love, she discovers a video camera trained on the bed — another instance of the private eye being eyed and objectified. She leaves before Logan can explain, and only later learns that the camera was his father's, not something Logan knew about — and that Logan's father used it to film Lilly while they had sex — Lilly, whom he later murdered. Thus the camera's eye positions Veronica in parallel to the victim of the murder that started the whole story of the series, a murder she has determined to solve. She could hardly be more entangled in the darkness.

The *noir* elements, however, go beyond the fugue of immoral relationships and the failed attempts to control with voice and eye. The relationship of the detective to the social structure is classic *noir* as well: Veronica cannot change the wickedness of the world. She may fight for the right but she never changes the system — though she can, on occasion, rescue individuals within the system. A good example of this kind of problem comes in the case of

Carmen, a fellow Neptune High student who wants to break up with a controlling boyfriend ("M.A.D.," 1.20). The boy, Tad, has drugged Carmen's drink and used his cell phone to shoot a lewd video of her which he threatens to make public if Carmen will not reconsider and stay with him. Veronica manages to retrieve the cell phone for Carmen, but Tad has by then made copies. Veronica successfully fakes a video of the homophobic Tad which implies that he is homosexual, and offers Carmen the Mutual Assured Destruction option in hopes that Tad will let Carmen go. Carmen is being threatened with the kind of undeserved reputation as a slut which Veronica has had to endure since Shelly Pomeroy's party at which she was date-raped (and thus Carmen is one of the many Veronica foils in the series). The gender assumptions under the system Veronica is struggling against mean Carmen and Veronica are socially damaged by their reputations while Tad is not damaged by his. When Carmen breaks up with Tad, his anger at losing her — at losing *control* of her — is such that he makes the lewd video of her public, and she suffers the mockery and disdain that follow (just as Veronica has). Veronica offers her the revenge option of releasing the doctored video about Tad, but Carmen refuses, saying, "I'd rather the whole world think I'm trashy than have a guy like Tad think he can push me around" ("M.A.D.," 1.20). *Noir* detective Veronica cannot change the social structure, but she has nonetheless given Carmen a choice, and helped Carmen reach a point where she has gained a measure of freedom, even if at a cost.

The interconnectedness of the shadows in the *noir* world can also be seen in this episode. When Veronica helps someone else, she often comes closer to her own truth. In the background of the video of Carmen, she sees lights that identify it as Shelly Pomeroy's party. Thus she also discovers that the drug used on Carmen was from the same batch that was used on her, leading to her rape. And, to her horror, she discovers that the drug was provided by Logan, who passed it around to his friends to have fun with. "Fun — like sex with unconscious people fun?" Veronica later asks him. "No — fun like going to a rave," he answers ("A Trip to the Dentist," 1.21). The fact that Logan had no idea of the uses to which the drug would be put works perfectly as a social metaphor: the privileged, rich male is unaware of the consequences of his prodigal actions, never thinking about the potential effect on young women such as Carmen and Veronica — until Veronica makes him think. And the series, one hopes, makes us all think.

The grimness of the *noir* plot belies the overall texture of the series, which modulates towards the positive when Veronica attains some small success or measure of control. One means of her control, mentioned earlier, is Veronica's voiceover — or, indeed, much of her language. The very stylized language is a traditional marker of the *noir* detective: as Alaine Martaus observes, language is "essential" in the series (81); and the use of dry humor and the power of observation is part of her heroism. "The best way to get over the pain of your best friend's murder is to have your mother abandon you as soon as possible," she tells us ("You Think You Know Somebody," 1.5), and the pain is *contained* in those words, the words themselves making it more possible for her to cope. She "turns to [her] discursive powers as a last resort against [her] troubles," as J. P. Telotte says of the *noir* narrator (35). In the last episode of the second season, having watched Lilly's murderer go free from the courtroom, she recites what might be the *noir* detective's credo: "So this is how it is: the innocent suffer; the guilty go free; and truth and fiction are pretty much interchangeable" ("Not Pictured," 2.22). But episode by episode, as she helps individuals along the way, her language flies. When a student says the secret society of the Tritons will destroy him if he gives Veronica information, she replies with vengeful zest, "I'll destroy you worse" ("Clash of the Tritons," 1.12). When she accompanies her friend Meg to a costume party to help Meg connect with Veronica's supposed half-brother Duncan, she says, "I look like Manila Whore Barbie" ("Ruskie Business," 1.15). When she, a teenager, is asked to be the foreperson of a jury so that deliberations will go faster, she mocks the "sacred ideal of drive-through-express justice" ("One Angry Veronica," 2.10). Or to put it in words of Pope that Veronica (who quoted him in the pilot) might know, "Wretches hang that jurymen may dine"—but not on her watch; in response to a lone Latina holdout, Veronica solves the case and sways the jury. When she helps a steroid-selling ex-boyfriend beat an unjustified rape charge at nearby Hearst College, she does it for the sake of justice, not fondness, telling him, "You're just water under the bridge — duplicitous, evil water" ("The Rapes of Graff," 2.16). And overall, she reminds us, "When I've had my fill of soul-mates, glitter, and puppy love, I always find a private detective's office a refreshing change of pace" ("Ruskie Business," 1.15). Veronica's father, Logan, Wallace, and other friends also entertain us with their linguistic wit, but Veronica is the master: she is the hero.

A central reason that the series is canonical television, then, is the character of Veronica: a young woman on a hero's journey; a daughter; a friend; a romance heroine; and a *noir* detective and language master. It is no accident that the series bears the character's name. But the series also gains power through its confrontation of larger issues: class; gender; sexual orientation; race; politics; and more. Many of these themes have already been suggested earlier in this introduction. The motivation provided by class disparity underlies many *noir* detective stories, and class is the subject of more overt comment in *Veronica Mars* than in perhaps any other television series. When, in the pilot, Veronica introduces her school, she famously says, "This is Neptune High. If you go here, your parents are millionaires, or they work for millionaires. Neptune High—the school without a middle class." When Veronica reports her rape, the sneering sheriff assumes she is seeking revenge on the wealthy friends who have dropped her, and asks if she wants him to arrest all the rich boys in town (simultaneously insulting her with the implication that she would sleep with anyone wealthy). In an early episode, the election for student body president is framed as "class warfare—the haves versus the have-nots" ("Return of the Kane," 1.6). And Veronica is told, "You more than anyone should understand that." Wanda, the outsider running for school president, says, "The rich kids, they run things around here. They're the minority and they're corrupt. They get away with murder"—which, in fact, does happen—though they *get* murdered, as well, in Lilly's case. While most of the rich kids do simply want to keep their privileges, Duncan Kane, pressured into running, actually changes the system once elected; but he is presented as the exception. As for Wanda, the lower class voice of democracy, she is revealed (by Veronica's biker friend Weevil) to be a narc—willing to sell out others in order to keep a good record and get ahead through a good college education for herself. "All I have to do is rob a bank and ace the SATs," Wanda says; but staying out of jail for a drug charge and becoming class president couldn't hurt.

In the same episode we see another class critique, with rich-guy Logan involved in paying homeless men to "box" each other. When one homeless ex–Marine refuses and asks Logan, "You find some sucker willing to make a bitch out of themselves for cash?," Logan is sitting in a convertible with his movie star father Aaron, listening to him agree by phone to star in a movie with what Aaron knows is a terrible script just for the eight-figure salary. Aaron, obviously, is just such a bitch. The two Echolls men are on their way to a homeless shelter so that they can try to reverse some of the bad press resulting from Internet images of Logan's boxing ring; the look on Logan's face shows that he understands that his father is selling himself, and in their next scene Logan surprises Aaron by announcing to the camera crews called together to the homeless shelter that his father is donating half a million dollars to the place—a gesture that might be equal parts recognition of class inequity and spite against his abusive father's control. Logan is also involved in another noteworthy first-season story with embedded class issues. He and Eli Navarro (a.k.a. Weevil), Veronica's biker boss ally, are both given detention by the same teacher, a black man who says to Eli, "Mr. Navarro, I wonder if you'll find Mr. Echolls so amusing ten years from now, when you're pumping his gas" ("The Girl Next Door," 1.7). (Eli, in fact, ends up as a janitor.) When

Logan and Eli play an extreme prank on the teacher, the upper class protection afforded the movie star's son becomes apparent when he is given minor punishment and Eli is expelled. Once again Logan, in spite of his flaws, recognizes the inequity. Without Eli's knowledge, Logan forces the vice principal to make Eli's punishment less — and both their punishments equal — purportedly on the grounds that Logan wants equal credit for the prank. In Logan and Duncan the audience is given the comfort of seeing rich white males who acknowledge some class inequities — but at least those inequities are shown.

Possibly the most significant representation of class, however, is tied up with the very central representation of gender. Above all, *Veronica Mars* is a series about a strong, intelligent young woman. It is also a fascinating example of television narrative: each episode contains a separate, small mystery, but season one contains a season-long mystery, apparently resolved in the last episode ("Leave It to Beaver," 1.22), and season two contains a related, second season-long mystery — whose resolution in its last episode rewrites the resolution of the first season ("Not Pictured," 2.22). The first season's major mystery addresses the question of who murdered Lilly Kane and who raped Veronica Mars (and, to a lesser degree, what happened to Veronica's mother). The second season's major mystery addresses the question of who caused a bus crash and thus murdered a group of high school students. Each represents in a different way the situation of a young woman in the class structure. By the end of the first season we have learned that Veronica is the biological daughter of Keith Mars, not of Jake Kane; and we have learned that a drunken and drugged Duncan slept with the drugged, barely conscious Veronica as she lay on a bed at Shelly Pomeroy's party. Having suspected that they were half-siblings, Duncan never spoke of the event to Veronica. In this version of the story, Duncan and Veronica both were of equally diminished capacity and had consensual sex; Duncan was unaware that Veronica's diminished capacity was involuntary. Thus one might argue that in this version none of the upper class males at the party directly raped the young woman of lesser status. Lilly, Veronica discovers, was involved in a sexual relationship with the father of her own boyfriend — Aaron Echolls, father of Logan — so the rich, sexually profligate girl is punished by death at the hands of the rich, sexually profligate male — an unpleasantly traditional outcome. For her part, our brave hero is in the end rescued from death at Aaron's hands by her brave hero father. Moment by moment, throughout the season, this series has invited us to examine class and gender issues; but the underlying narrative's main lines have brought us to a rather traditional, comfortable, conventional conclusion at the end of season one.

By the end of season two, however, we have discovered that the person responsible for the bus crash — a crash that killed students who might have told the truth about him — was the wealthy teen Cassidy "Beaver" Casablancas; recall the foreshadowing title of the last episode of the first season: "Leave It to Beaver." And Beaver Casablancas, on the night of Shelly Pomeroy's party, raped the unconscious Veronica Mars.

It would have been a very different story if Veronica had not been raped by a rich boy. Consider what the story would have meant if Rob Thomas had chosen to have the biker gang boss Eli be the rapist, for instance. The narrative would clearly be freighted with a different message about class. Cassidy's resources are such that it takes two years for even a person as smart and determined as Veronica to discover him, and she is almost killed in the process. Furthermore, consider the effects of Cassidy's raping Veronica on her interaction with the legal system. She discovers his guilt in part because he gives her a sexually transmitted disease. When she testifies against Aaron Echolls in the Lilly Kane murder trial, her testimony against him is undercut when the defense lawyer reports in open court that she is being treated for an STD, implying that she is a person of poor character. Thus her rape by an upper class male means that the upper class male who killed her best friend goes free. The narrative lines have turned, and the gender/class implications are unnerving. The capper is that the most virtuous upper class male of the series — Duncan Kane, who is now out of the country — arranges for the immediate death of his sister's killer at the hands of someone in Duncan's pay. Perhaps this can be seen as justice, but it is also another example of a wealthy man who kills outside the law. When, in parallel, Eli brings about the death of a murderer of one of *his* own, he ends up going to jail for it.

If even a strong, blonde, beautiful young woman like Veronica — or a strong, blonde, beautiful young woman like Lilly — or like Meg — is vulnerable in this class and legal system, it should be no surprise that the series shows us the raw side of race relations as well. The series presents social challenges in many categories — class, gender, and race (cf. Naremore 223–24). One of Veronica's admirable qualities is that she crosses not only class but also racial and ethnic lines in her friendships. This is the more impressive because the series is far from color-blind. Overt remarks about race are made from the pilot on. Eli "Weevil" Navarro calls Veronica's soon-to-be-be-friend Wallace "that skinny Negro" when the biker gang threatens Wallace. In the second episode, Logan taunts the Latino Weevil with the fact that his grandmother works as a domestic in the Echolls household. At a Christmas holiday high-stakes poker game at the Echolls house that Weevil talks his way into, a young movie star who is another one of the players complains to Logan, "That's like the tenth racist thing you've said" ("An Echolls Family Christmas," 1.10). Of course, this is shortly after Logan has realized that Eli might have been involved with his beloved Lilly before her death, but the fact that he can use race as an emotional weapon to support his jealousy is only too believable. Three episodes later, Wallace asks Veronica if she wants help with her "cred with the urban demographic" in an episode that highlights a black music millionaire's need to use a phony reputation for violence (and his dissatisfaction with a smart but nerdy son) ("Lord of the Bling," 1.13). And Carmen (of sexy video fame) notes that when she or other Latinas date white (as she puts it) or join the honor society, they are called "coconuts"—brown on the outside and white on the inside ("M.A.D.," 1.20). As for Jackie, the beautiful young black woman who becomes Wallace's girlfriend in season two, she (like so many others) needs help from Veronica when accused by a teacher of theft on the grounds of "lurking"—which she defines as "standing while black" ("Ain't No Magic Mountain High Enough," 2.13). Racial and ethnic difference are not as pervasively problematic in *Veronica Mars* as class and gender issues, but they are not simplified either. Wallace and Veronica's friendship as well as her father and his mother's dating are happy examples, but not presented in a gleaming racial vacuum.

As for the government and legal system, the series does not shy away from showing their flaws as well. Elections are shown as problematic, from the high school students up through the adults. Veronica demonstrates the election of Wanda vs. Duncan Kane to have been originally rigged in Duncan's favor, necessitating a new election. Keith Mars, clearly the best candidate for sheriff, loses the election because of bad press unfairly tying him to the bus crash. In season two, the amazingly wholesome little league coach "Mayor" Woody invites Keith to serve in an appointed position, should Woody be able to succeed in getting a vote to incorporate part of the county — but others note that this would be "a wall between the economic classes" or in other words "an ultra rich center surrounded by the crime capital of America" ("The Quick and the Wed," 2.15). Certainly, *Veronica Mars* connects government with class. Furthermore Woody, whose good sense in inviting Keith to join his administration at first recommends him, gradually reveals more and more questionable qualities. We learn he has an almost manically clean and intimidating wife who seems to emotionally abuse his son. Then he asks Keith to help him deal with a sex scandal — and proceeds to pin the scandal on Keith — and finally he turns out to have been molesting the boys on his little league team for years — including Cassidy Casablancas, to whom he gave the STD that Cassidy passed on to Veronica. Cassidy's sociopathic character is the product of a neglectful, financial scam artist father, an absent, uncaring mother, and a macho, selfish brother — the eloquently named Dick. But he is also the product of the baseball-and-apple-pie-touting public hypocrite, the faker of virtue who tries to justify his actions as caring. This public fakery (as American voters have seen time and again) is an endemic part of a system that can hurt so many — even someone like Veronica, the ultimate recipient of the social disease that Woody represents. This male power figure defines yet another social force pressing on the individual, an individual made real to us in the form of Veronica. And when Veronica tries to use the system to bring a murderer, Aaron Echolls, to justice, the very class and political power structure that enabled Cassidy's suffering and Veronica's rape is used to blame and disempower her in court: she is represented as the one who is diseased.

"Underneath that angry young woman shell, there's a slightly less angry young woman," says Wallace to Veronica (Pilot). And Veronica's strength is such that she does survive this dark world — though she does not do so undamaged. Veronica's anger is a righteous anger, if not always a healthy anger. But her character, and the other vivid characters in the series, believably embody the larger issues. The first two seasons present a remarkable balance of intimate psychological portraiture and sweeping sociological implications. The episodic mysteries show Veronica sometimes winning, sometimes losing; the season-long narrative arcs show her winning in the sense of gaining truth, but not power to change the system (a very *noir* result).

In the third season, however, the balance shifts. With episode-long mysteries continuing, the longer narrative arcs no longer last the whole season, but run through several episodes instead. Even more significantly, the arc narratives are no longer directly about Veronica, thus weakening the emotional balance. Rape represents a very intimate damage — the entry of society's violence into the body of a single individual. Veronica's grappling with this crime over the course of two years is genuinely heroic. It is somewhat dismaying, therefore, that season three presents rape in wholesale fashion, in the form of a serial rapist at Veronica's college, Hearst (cf. Joyrich). One might argue that the third season suggests that such damage is in fact spread among far too many women. In fact, Veronica encounters victims of the Hearst rapist in the second season, when she saves a former boyfriend from false accusations of the crime and causes a fraternity house to be given a semester of probation for their sex pursuit score board ("The Rapes of Graff," 2.16). The third season focus on the Hearst rapist could be seen as continuity, and a recognition that such problems do continue in the world; but for some viewers the re-use of the subject seemed to be exploitation.[5] What makes the difference? Along with the change of Veronica's role, there is another problem. In the third season DVD "Do-Overs" feature, Rob Thomas comments on another subject (a bone marrow transplant for the Hearst dean's stepdaughter), saying, "We cannot have stories of this density as a B story ... [it becomes] maudlin ... because we haven't invested enough screen time." He even notes that "it reaches a level of melodrama." He has also noted (in the "Favorite Veronica and Logan Moments" feature) that "one of the justifiable criticisms of season two ... [is that for] Duncan and Veronica there is not much screen time" so the emotion of their separation is hardly earned. Similarly, for the third season Hearst rape victims, there is "not much screen time," unlike our intense investment in Veronica herself throughout seasons one and two. True, one of the victims is Parker, the gregarious roommate of Veronica's friend Mac; but she is a secondary character, not present in every episode. The effect is also oddly weakened by multiplication: Mac herself was sexually traumatized by the person she thought of as her boyfriend — Cassidy Casablancas; she refers to herself as "frozen from the waist down" ("Welcome Wagon," 3.1). The parallel situations of Parker, Mac, and Veronica put together unhappily give the effect of overplotting rather than emotional power.

In general, the third season seems to suffer from statistical improbabilities beyond the Parker/Mac/Veronica trio. The normally virtuous Keith is tempted to enter into an adulterous relationship with Harmony Chase (whose name joins those of two *Buffy* characters),[6] who makes a persuasive carpe diem argument. (She also has a curious extratextual persuasive power, in that the actress, Laura San Giacomo, was the love interest of Enrico Colantoni in another series, *Just Shoot Me* [1997–2003]: as Richard Gess says, in the world within the television, the two characters were involved in another life.) Keith nonetheless refuses, and drives off into the night — only to be hit by a car, reminding of him life's brevity, so that he runs back to her arms. Who could blame him? Blaming the writers, however, is another matter. Or consider Logan's rescue of Veronica when she herself is drugged and endures the beginning of the head-shaving that constitutes part of the Hearst rapist's method. In seasons one and two, Logan came to Veronica's rescue on more than one occasion, but it normally involved a degree of teamwork. For instance, in "Weapons of Class Destruction," she leaves her cell phone on so that he can hear her say where the bad guy is taking her; in "Not Pictured," she sends Logan a text message so that he knows to come to the roof, where the bad guy has her trapped. But in season three, Logan, out of every person at Hearst College, by purest chance, happens to be walking by the parking garage at the very moment when Veronica is being attacked. Moments such as these cheapen the carefully-built set of connections we have seen laid in place over the previous two years. Whatever the cause — whether it was the result of pressure from the network for ratings, or misjudgment on the part of the unquestionably stressed writer-producers—the third season does not match the quality of the first two—which, in fact, form a narrative unit of their own.

One of the jobs of scholars is to try to help establish the canon. We would argue that for television, this task needs in many instances to go beyond recommending for and against certain television series; these recommendations should be as specific as noting certain seasons or "vintages" of television—or sometimes even specific episodes. Anyone who has taken a literature survey course will have encountered a literary anthology (most likely a Norton anthology) and is familiar with the fact that introductory students often study excerpts: they may read Plato's Allegory of the Cave rather than the entire *Republic*; or only the first two books of *Paradise Lost*. More specialized scholars will study the entire work, but those attaining a survey of knowledge will read only part. We predict that a similar practice may be necessary in television studies. A series like *Dollhouse* (2009–10), for instance, has glorious episodes like the Whedon-written original pilot or "Man on the Street," but probably few other than serious Whedon scholars will watch the entire series a hundred years from now. *Veronica Mars* is a parallel instance. Though the contributors to this volume analyze all three seasons for the sake of scholars to come, the editors of this volume evaluate the first two seasons as those that should last. We hope that this introduction and the essays that follow successfully make the case that while seasons one and two are indeed canonical *Veronica*, an investigation of the series as a whole might be an illuminating and worthwhile enterprise.

To make that argument, we propose a triangulation of approaches. Triangulation, as social scientists know only too well, involves choosing at least three different research methods to investigate the same phenomenon based on the premise that considering the same object from a range of different perspectives will provide a more holistic and rigorous account. As will be evident from a brief survey of the contents of this collection, the essays presented here endeavor to achieve just that by investigating *Veronica Mars* from a number of different angles. These include attention to the ways in which the operations of the television industry might impinge on the text; the concept of auteurism; close analyses of the text itself in a series of attentive readings with reference to a diverse range of theoretical and critical approaches; as well as a discussion of the audience and their engagement with the show. For those with a background in media studies, this recipe involves the familiar triad of industry, text, and audience with a dash of auteurism borrowed from Film Studies combined with a good dollop of the kinds of textual analysis which have long been standard in Literary Studies, not forgetting Cultural Studies' attentiveness to the key issues of race, class and gender.

David Lavery's essay, "Rob Thomas and Television Creativity," beautifully illustrates the magpie and eclectic nature of contemporary television studies as it ranges across a variety of televisual and filmic texts while poaching literary theorist Harold Bloom's concept of the "ephebe," or newcomer, in order to describe the emergence of Rob Thomas as a televisual auteur. As Lavery makes clear, *Veronica Mars* marks the culmination of a whole series of diverse experiences for Thomas, including his various careers as a high school teacher, a successful teen novelist, a screen writer, a show runner and a TV watcher who always knew what he liked, from *Twin Peaks* to *Freaks and Geeks*. Like *Buffy* auteur Joss Whedon, Thomas clearly knows his popular culture "stuff," and part of the pleasure to be derived from both of their work involves intertextual trainspotting as well as the shock of the new, although Lavery is careful to make a distinction between their respective achievements. In this latter regard, Lavery considers the network forces beyond Thomas's control which, as we have suggested above, severely compromised the quality of season three, leaving the series, the audience, and Thomas's own career, somewhere up in the air.

Co-editor Sue Turnbull also approaches *Veronica Mars* from what might be considered an industry angle in "Performing *Veronica Mars*." Here the focus is on the actors and the ways in which their onscreen performance impacted on the choices Thomas and his co-writers made about the development of the characters and the direction of the narrative. Like Lavery, Turnbull also cheerfully poaches from both literary and film theory, "borrowing" the concept of ekphrasis as elaborated by Stern and Kouvaris as well as Andre Klevan's discussion of film performance in relation to comedy, melodrama, and the psychological thriller in order to offer a close reading of the onscreen performances of Kristen Bell, Jason Dohring, and Enrico Colantino. As Turnbull points out, one of the major accomplishments of *Veronica Mars* as a series is the ways in which it could move across these three modes, not only within a season or an episode, but also within the parameters of a single heart-stopping scene. The issue of performance is thus related to questions of audience affect.

Co-editor Rhonda V. Wilcox ends her essay "So Cal Pietà: Veronica Mars, Logan Echolls and the Search for the Mother" with two different heart-stopping moments. The first of these occurs in the first episode of season two when Veronica cradles Logan in her arms, and the second in the final episode of the same season when Logan cradles Veronica in a mirrored reversal of the usual gender roles. These two scenes frame Wilcox's discussion of Veronica as a Campbellian hero on a quest aided by a series of significant helpers, including Weevil as the "deus-ex–Mexican" (Wilcox poaches and she puns).

The notion of the quest is further elaborated with reference to Janice Radway's discussion of the romance heroine embarked on a search for the lost mother. Along the way, through her close reading of the series as a whole, Wilcox demonstrates just how many lost mothers there are in *Veronica Mars* and how skillful Thomas and company can be at manipulating the power of the image to heighten our awareness of both narrative and character.

From mothers to fathers. Daughter and father team Sarah A. Leavitt and Lewis A. Leavitt pick up on the relationship between Veronica and her father Keith in their essay "'Who's Your Daddy?': Issues of Fatherhood" in order to examine what fatherhood might mean in the series. To put the theme in context, Leavitt and Leavitt discuss a range of other TV teen dramas, from *Gidget* (1965–66) to *Beverly Hills 90210* (1990–2000) to *The OC* (2003–07), to arrive at the conclusion that, in the teen drama genre as a whole, good parenting is a rare phenomenon. The celebrated "good" relationship between Keith and Veronica is therefore the exception, not only within the teen drama as a genre, but also within the show in which it occurs. It is, however, as Leavitt and Leavitt elucidate in their careful delineation of Keith and Veronica's ups and downs, secrets and lies, moments of betrayal, self-sacrifice and forgiveness, far from perfect.

In "Family Matters: Antigone, Veronica, and the Classical Greek Paradigm," Stan Beeler invites us to take a step back from the intensity of family relationships in the contemporary teen drama series in order to consider how these might relate to the fraught family relationships in classical Greek tragedy. Although Beeler is careful to point out that classical Greek drama and contemporary long-form television drama are very different in form and structure, he presents us with a vivid illustration of how G.W.F. Hegel's (1971) account of the Greek tragedy *Antigone* is applicable here. Antigone's family troubles, Beeler argues, might usefully be compared with those of Veronica in season one. Beeler makes his case in a reading of Veronica's role as a "fury" and the ethical dilemmas which she faces. Teen drama, he concludes, can thus embrace the highest artistic standards in complex narratives which engage with the fundamental questions of human existence.

As Tamy Burnett and Melissa Townsend point out in their essay "Rethinking 'The Getting Even Part': Feminist Anger and Vigilante Justice in a Post-9/11 America," this could include questions of justice within the particular context of a post–9/11 America. To make their case, Burnett and Townsend draw a parallel between Veronica's personal 9/11, the rape at Shelly Pomeroy's party, and America's metaphorical experience of violation in the 9/11 attacks. Responding to a suggestion that the best response to such violations would be to forgive and forget, Burnett and Townsend demonstrate that Veronica's vigilantism is both justifiable and necessary given that she is up against official corruption in Neptune at a number of levels within the political structure. These include the official justice system as represented by the incompetent Sherriff Lamb; the governmental authorities as represented by inexcusable Mayor Woody Goodman; and the operations of her primary social worlds, both high school and college, where the figures in authority fail dismally in their duty of care towards Veronica and her peers. As Burnett and Townsend argue, in getting tough and getting even in her pursuit of revenge, Veronica stays true to her feminist roots, offering a much needed alternative model of feminist agency in the battle against corrupt political officialdom.

Paul Zinder also takes up the theme of revenge in a discussion of Veronica as a tragic archetype whose actions never quite satisfy her own psychological needs. Like co-editor Wilcox, Zinder draws on Joseph Campbell's concept of the hero's journey in his essay "'Get My Revenge On': The Anti-Hero's Journey," but in contrast to Wilcox, he casts Veronica in the mold of the postmodern *anti*-hero whose journey is marked by a number of stages. In season one this constitutes a "Departure," in season two an "Initiation," and in season three a "Return" which, in contradiction of the structural archetype of success, is far from triumphant (and more problematic than what Campbell calls the "difficult" return [36]). It is in this final section that Zinder demonstrates just how far Veronica's hero's journey differs from that of Campbell's archetype, leaving the audience with an image of "stormy despair" and far from satisfied.

Lisa Emmerton is also concerned with the audience and its relationship to the series in her essay "This Teen Sleuth's Tricks Aren't Just for Kids: Connecting with an Intergenerational Audience." The first part of this essay locates the series within the history of the teen television genre, the only genre to be defined by its audience rather than by its content. Referencing Davis and Dickinson (*Teen TV*), Emmerton points out that *Veronica Mars* has all the hallmarks of the contemporary teen drama series including sophisticated language, intertextual references, a melodramatic use of emotion, and a prominent pop music soundtrack. It is these qualities in combination with the clever writing, complex narratives, highly developed characters and unique experiments with genre which — and this is Emmerton's key point — lift the appeal of the series to include not only teens but multiple audience sectors including Generations X, Y, and the infamous Baby Boomers.

A major part of that appeal, as Sophie Mayer argues, is Veronica's embodiment (like that of her predecessor in Joss Whedon's *Buffy the Vampire Slayer*) of mainstream America's idealized image of girlhood as white, blonde, slim, attractive and able-bodied. In "'We Used to Be Friends': Breaking Up with America's Sweetheart," Mayer considers *Veronica Mars* in relation to other recent cultural texts which appear to represent a "girlhood that truly serves girls" but which are at the same time complicit in sustaining the ubiquitous idealized image of the "American Sweetheart." Mayer argues that this ideal, from Shirley Temple to Buffy, constitutes an empty signifier just waiting to be filled up with consumer goods and adult male desire. Five versions of this ideal are identified in *Veronica Mars*, including: the American Beauty; the Girlfriend in a Coma; The Virgin Suicides; Girls Gone Wild; and The Bionic Woman. In the ensuing discussion of the various appearance and significance of these specific tropes, Mayer invites us to consider the ways in which power is avowed and disavowed during the course of Veronica's investigation into what it means to be young, blonde and female in America today.

Sarah Whitney's "No Longer That Girl: Rape Narrative and Meaning in *Veronica Mars*" returns to the theme of rape in order to discuss how the theme of rape might operate as a narrative device across the series as a whole at the same time as it underlines the materiality of sexual violence against women. In the first part of her essay, Whitney discusses the representation of rape within an historical context which encompasses both feminist interventions in the debate and recent onscreen depictions, with particular attention to the television crime drama. In her unravelling of the rape narratives in seasons one and two, Whitney argues that these eventually become "about" something else: in this case, class warfare. The season three rape narrative, unfolding within the halls of the fictional Hearst College, is also "about" something else, in this case the politicization of rape itself. While Whitney finds some of these transformations "maddening," she also find them "thought-provoking," and as such well worthy of our attention.

The final essay in this collection, a discussion of *Veronica Mars* fandom, also deals with the theme of rape, demonstrating in the process the centrality of rape as a thematic in the series. Tanya R. Cochran's particular intervention demonstrates the ways in which *Veronica Mars* fans came to experience themselves as metaphoric rape victims at the mercy of UPN, which not only messed with their show but eventually cancelled it. In her essay, "Neptune (Non-) Consensual: The Risky Business of Television Fandom, Falling in Love, and Playing the Victim," Cochran begins by relating fan investment in *Veronica Mars* to theories of fandom derived from other areas, noting that it is usual for fans of all kinds (whether of sports or television) to care deeply and personally about the object of their passion. Cochran then proceeds to elaborate some of the more specific and memorable characteristics and activities of the *Veronica Mars* fandom, including the organization and management of *Veronica Mars* viewing parties and the resourceful but doomed Cloud Watchers campaign to save the series from cancellation. Cochran's central argument, however, concerns the ways in which fans came to increasingly identify with the character of Veronica through the metaphoric function of her initial rape. As Cochran points out, following Lakoff and Johnson, metaphors shape the way we think, and in imagining themselves as victims, fans constructed the television industry as all-powerful while denying their own agency and power as an audience. The cancellation of *Veronica Mars* was, in the end, all about the ratings.

Tanya Cochran's paper thus returns us to the operations of the television industry and the ways in which these inevitably influence what audiences will get to see and when. As *Veronica Mars* illustrates, no investigation of its successes and failures, innovations and limitations, would be complete without attention to all the possible avenues of inquiry, both textual and meta-textual, which came to bear on its creation and demise. Like the best kind of detective story, we hope that our investigation has suggested not only whodunnit, but also how and why. However, unlike the best detective stories, we hope that the case of *Veronica Mars* is far from closed, and that as the reader of this book you will feel both encouraged and inspired to investigate *Veronica Mars* for yourself. Happy televisual sleuthing.

## Notes

1. For a close visual analysis of the pilot, see Mittell.
2. On Rob Thomas's response to the Bell/Dohring acting combination, see Turnbull in this volume.
3. John G. Cawelti covers many of the qualities of the hard-boiled detective typical of *noir* stories in his classic *Adventure, Mystery, and Romance: Formula Stories as Art and Popular Culture*. Among the many books on *noir,* J. P. Telotte's *Voices in the Dark* is particularly helpful on narration, and James Naremore's *More Than Night* on the flexibility of the genre. For a more recent assessment of *noir* elements and their modern gender translation, see Priscilla L. Walton and Manina Jones's *Detective Agency: Women Rewriting the Hard-Boiled Tradition.* Alaine Martaus does a thorough job of evaluating *Veronica Mars* in terms of *noir* generic elements in combination with other genres.
4. Joy Press described the series as a cross between the films *Heathers* (1989) and *Chinatown* (1974).
5. On the Hearst feminists, see Whitney in this volume; and see Joyrich.
6. See Emmerton's note 8 in this volume on the details of the name allusion.

## Works Cited

Bloom, Harold. *A Map of Misreading.* New York: Oxford University Press, 1975. Print.

Campbell, Joseph. *The Hero with a Thousand Faces.* 2 ed. Princeton: Princeton University Press, 1968. Print.

Cawelti, John G. *Adventure, Mystery, and Romance: Formula Stories as Art and Popular Culture.* Chicago: University of Chicago Press, 1976. Print.

Davis, Glyn, and Kay Dickinson. "Introduction." *Teen TV: Genre, Consumption and Identity.* Ed. Glyn Davis and Kay Dickinson. London. BFI, 2004. 1–13. Print.

"Do-Overs." DVD Feature. *Veronica Mars: The Complete Third Season.* Warner Bros., 2006, 2007. DVD.

"Favorite Veronica and Logan Moments." *Veronica Mars: The Complete Third Season.* Warner Bros., 2006, 2007. DVD.

Gess, Richard. Conversation with Rhonda V. Wilcox. 7 Nov. 2006.

Gallo, Phil. "*Veronica Mars.*" *Variety.com.* Variety, 19 Sept. 2004. 29 Mar. 2010.

Havrilesky, Heather. "Mars Attacks." *Salon.com.* Salon, 29 Mar. 2005. Web. 29 Mar. 2010.

Hegel, Georg Wilhelm Friedrich. *Vorlesungen über die Ästhetik: Dritter Teil, Die Poesie.* Ed. Rudiger Bubner. Stuttgart: Reclam, 1971. Print.

Joyrich, Lynne. "Women Are from Mars?" (Part 2). *Flow* 5.9 (9 Mar. 2007). n. pag. Web. 15 Aug. 2009.

Klevan, Andrew. *Film Performance: From Achievement to Appreciation.* London and New York: Wallflower, 2005. Print.

Lakoff, George, and Mark Johnson. "The Metaphorical Logic of Rape." *Metaphor and Symbolic Activity* 2.1 (1987): 73–79. Print.

Martaus, Alaine. "'You Get Tough. You Get Even': Rape, Anger, Cynicism, and the Vigilante Girl Detective in *Veronica Mars.*" *Clues: A Journal of Detection* 27.1 (2009): 74–86. Print.

Mittell, Jason. "'These Questions Need Answers': Narrative Construction and the *Veronica Mars* Pilot." *Just TV.* Jason Mittell, 10 Aug. 2009. Web. 28 June 2010.

Naremore, James. *More Than Night: Film Noir and Its Contexts.* Berkeley: University of California Press, 1998. Print.

Poniewozik, James. "6 Best Dramas on TV Now." *Time Magazine Archive 1923 to the Present. Time.com,* 4 April 2005. Web. 29 Mar. 2010.

Pope, Alexander. *The Rape of the Lock.* 1714. *The Norton Anthology of English Literature.* 8th ed. Vol. I. Ed. Stephen Greenblatt. New York: Norton, 2005. 2513–2532. Print.

Press, Joy. "The Teen Beat: Regarding the Geekiness of High Schoolers." *VillageVoice. com.* The Village Voice, 30 Aug. 2004. Web. 29 Mar. 2010.

Radway, Janice. *Reading the Romance: Women, Patriarchy, and Popular Literature.* Chapel Hill: University of North Carolina Press, 1984. Print.

Roush, Matt. "Give This P.I. an A: Was Nancy Drew Ever This Scrappy and Savvy?" *TVGuide.com.* TV Guide, 29 Nov. 2004. Web. 29 Mar. 2010.

Stanley, Alessandra. "A Junior Detective at Hard-Boiled High." *New York Times Online.* New York Times, 26 Sept. 2004. Web. 29 Mar. 2010.

Stern, Lesley, and George Kouvaris. *Falling for You: Essays on Cinema and Performance.* Sydney: Power, 1999. Print.

Telotte, J. P. *Voices in the Dark: The Narrative Patterns of* Film Noir. Urbana and Champaign: University of Illinois Press, 1989. Print.

Thomas, Rob. "Notes for the Series." *slaverats.com.* Rob Thomas, n.d. Web. 29 Mar 2010.

_____. "The Origins of *Veronica Mars.*" *robthomasproductions.com.* Rob Thomas, n.d. Web. 27 June 2010.

_____. *Rats Saw God*. New York: Simon & Schuster, 1996. Print.

Walton, Priscilla L., and Manina Jones. *Detective Agency: Women Rewriting the Hard-boiled Tradition*. Berkeley: University of California Press, 1999. Print.

Whedon, Joss, writ., dir. "Echo [Unaired Pilot]." *Joss Whedon's* Dollhouse*: Season One*. Special feature. Twentieth Century Fox Home Entertainment, 2009. DVD.

_____, writ. "Man on the Street." Dir. David Straiton. *Joss Whedon's* Dollhouse*: Season One*. Episode Six. Twentieth Century Fox Home Entertainment, 2009. DVD.

# 1

# Rob Thomas and Television Creativity

## DAVID LAVERY

> MAC: Hey, did anyone else hear there's gonna be a Matchbox 20
> reunion show?
> PIZ: [dismissively] So? Rob Thomas is a whore.
> MAC: Yeah.
>
> > "Weevils Wobble but They Don't Go Down"
> > [*Veronica Mars* 3.19]

In the relaunch of the *Friday the 13th* franchise (Marcus Nispel, 2009),
we encounter an idiotic character named Nolan, one mindless member of a
group of pre-doomed partiers headed for a wild weekend in a house unfor-
tunately located in Jason Voorhies's backyard. The cypher is interested only
in booze and women, and, less than fifteen minutes after we meet him, he is
killed by Jason's arrow while piloting a power boat with his water-skiing
woman in tow (his would-be conquest dies at Jason's hands soon after).

At first glance, neither the movie nor the death scene would seem to
have any relevance to a consideration of *Veronica Mars*. But Nolan is played
by Ryan Hansen, *Veronica*'s wonderfully obnoxious, meta-vacuous 09er Dick
Casablancas, in a performance that makes *Veronica* devotees wonder if the
progeny of real estate scammer Richard Casblancas, Sr. hasn't emigrated from
small screen to big, from Neptune to Crystal Lake.[1] In reality Nolan and Dick
have little in common but the actor who plays them. Doomed from the outset,
Nolan is two-dimensionally movie shallow. Dick, who appeared in 52 episodes
of *Veronica*, is three-dimensionally quality television shallow — profoundly
shallow. (The quantity of narrative time available to a television storyteller
enables full exploration/development of complex and shallow characters alike.)

In *From Mao to Mozart: Isaac Stern in China* (Murray Lerner, 1981) one of the virtuoso violinist's Chinese pupils plays a passage from Mozart on his instrument. It's perfectly done in a way, every note exact, and yet it has no resonance, no soul. Then Stern plays the same notes — exquisitely, soulfully. The difference between the two renditions is much more than day and night — let's call it the difference between winter and spring. The Chinese violinist's version is austere, lifeless, cold; Stern's brings the music to life. The same might be said for the difference between *Friday the 13th*'s Nolan and *Veronica*'s Dick. Dick is wonderfully, repulsively alive, real. And the animating force, the Isaac Stern of the analogy? Rob Thomas, the former teacher, novelist, and screenwriter who brought *Veronica Mars* out of his mind and imagination and into our world.

## Rob Thomas, Ephebe

To begin an examination of a creator of television with a discussion of a major literary theorist may seem a bit incongruent, but bear with me.

According to the post-structuralist, bestselling, prolific author Harold Bloom, every great writer (and, by extension, every work of the imagination) must struggle to escape from the influence of the writers (and works) that came before. According to Bloom's "map of misreading," the newcomer, or "ephebe," must, in order to be original, simultaneously borrow from "ancestor texts" and depart, "defensively," from them in order to become unique and innovative. In Bloom's "antithetical" system (in keeping with the *Oxford American Dictionary*'s definitions for the word: "directly opposed or contrasted; mutually incompatible"), this rewriting is anything but mere borrowing from a "precursor" poet or text. Rather, it "always and inevitably involves some form of 'misprision,' a kind of misreading that allows the later writer's creativity to emerge" (Murfin and Ray 18).

The ephebe, forever belated, forever defensive, must do battle with its ancestor texts, its precursors, those "strong" works that come before and must be overthrown by the newcomer as it strives for originality. In Bloom's undisguised Freudianism, the father text must be slain in order for the novice to make a new kind of music. Just as no one gets to select his or her own parents, "the ephebe poet encounters a precursor whom he can't choose at will" (Renza 188).

When the ephebe is successful in creating a "revisionary space" for the new work of imagination — Bloom deems such works "strong" — an "illusion of priority" may be created: the impression that they are original when in fact they are belated.

Now Bloom's critical topography does not, of course, extend to the terra incognita of popular culture — our map maker, after all, is an unrepentant highbrow elitist. Its relevance for considering authorship in television and film, as I have argued elsewhere (Porter and Lavery, *Unlocking* Lost; see in particular the chapter "Is There a Text on This Island?"), is nonetheless apparent. As an ephebe television series in an ephebe medium (woefully belated, TV must make a place for itself against long-established, more respected ancestral media like the book and the cinema), *Veronica Mars* found itself in primary contention for imaginative space with another So Cal narrative about an outcast blonde teenager, Joss Whedon's *Buffy the Vampire Slayer* (The WB, 1997–2001; UPN, 2001–2003).

Both set in the Golden State, both in their early years unsparing depictions of caste and class in an American high school, both wonderful amalgams of exciting narrative and pop culture–savvy wit, both very adult in their themes and their very naughty double-entendres,[2] both adept at mixing stand-alone episodes with season-long (and season-contained) story arcs, both generally snubbed by the Emmy Awards, both broadcast for a time on UPN (where *Buffy* aired in its last two years), *Buffy* and *Veronica* also had in common a failure to secure the sort of large audiences their networks hoped for.[3] As *Television without Pity*'s Couch Baron notes in his interview with Thomas (Part I), both series are a tough sell to the unreceptive viewer:

> I recently read an interview with Enrico Colantoni where he conceded that the short version of the premise, "teen-girl PI in training," is a bit of a tough sell, and a lot of our posters who have tried to hook their friends on the show have found the same thing. I'm reminded of my own experience telling people about *Buffy the Vampire Slayer*, which I watched from the very beginning. It was like, you started out saying, "It's a show about a sixteen-year-old girl who fights vampires," and before you could get to the characterization or the storytelling, there was a dust cloud in front of you and your friends wouldn't return your calls.

In the Bloomian take on influence, on the historical relations of ancestor and newcomer, the relationship, whatever the commonalities, is supposed to be congenitally adversarial. Other than in crossover fanfic, Buffy and Veronica, *Buffy* and *Veronica*, never met, but they got along just fine.

In the history of misprision, from Virgil's wrestle with Homer, say, to Blake's vanquishing of Milton, and Whitman's superseding of Emerson, I cannot recall a single incident where the precursor wrote an adulatory essay in praise of the ephebe — as Whedon did of *Veronica* in "Ace of Case" — or agreed to an hilarious cameo in the belated's narrative — as Whedon did in his turn as a German-speaking, geeky, pedantic, and officious "employee of the month" rental car salesman in "Rat Saw God" (2.6).[4]

Thomas has reciprocally acknowledged his admiration for *Buffy*—most emphatically in a posting about Whedon's praise for *Veronica*:

> The things he complimented about our show—the plotting, the dialogue, the relationships, the acting—are all elements I've admired in *Buffy* ["Joss Whedon to guest star on Veronica Mars?"].

But at the same time (September 2005—just as *Veronica* began its second season), we learn that Thomas was, in reality, not terribly familiar with *BtVS*. Whedon's praise had inspired him to Netflix Season Two of the seven season series, and over a year later (responding in *Neptune Noir* to Samantha Bornemann's discussion of *Buffy* in "Innocence Lost: The Third Wave of Teen Girl Drama"), Thomas would appear not to have made much progress in his *Buffy*-watching marathon:

> Veronica and Buffy may have a few things in common, but until I read Samantha's essay I didn't know Buffy received an award and ovation at her prom [184].[5]

In other words, he had not progressed as far as "The Prom" (*BtVS*, 3.20). Thomas, of course, has a ready explanation for his neglect of *Buffy*:

> I think I never let myself get fully-hooked by *Buffy* for the same reason that I feel a lot of people don't watch *Veronica*. By the time the enthusiastic word-of-mouth reached me, I felt like I'd already missed the bus. I was afraid of being so far behind in the mythology that I couldn't follow the ongoing storylines, though I would occasionally see episodes and admire the snappiness, the pacing, the angst.

It's difficult not to see this as the rationalization, "defensive" in Bloomian terms but perfectly understandable, of an ephebe anxious not to know too much about his father's business.

*Buffy* was not, of course, *Veronica Mars'* sole television ancestor. That splendid failure *Twin Peaks* (ABC, 1990–1991), as Thomas has more than once observed ("Veronica Mars, Not Your Average Teen Detective"; *TWoP*, Part I), has always been a looming televisual presence, as it has been for almost all those seeking to produce quality television in the years since it aired. (Sophie Mayer addresses *Twin Peaks'* influence in her essay in this volume.) Thomas evokes other ancestors—yet another quirky 90s show and one of this decade's biggest hits—when he insists (in the *TWoP* interview, Part I) he sees himself "as a *Northern Exposure* [CBS, 1990–1995] writer in a *C.S.I.* [CBS, 2000– ] world." Movies, too, are part of the ancestral mix: Thomas proclaims his fondness for *The Village Voice's* characterization of *Veronica* as "*Heathers* [Michael Lehmann, 1988] meets *Chinatown* [Roman Polanski, 1973]" ("Veronica Mars: Not Your Average Teen Detective"). The story of *Veronica's* genesis is complex.

## *The Origin of* Mars

Like many quality television series, *Veronica Mars* has an intriguing origin story. In a Paley Center forum and elsewhere, Thomas charts the history. *Veronica* began as a novel, one of five Thomas owed Simon and Schuster. Like many of its kindred, it ended up "in a drawer." Thomas had already considered it as the possible foundation for a TV series, but not for the networks. Its subject matter and tone, he was certain, predestined it for HBO or perhaps cable. After a period of dormancy, however, the manuscript nevertheless emerged, at a point in his career when Thomas had, by his own admission, come to see himself as a failure in the TV world (*Neptune Noir* 2) as a potential basis for a network (UPN) series. Inspired by ancestors like *Buffy*, then ending its run on the same network, Thomas knew he wanted to do a teen show, but he needed a better hook: "I've said it before, and I'll say it again, if I could get away with doing a completely grounded teen series like *Freaks and Geeks*, I'd be doing it" (*Neptune Noir* 94).[6]

With *Buffy*'s recombinant splicing of high school and horror in mind, he hatched the idea of infusing the high school genre with the conventions of *noir*. Thanks to the mediation of Ari Emmanuel (the super-agent, brother of President Obama's Chief of Staff, who inspired Jeremy Piven's *Entourage* character), über-producer Joel Silver, anxious to score in the television world, got on board.[7] (We have Silver to thank for the stuntcasting of Paris Hilton in Season One.) With the lead now undergoing a sex change, primarily to make it more appealing, Thomas turned his now out-of-the-drawer idea around over a weekend and was greenlit almost immediately.

In the *TWoP* interview (Part I) Thomas again mentions, in the context of a discussion of censorship by Standards and Practices — its refusal to allow Logan to have a very phallic bong in his locker at Neptune High — an all-important detail about *Veronica*'s genesis: "I originally envisioned *Veronica Mars* as a cable show, where I could have gotten away with that." To do the show he really wanted to do, Thomas would have needed the creative license cable provides. On UPN and, later, the CW, he would have to do battle constantly with interference from above.

## *The Journey to* Mars

The Rob Thomas origin myth is yet another story. The paths to success of television auteurs are many and varied: David Milch was supposed to become a great novelist (according to his mentor Robert Penn Warren) before

*NYPD Blue* and *Deadwood*; Alan Ball was an Oscar-winning Hollywood screenwriter (*American Beauty*) before *Six Feet Under* and *True Blood*. Joss Whedon wanted to be a great movie auteur, "Spielberg by way of George Romero or Wes Anderson, or a strange combination of the two" (in his own words) ("An Interview with Joss Whedon"), but found his niche (like his father and grandfather) in television.

As we have already seen, Thomas was, pre–TV, an aspiring novelist, but even before that, as he told *Television without Pity*'s Couch Baron,

> I taught high school in San Antonio for two years, then advised the University of Texas student magazine for a year, and then taught high school again in Austin for two years. Then I moved to L.A. to work for Channel One, the teen news network, which got a lot of criticism, because some people thought we were just shoving Doritos down kids' throats. Not that there weren't a lot of great creative jobs at Channel One — I just didn't have one of them [Part I].

He learned a great deal as a teacher that would prove useful later both as a novelist and television writer:

> Working with kids in journalism is different from teaching them Math or English. I worked with them after school, on yearbook, in a different setting than the classroom. They'd talk about their relationships and their lives, and those conversations stayed in my mind [Part I].

The absence of an outlet for his creativity in his day job (his nine years in a rock-and-roll band was evidently not satisfying enough) inspired him to start writing, generating a page a day.

The result was *Rats Saw God*, a clever 1996 novel that would inspire the title of a second season episode of *Veronica*. Its allusionary breadth presages *Veronica*'s later rich intertextuality. *Rats* is peppered with references of all kinds. Art and artists —*American Gothic*, Dada, Marcel Duchamp, Norman Rockwell, Tristan Tzara; literature and books — *The Color Purple*, D. H. Lawrence, *Dubliners*, Gore Vidal, J. D. Salinger, Kurt Vonnegut, Jr., *Lolita*, *Poor Richard's Almanac*, *Slaughterhouse-Five*, William Faulkner; music and musicians — AC DC, Alice Cooper, Bread, Garth Brooks, Led Zeppelin, Lenny Kravitz, Madonna, Neil Diamond, U2; popular and material culture — Lucky Charms, *Phantom of the Opera*, Piggly Wiggly, Taco Bell, Transformers; and, of course, television and film —*A Charlie Brown Christmas*, *Backdraft*, *Easy Rider*, *I Dream of Jeannie*, Julie Christie, *Saturday Night Fever*, *Shampoo*, *Sleepless in Seattle*, *Texas Chainsaw Massacre*, *The People's Court*, *The Right Stuff*, *This Is Spinal Tap*, Uma Thurman ... all play a role in Thomas's witty and readable fiction. He would publish four more novels —*Slave Day* (1997), *Doing Time: Notes from the Undergrad* (1997), *Satellite Down* (1998), and *Green Thumb* (1999) — before heading off to Hollywood.

Thomas would write a free-lance solo script — oddly enough for Cartoon Network's *Space Ghost: Coast to Coast* (1996)[8]— before eventually finding his way into a television writers room for *Dawson's Creek* (The WB, 1998–2003), where he would pen important episodes in the series' first season: "Kiss" and "Road Trip." He would leave the show after one season, however, admitting to *TWoP* (Part I) in 2005 that he has still never seen a full episode of the *Creek*. Writing for *Dawson's* he would learn that sometimes earning a paycheck can be as important as creative fulfillment: "it enabled me to pay off some large credit-card debt and buy a house. I was making three thousand bucks a week to be on staff."[9] Besides, the "atmosphere" was not especially conducive in the first place: "There was a lot of upheaval at the top of the show — Kevin Williamson [Dawson's creator — and author of the *Scream* trilogy] was in and out and working on movies and was very involved at some points and not involved at all at others, and they fired the first showrunner they brought in — it didn't make for a good working environment." Lesson learned: a showrunner needs to be involved in every phase of production.

On the *Creek*, he recalls in *Neptune Noir*, Thomas also learned something about making his female characters strong. A script that had Joey responding in kind to a vicious rumor was rejected by The WB because they thought the audience would condemn her thereafter as mean. Thomas resolved in the future to have his heroines "go down swinging" (72).

With *Cupid* (1998–1999) Thomas was at least working on his own creation, but he admits that may have been as well one of its many weaknesses since he had no experience managing a series. After scheduling it in a graveyard timeslot (on Saturday night), ABC micromanaged — "The network brought in a writing team, plus two executive producers..., but by Episode 8, they had fired the EPs" (Couch, Part I)— which left Thomas in charge. He admits to not being heartbroken when the plug was pulled (Couch, Part I).[10] Lessons learned: (1) a showrunner needs to know what he is doing; (2) top-down network interference can be debilitating.

Working on *Snoops*, a short-lived 1999 series from the pen of the prolific, and prolix, David Kelley, Thomas had another less-than-optimal creative experience. Though he acknowledges that he "bear[s] him no ill will," Thomas deems the creator of *Picket Fences*, *Ally McBeal*, *The Practice*, and *Boston Legal* "an odd duck" and, with real cogency, explains why to *TWoP* (Part I):

> The way David runs a show is that he writes it, and he lets other people cast and edit and run the production. He writes, and more power to him. He certainly cared about *Snoops*— if he hadn't, he would have just handed it off to me. But it's like he's autistic — he's off in script world. He writes faster and more than any writer I've ever seen, but I think the tradeoff in that is that he's not present in

the room in which he's in. You can have these conversations with him where you don't think he's talking to you — he's writing the third act of next week's *Ally McBeal* [Couch Baron].

Always fair-minded, Thomas goes on to suggest that his clash with one of television's major auteurs simply came down to creative differences, but he still cannot forgive Kelley's unwillingness to place blame where blame was due:

> [A]fter the series ended, he told the *Hollywood Reporter* that the lesson he learned from *Snoops* was not to hand over a show to other producers. That's so offensive to me, because he didn't hand off the show. I was like, "That's your bomb, David. That's all you. Please step up and take responsibility for the show you did" [Couch Baron].

Thomas had been reminded again that showrunning your own creation should always be option one, and once more his sense of disappointment was ameliorated by the conviction that "I think I came up with the better detective show, so I feel like I won."

## An Education on Mars

Rob Thomas may be the only television auteur to have co-edited a critical book on his own show. Although it seems dubious that he actually compiled BenBella's Smart Pop collection of "Unauthorized Investigations into *Veronica Mars*" as the "Edited by" designation would suggest (I suspect his "with" collaborator Leah Wilson did much of the work), the book does offer Thomas' often insightful responses to each of the essays. Both *Neptune Noir*, and Thomas's extended *TWoP* interview, offer candid backstage glimpses into the making of *Veronica*.

We learn, for example, that, in sharp contrast to David Chase — whose *Sopranos*' run (1999–2007) partially overlapped with *Veronica*'s — Thomas and his creative team were "not trying to do a little art house film each week." Chase aspired to make one hour feature films for "not TV" HBO. Thomas' goal was more modest: "to be the thinking-man's (or–woman's) popcorn show" (*Neptune Noir* 8).

Ready and willing to point out narration in *Veronica* at both its best and worst, Thomas nevertheless expresses his irritation that the best film schools in the land, from USC to NYU, are wrongly teaching that the practice is always wrong, an uncinematic "crutch." (With typically sardonic humor, Thomas adds that, since he was rejected at all these schools, he is only guessing.)

We discover, too, that like its Bloomian precursor *Buffy*, *Veronica* hoped to offer what Joss Whedon deemed "emotional realism" (Wilcox and Lavery xxiv). Trying to respond to the unjustness of a posting board complaint that Season Three's dorm rooms were unrealistically large with an explanation of televisual production exigencies and the space necessary for camera angles, Thomas speaks of his perpetual aspiration to find and present a "nexus of escapist entertainment and emotional truth" (*Neptune*, 94).

Though initially, pleasantly surprised by UPN's willingness to allow him to have his way with certain narrative developments — allowing Veronica's rape to stand in the pilot, for example (Couch, Part I), and even receiving good advice in the customarily dreaded "notes" from above — it was UPN's suggestion that Veronica and her father remain very close and supportive (his approach was to have them more estranged), Thomas would come more and more to clash with the network. As previously mentioned, he was annoyed by Standards and Practices censorship, and he was especially upset over UPN's idiotic practice of revealing key plot development in promotional teasers: "I about hit the roof, and I think they gave away our huge twist for next week's episode ["Ruskie Business," 1.15]. I am so angry with them today. It's been a constant battle, like, *tease the red herring — don't tease the actual ending*" (Couch, Part I). Thomas has also complained about the network's imposition of what he took to be unnecessary voice-over narration.

## *Life After* Mars

In the introduction to *Neptune Noir*, revealingly called "Digressions on How *Veronica Mars* Saved My Career and, Less Importantly, My Soul," Rob Thomas ruminates that perhaps the major lesson he has learned from over a decade in Hollywood is that "it's a minor miracle when any finished product doesn't suck" (1). Back when he was a high school teacher he had been puzzled why all television wasn't as good as *Seinfeld, Moonlighting,* or *Northern Exposure*; now, a veteran of multiple series, Thomas knows the odds are long against any show's success. Miscasting, the wrong ending, network interference — all can doom a promising series, and often do. (Thomas' essay is especially revealing concerning the fluctuating power struggle between creator and network from pitch, to series development, to actual showrunning.)

For all his obvious talent, Thomas has yet to know complete success. *Cupid* had its critical admirers but has been canceled — twice. *Veronica Mars* was a critical darling but never gained a large-enough audience to appease Thomas' masters and was not renewed past its uneven third season. As I write, the half-hour sitcom *Party Down*, Thomas' latest creation, is slated to reappear on STARZ' schedule sometime in 2010, with the cable movie channel hopeful of replicating AMC's original series success with *Mad Men* and *Breaking Bad*. Revealingly, Thomas is not showrunning his latest but has turned the assignment over to key *Veronica* collaborator John Enbom.[11] *Variety* reports that Thomas is also developing another series, *Waterloo*, for STARZ, this one to be based on his days in a rock band (Littleton).

What does the future hold for Rob Thomas? He may continue to toil, probably with constant frustration, in television. That Thomas — who, recall, knew that *Veronica* was genetically meant for cable — has moved further down the channel spectrum with *Party Down*, away from the restrictiveness of the lower digit niches and into the more open imaginative spaces of the higher numbers, indicates the path Thomas may be on.

If Thomas stays in television, it will be primarily as a writer not a director. Both episodes of *Veronica* helmed by Thomas — "Donut Run" (2.11) and "Spit and Eggs" (3.9) — are workman-like hours of television, and both pivotal *and* exciting: Veronica helps Duncan escape with his child; Veronica discovers the identity of the Hearst rapist(s), narrowly escaping herself, and Dean O'Dell is murdered. He shows no signs, however, of the sort of brilliant directorial innovation with which Whedon revolutionized television as an art form in *Buffy* episodes like "Hush," "The Body," and "Once More with Feeling."

Perhaps Thomas will return to the life of the novelist — a consummation he contemplated pre–*Veronica* if the series had not made it to air (*Neptune Noir* 7), or move back and forth between literature, film, and television. Wherever he ends up, his work will no doubt exhibit his usual integrity and originality. Rob Thomas is no whore — whatever Piz says — and he is no longer an ephebe.

## Notes

1. Not surprisingly, Thomas would put Hansen back to work in his new series *Party Down*. Editor's note: *Party Down* ran from 2009 to 2010.

2. Both series took delight in being naughty in ways too clever for literal TV censors. Compare these very similar instances of getting away with obscenity in prime time.

- On *Buffy* ("Family," 5.6 — an episode written and directed by Whedon):
  Spike baits Buffy — about whom he is now having vivid fantasies — to "come and get it," and she responds, "I'm coming right now" — all of which turns out to be taking place in the vampire's mindscreen during sex with the airhead vampire Harmony.
- On *Veronica* ("Donut Run," 2.11— an episode written and directed by Thomas):
  Logan and Veronica find Kendall Casablancas in a towel in Duncan's hotel suite, resulting in the following exchange:

KENDALL: Oh, quit standing there so smug. Tomorrow you're just gonna call me at two in the morning saying you want some company. For your information, that really doesn't satisfy me, Logan.
LOGAN: Really? You always come.

3. The two series also had actresses in common. *Buffy*'s Alyson Hannigan (Willow) would appear as Trina Echolls in three episodes, and Charisma Carpenter would have a major recurring role as Kendall Casablancas in Season Two. Interestingly, the *Buffy* connection almost prevented Hannigan's role. As Thomas tells *TWoP*'s Couch Baron, Hannigan, a fan of *Veronica*, was concerned that playing Logan's sister would not advance her career: "You guys are kind of the new Buffy, and will that be a real sideways move in my career if I come on the show?" Her eventual major role on *How I Met Your Mother* would end her involvement in *Veronica*.

4. Emerson's generous epistolary response upon reading the manuscript of the first edition of *Leaves of Grass*, "I greet you at the beginning of a great career," does comes to mind, but Whitman's advertisement-for-myself publication of his patriarch's letter of praise in *The New York Tribune* in October 1855 was done without permission.

5. Thomas, we learn, had toyed with having Veronica become prom queen.

6. By the middle of the new century's first decade, Thomas had realized, there was no room on television for "these tiny moments with teenagers having these small epiphanies and very real life lessons. It had to be in *The O.C.* territory of lesbians and affairs and fucking the pool boy" (Couch Baron).

7. Thomas' partnering with Silver marks yet another synchronicity with "patriarch" Joss Whedon, who in 2005 would sign on with Silver to write and direct a big screen version of Wonder Woman, a project which would come to nought when Whedon's ideas for the blockbuster-in-the-making never satisfied the producer.

8. Although Thomas is seldom thought of as a compatriot of comic book geek creators like Whedon, it is important to note that his *Space-Ghost* was the work of a man who goes on at some length to *TWoP* (Part I) about the large impact of *Spider-Man* comics on his favorite themes as a writer (Couch Baron).

9. For more on the central role of money for 1990s television writers, see Jeffrey Stepakoff's *Billion Dollar Kiss*. Like Thomas, Stepakoff would write for *Dawson's Creek*—beginning the year after Thomas had left the series.

10. Inexplicably, ABC would bring *Cupid* back under new management for an abortive second try in March 2009. It was cancelled after airing seven episodes.

11. In a similar, contemporary development, Joss Whedon delegated *Dollhouse*'s showrunning to Sarah Fain and Elizabeth Craft in Season One and Tara Butters and Michele Fazekas for Season Two.

## *Works Cited*

Bloom, Harold. *The Anxiety of Influence: A Theory of Poetry*. New York: Oxford, 1973. Print.

_____. *A Map of Misreading*. New York: Oxford University Press, 1975. Print.

Couch Baron. "Sometimes Those Who Teach Can Also Do: The Rob Thomas Interview, Part I." *TelevisionwithoutPity*. Television without Pity, 2 Mar. 2005. Web. 20 Apr. 2007.

_____. "'Veronica Mars' Just Rolls Off the Tongue: The Rob Thomas Interview, Part

II." *TelevisionwithoutPity.* Television without Pity, 8 Mar. 2005. Web. 20 Apr. 2007.

"Joss Whedon to guest star on *Veronica Mars?*" *Whedonesque.com.* Whedonesque, 15 Sept. 2005. Web. 25 Apr. 2007.

Littleton, Cynthia. "Starz adds 'Fly' to original slate." *Variety.com.* Variety, 28 July 2009. Web. 25 Apr. 2007.

Murfin, Ross, and Supryia M. Ray. *The Bedford Glossary of Critical and Literary Terms.* Boston: Bedford 1997. Print.

Porter, Lynnette, and David Lavery. Lost*'s Buried Treasures: Everything the* Lost *Fans Need to Know.* Napierville, IL: Sourcebooks, 2009. Print.

Renza, Louis. "Influence." *Critical Terms for Literary Study,* 2d ed. Ed. Frank Lentricchia and Thomas McLaughlin. Chicago: University Chicago Press, 1995. 186–202. Print.

Stepakoff, Jeffrey. *Billion Dollar Kiss: The Story of a Television Writer in the Hollywood Gold Rush.* New York: Penguin, 2007. Print.

Thomas, Rob. *Rats Saw God.* New York: Simon Pulse, 2007. Print.

_____, ed. *Neptune Noir: Unauthorized Investigations into* Veronica Mars. Smart Pop Series. Dallas: BenBella, 2007. Print.

"*Veronica Mars.*" Paley Center for Media (2005). Forum.

"Veronica Mars: Not Your Average Teen Detective." DVD Feature. *Veronica Mars: The Complete Second Season.* Warner Bros., 2006. DVD.

Whedon, Joss. "Ace of Case." *EW.com.* Entertainment Weekly, 14 October 2005. Web. 20 Apr. 2007.

_____. "An Interview with Joss Whedon: The *Buffy the Vampire Slayer* creator discusses his career." *Ign.com.* IGN Filmforce, 23 June, 2003. Web. 24 June 2010.

Wilcox, Rhonda V., and David Lavery, eds. *Fighting the Forces: What's at Stake in* Buffy the Vampire Slayer. Lanham, MD: Rowman and Littlefield, 2002. Print.

# 2

# Performing *Veronica Mars*

## SUE TURNBULL

I find it impossible to imagine Veronica Mars played by anyone other than Kristen Bell. We had some fantastic actresses audition for the part, but Kristen was in another league.... After Kristen auditioned at the studio, the first comment from an executive was that "she might be good in the best friend role, but not as a lead." It almost seems ludicrous now, but we had to fight to convince our studio to let us take Kristen to the network audition. Had we lost that argument there would be no show today.

— Rob Thomas (*Neptune Noir* 6)

Without the performance of Kristen Bell, according to creator Rob Thomas above, *Veronica Mars* the TV series would not have existed. It's quite an assertion, suggesting that by an early stage in production Bell had become so central to the concept of the show that Thomas was prepared to sacrifice the entire enterprise on the basis of a casting decision. This may explain, or maybe not, why Thomas was willing to make other compromises in getting *Veronica Mars* up and running on the UPN network, including the decision to cut the original pre-title sequence featuring junior private eye Veronica on a stake-out at the seedy Camelot motel waiting for the "money shot" of a couple *in flagrante* in the long lens of her trusty camera. But then the business of television would seem to be fraught with compromise and tactical decisions made in the exigency of the moment.

Whatever the backstory, it is clear that Bell's performance carries the show from that very first moment (now happily restored in the DVD release) when we hear the unmistakable voice of Veronica telling us, the audience, how she sees the world from her prematurely jaded point of view: "Sooner or later, the people you love let you down ... betray you" (1.1). Except, of course, they don't always. Veronica, despite her assertiveness, is not always right in her assessments of people or events. But that revelation will come later in the series as we learn more about her world, as realized by the many actors who bring the community of fictional Neptune, the "town without a middle class," to life.

But how to talk about those performances? How is it that the representation of bodies and emotions on screen comes to move the body and emotions of the viewer in sympathy? What ignites that affect? How can we elucidate the manifold ways in which the actors convince us of the "truth" of their emotions and the "reality" of the fictional world which they inhabit in such a way as to move us to laughter or tears, to nail-biting anxiety, utter frustration or anger? And why, here's the killer, has so little attention been paid to the issue of performance in television studies since without the performance of the actor in the frame, there would be nothing to look at but the set, artfully constructed though it may well be?

Film critics and commentators have paid some, but not much, attention to performance in cinema. James Naremore's *Acting in the Cinema*, for example, provides a "classification of different types of cinematic performance according to theatrical traditions and approaches" ("Falling for You" 13). What it doesn't do, as Stern and Kouvaris point out, is explain why some performances affect the viewer more than others. In order to do that, they argue, the film critic has to move towards a practice which they describe as "ekphrasis." This is a rhetorical term borrowed from the Greek, and one which I earlier employed in an endeavor to discuss aspects of performance (particularly that of James Marsters as Spike) in *Buffy the Vampire Slayer* ("Moments of Inspiration").

The practice of ekphratic film criticism, as outlined by Stern and Kouvaris, involves trying to capture the ephemerality of film in the words on a page:

> In order to set the scene before the eyes of the reader the writer needs to deploy a notional ekphrasis, or a degree of fictionalization. This is not to turn the film into fiction; but in order to turn the film into writing, in order to convey movement, corporeal presence, performative modalities and affective inflection, a certain refiguring is required... [17].

According to Stern and Kouvaris, this refiguring involves the writer using description in an effort to recreate the intensity of the original experience in order to ... well, what? Share? Persuade? Convince? Or simply to re-create and re-live that moment again in their own creative endeavor?

Whatever the impulse, and there may be many, it would seem that writing about cinematic performance involves an act of translation from one language (the language of film), to another (the language of film criticism) which has always had a somewhat uneasy relationship to the practice of description. "Too much description, not enough analysis" might be the accusation voiced by a generation of film scholars versed in the practice of film theory post 1970 in any institution of higher learning in the Western world. And yet, as Stern and Kouvaris make clear, there can be no film criticism without some degree of description to make the context of the analysis clear (12).

In his recent book, *Film Performance: From Achievement to Appreciation*, Andrew Klevan picks up where Stern and Kouvaris leave off, arguing that although film criticism has paid some attention to performance with regard to the phenomenon of stardom or acting, it has tended not to pursue "the complexity of a performer's internal relationships within a film" (Preface). In order to demonstrate how this might be achieved, Klevan considers a number of performances on film, "treating performance as an internal element of style in synthesis with other aspects of film style" (Preface). This involves an exquisite attention to the detail of specific performances rendered through extensive description. In the process, Klevan arrives at three analytic frames which conveniently coincide with three different genres of film.

The first of these is comedy and involves the relationship of the performer to the camera, their position and perspective within the shot. Klevan elucidates these relationships through an account of Charlie Chaplin's performance in *City Lights* (1931) as well as the comedic performances of Stan Laurel, Oliver Hardy, and Cary Grant in a number of other films. The second genre, melodrama, involves an exploration of the performer's relationship to place, including location, décor, furniture and objects. Klevan's descriptive analysis here includes Marlene Dietrich's performance in Von Sternberg's *The Scarlet Empress* (1934) and that of Fred MacMurray in Douglas Sirk's *There's Always Tomorrow* (1956). Lastly, Klevan turns his attention to the thriller and the relationship of the performer to plot in a discussion of Fritz Lang's *Secret Beyond the Door* (1948) and Hitchcock's *Shadow of a Doubt* (1943).

Of particular interest to students of *Veronica Mars* is Klevan's discussion of the use of the voice-over in the Hitchcock film. In *Shadow of a Doubt*'s thriller narrative, Celia, the central character, meets and marries a man who she begins to fear is planning to kill her. The viewer of the film is privy to her thoughts right from the very first moment in the film, thus placing her in a very different relationship to the viewer than any of the other characters in the film. Here's how Klevan describes it:

> Her vocal manner is deep and breathy, rounded and smooth, and never high-pitched. Sensuously rhythmic, it modulates, caresses and nurtures even her most anxious thoughts. She contains the turbulence as if relishing her passion on the

verge of release. The voice over allows her to keep thoughts courteously to her-self while she impolitely whispers: eagerly murmuring, illicitly, close to the viewer's ear [76].

Now think of Veronica's voice in either the first or the second of the two voiceovers which open the first episode of Veronica Mars.

Veronica's voice is not breathy or whispery; it's confident, matter of fact, somewhat terse. Veronica sounds sure of herself, telling the viewer exactly what she thinks about her world and what is wrong with it. And Veronica's voice is the first thing we hear, no matter which version of the first episode we watch: Thomas's original stake-out at the Camelot motel or the crane shot of the car park at Neptune High preferred by the network. In both contexts, it's Veronica's voice and its vocal inflections which orient us not only towards the character of Veronica, but also towards all the other characters we are about to meet who are framed within the story she is telling. Veronica's voice initially and repeatedly focuses our attention on the various plots which are unfolding, both in terms of what Veronica knows, or thinks she knows, and what she doesn't.

But a television series isn't a film, although, as has often been remarked upon over the years, "quality" television has often looked like very like film and is now gradually being treated with the respect which film, as an already established art form, has commanded. Film achieved this respect, it might be recalled, with the assistance of some timely and strategic film criticism from the nineteen sixties onwards, the kind of criticism which television is increas-ingly attracting as the younger medium gradually emerges from the shadow of big brother film, to be recognized as its own particular kind of art form.[1] The relationship between film and television and their relative status has always been a complex one, as historians of television reveal the blurring of the edges between the two media forms. This blurring was an inevitable result of the early and continuing cross-over in personnel from film to television, as well as the development of a number of televisual dramatic genres with their origins in film (and indeed radio). Such genres would include the West-ern, the family melodrama, and the crime series. In the case of the latter, Jack Webb's *Dragnet* provided some stunning examples of film noir stylistics on the small screen in the early years,[2] stylistics of which the producers of *Veronica Mars* would appear to be well aware.

In terms of television genres, *Veronica Mars* might best be described as a not entirely original hybrid, the teen melodrama crossed with the television crime series. In the late 1980s, producers Patrick Hasburgh and Stephen J. Cannell came up with a similar concept for the fledgling Fox network in order to cater for a teen audience. The result was *21 Jump Street*, which launched the career of Johnny Depp as a fresh-faced policeman going undercover on the high school beat to deal with the kinds of problems with which Veronica routinely deals. Note the allusion to *21 Jump Street* by Logan (see Wilcox in this volume) when addressing a federal agent who has been undercover at Neptune High. The writers of *Veronica Mars* clearly know their television antecedents. Like *Veronica Mars*, *21 Jump Street* veered from comedy to melodrama to action series during its run (with Depp only present in the first four seasons). Unlike *21 Jump Street* (1987–91), *Veronica Mars*, at least in its first two seasons, also developed a thriller element in terms of a season-length narrative arc involving the central character, Veronica.

Any attempt to discuss performance in the narratively complex, generically hybrid *Veronica Mars* therefore requires attention to all three of Klavan's dimensions of film performance,

- the narrative — involving the relationship of performance to plot;
- the melodramatic — involving the relationship of performance to place;
- the comedic — involving the relationship of performance to the camera.

What also has to be considered is how these various elements play out within the medium of television as opposed to that of film. For example, a longform drama series like *Buffy the Vampire Slayer* or *Veronica Mars* may also involve an evolution in the performance of the actors across an extended period of production as well as an evolution of the character as necessitated by narrative choices on the part of the writers. A performer might be required to shift from being a jerk to being a romantic hero, from being a hard-nosed teen private eye to a vulnerable victim.

There are other factors to be accounted for too, such as the ways in which the narrative trajectory of a show might change depending on the nature of the performances themselves, and the direction the writers choose to take as a result. Here the parallels between the case of James Marsters as Spike and Jason Dohring as Logan immediately come to mind, since it was what they saw on screen which caused their respective creators (Joss Whedon and Rob Thomas) to change the direction of the characters, especially in their relation to the central female character in each show.

Of course there may also be factors beyond the producer's control, as was sadly evident in the case of *Veronica Mars* when the show was moved from the UPN to the new CW network, with all sorts of repercussions in season three. Or take the case of an actor falling pregnant causing her to be swiftly written out of the show, as was true for Paula Marshall, who played Keith Mars' love interest for a brief time in season one.[3] Or, and I'm quite serious here, consider the case of producer Thomas's problems with the trainer of the original brown and white pit bull playing the Mars family's Back-Up, which led to a change of dog (yes, I count pit bulls as performers too), a switch with which I have never fully managed to come to terms.

Despite, or even because of, all the above, it is possible to focus our attention on the performances in *Veronica Mars* exclusively in terms of how they are unfolding on screen. Taking the lead from Klevan, it is then possible to consider these performances in relation to the elements of plot, place, and position in the frame while recognizing that as a long-form television series, *Veronica Mars* frequently changes mode from thriller to melodrama to comedy not only across a season, but also within an episode, and sometimes even within a scene, requiring considerable dexterity on the part of the performers.

## Performing Veronica

> At the center of it all is Veronica herself. Bell is most remarkable not for what she brings (warmth, intelligence, and big funny) but for what she leaves out. For all the pathos of her arc, she never begs for our affection. There is a distance to her, a hole in the center of Veronica's persona. Bell constantly conveys it without even seeming to be aware of it. It's a star turn with zero pyrotechnics, and apart from the occasionally awkward voice-over, it's a teeny bit flawless.
>
> — Joss Whedon

Sure it begins with the voice, a voice which Bell has since conferred on the character of *Gossip Girl* (2007– ) in the subsequent eponymous series in which she does not appear, to the regret of at least one fan on the Television Without Pity website who has compiled a comprehensive assessment of Bell's career post *Veronica Mars*.[4] The disembodiment of Bell is indeed a shame in terms of what else the actress Kristen Bell might have brought to the show. The taut, compact figure of Veronica striding towards, or away from, her school locker is one of the iconic punctuation marks in the series, at least in the first two seasons. Her shoulders slightly hunched, her head ducked down as if ready for a fight, her eyes darting sideways, Veronica walks through her world on the alert, and it's a terrific walk, right up there with other iconic screen walks such as the Humphrey Bogart shuffle in any film you care to mention, or the Seth Bullock lope as performed by Timothy Olyphant in the HBO series *Deadwood* (2004–06), to recall just one other recent memorable televisual performance.

In describing Veronica's walk, I'm thinking of her confident stride through the school yard and down the school halls in her incarnation as Veronica, girl detective, remembering at the same time that this is the walk that Veronica has learned to perform in self-defense. As the flashbacks gradually reveal, Veronica didn't use to walk this way when she went out with Duncan Kane, when she partied with the rich kid '09ers, after she was raped at Shelly Pomeroy's party and before Lilly was murdered. Veronica's assertive stride is the walk of Veronica Mars on a mission to discover the truth, not the vague lost meanderings of Veronica Mars, the rape victim. Veronica's walk is thus impossible to discuss without reference to its narrative significance, what came before and why it is the way it is.

Veronica, as we come to discover, is quite a performer for the purposes of the narrative. She can if required disguise her walk, her appearance, and even her voice in ways to which we as the audience are usually privy, allowing us to delight in the subterfuge, and sometimes not, when the precise nature of Veronica's talent for misdirection is hidden even from the audience until the last minute. I'm thinking here of the episode "Donut Run" in season two, when Veronica fools everyone, including her father, in her efforts to secure the escape of Duncan and his baby daughter (2.11).

Given that we are made so aware of Veronica's capacity for performance, one of the delights in watching Bell perform Veronica is catching the moment when the character's self-confident mask drops, and Bell performs what in the moment we are encouraged to believe is the "real" Veronica. In the discussion of reality TV, this is the moment which has been described as revealing "the flicker of authenticity"; the moment when we are convinced that what we are watching as an audience is emotionally "real" (Roscoe). Watching season one of *Veronica Mars* for the third time, paying particular attention to performance, I discovered anew that "flicker of authenticity" in the moment when Veronica kisses Logan on the balcony of the Camelot Motel in the episode "Weapons of Class Destruction" (1.18). It's a moment in which the characters themselves appear surprised, caught off guard. It's therefore a moment when the performers completely convince me of the reality of their characters' situation, at that moment, in that space, in that frame. It's also a moment which changes everything for them. Let me try to describe how and why it does this.

After Veronica impulsively kisses Logan, who has just come to her aid, she makes as if to turn away. Logan pulls her back and kisses her with serious intent. It's a long kiss, shot from two different angles, the second involving a laborious (and expensive) crane shot as the camera swings from right to left and then zooms in to catch them on the balcony in mid shot where — it might be remembered for those who saw the original opening scene — it all began on that first stake-out, as Veronica's voice told us to forget the "primal drive," the "hormonal surge," and "ride it out." There's a nice irony being played out here in that Veronica is clearly experiencing what a primal drive might actually feel like in the exact location where she once denied it. This time, there's no ironic voiceover. Veronica is silent as she looks at Logan post-kiss before rushing back to her car where they exchange yet another set of startled and unsure glances.

This is a significant moment for all sorts of reasons, some of which may depend on the knowledge that the viewer may or may not bring to the scene in terms of their familiarity with the show. At the very least, this moment acknowledges an intense connection and attraction between the two characters. And yet there's what Whedon might call a "hole" in it. The faces of Logan and Veronica as they draw apart are stunned, enigmatic, leaving the viewer to speculate on what this kiss might mean, for the characters and for the narrative. It's a kiss which therefore sutures the spectator into the narrative in much the same way that the kiss before an advertising break in a daytime soap opera, followed by the intense close-up on the actors' impassive faces, leaves us free to draw our own conclusions as to how it might play out. In the absence of dialogue and obvious emotion, the viewer at home has to do the work of filling the "hole" which may have been deliberately left in the performances.

Creator Rob Thomas wasn't entirely happy with the kiss:

> Now I may have been wrong on this front, but it wasn't what I imagined, or really what I think was described in the script. The line of description called for Logan to "devour" Veronica. I wanted it to be — I don't know if sexual is the right word, but-hungry, or a release, or mixed with some self-loathing and confusion. Instead it came off as singularly romantic. Now the post-kiss moment of the two of them regarding each other — that was everything I hoped for [*Neptune Noir* 170].

What's interesting about Thomas's reading of this moment is how the performance of the kiss changed the meaning of the scene, even for its creator. For Thomas, it wasn't intended to be about romance, but a "primal urge" kind of affair. As Thomas has noted, he originally "didn't foresee a Veronica/Logan romance until we started seeing them on screen together." Evidently, actor Jason Dohring changed the direction of the narrative through his performance.

## Performing Logan

> When Jason Dohring came in to audition for the first time, it was one of the most powerful auditions I've ever witnessed. Because we didn't have that much dialogue for him in the pilot, I wrote an additional

audition scene in which Aaron picks Logan up from school after Veronica gets him expelled for the bong in his locker. In the scene, Aaron has Logan push the cigarette lighter, and the audience realizes as Logan loses his composure what Aaron plans to do with the lighter. Jason was spellbinding. (He always wanted to perform that scene in the show. It was replaced by the scene of choosing a belt with which to be whipped.)

　　　　　　　　　　　　　　　　　　— Rob Thomas (*Neptune Noir* 171)

It's interesting to note that the scene chosen as the audition piece for the actor intended to play Logan was an intensely melodramatic one, depending as it did on the character's relationship to a specific object, the cigarette lighter. The scene as eventually written is also intensely melodramatic and is worth revisiting here in order to explore how the characters of Logan and Aaron Echolls are performed in this moment.

In his discussion of performance in film, Klevan draws attention to the ways in which "aspects of a character's psychology in melodrama are indirectly revealed by the performer's relationship to other aspects of the film's presentation" (Preface). As a result of this shift, performers are relieved of the need "to overtly or openly express their psychological states" (14). As will become obvious, all of the performers involved in this particular sequence are defined by their relationship to the objects in the frame rather than by what they say, since none of them speaks. Instead the soundtrack is occupied by the song "Ventura Highway" as recorded by the band America in 1972. It might be noted that the lyrics, which are somewhat nonsensical, suggest a yearning for liberty while what we see is a family imprisoned in an unhealthy relationship. The "melos" of this particular melodrama is ironic, but also apt.

We first hear "Ventura Highway" at the start of a sequence which involves Logan and his father Aaron in the latter's expensive sports car. And yes, there is a close-up of the cigarette lighter as Aaron starts the car after filling up at the station, but that's as far as it goes. As we discover, they are on their way to a soup kitchen where Logan will serve a meal and Aaron will make a speech carefully staged for the assembled press in which he asks the inmates to forgive his son for staging boxing matches with homeless men for kicks. It's also the moment when Logan will take his father aback by announcing that Aaron plans to donate half a million dollars to the Neptune soup kitchen.

"Ventura Highway" takes over the soundtrack once again when we discover ourselves, since this is where the camera is positioned, inside a cupboard with glass fronted doors. The inside of the cupboard is predominantly dark red, the outside is cast in shadow but with just enough light to perceive a figure walk from right to left. As the double doors slide open, Logan is revealed front and center in the frame. His face is thoughtful, and oddly vulnerable. It's not the cocky, smirking Logan we know from the schoolyard, nor the coy, fake Logan we have just seen in the soup kitchen buddying up with his dad for the camera. Logan's face is impassive as he looks at the rows of belts on either side of the cupboard. Slowly he chooses one, takes it down and runs it through his hands. There's a long pause as he regards it contemplatively, before obviously coming to some sort of a decision, folding the belt, and shutting the doors, effectively leaving us trapped in the dark.

The next shot is of Logan walking towards the camera, which follows him as he swings right into his father's study where we are immediately confronted with two large posters on the opposite wall of the impossibly handsome Aaron Echolls, film star. The still handsome, but now much older, Echolls, is looking out of the window. He turns and walks towards Logan, whose back is to us. Aaron takes the belt from Logan and walks towards the camera, closing the door on us yet again as we see Logan begin to lift his shirt to reveal his naked back. It is now quite clear, if it wasn't before, that a child is about to be beaten.

With what is happening in that room now denied to us in a very Freudian way, the camera slides away from the shut door, back to the hallway and tracks right (there's a sneaky cut in there but it doesn't really matter) in order to discover Lynn Echolls sitting in a chair with a large glass of what looks like alcohol. She sips/gulps it twice, her face in shadow, her eyes glistening in the gloom.

It's a powerful sequence, which even as I try to describe it begins to take a different kind of shape on the page as I try to elucidate the ways in which the objects in the frame help to define the performances and our relationship to what is happening. The belt is the object which defines Logan's relationship with his father, first in the way in which Logan looks at it, then in the way in which he passes it to him and Aaron takes it, suggesting that Logan is still very much under Aaron's control. In this house of many rooms, doors are used to frame, to reveal and then to conceal what is being played out in them. And then there's the use of the glass in Lynn Echolls' hand which reveals that she would rather drink than intervene in the relationship between father and son. She too is held captive by Aaron, whose narcissism is revealed by the posters of himself in his prime which he has hanging so prominently in his study.

Of course, none of these objects would mean anything without the performers whose actions imbue them with meaning within the narrative. However, as Klevan points out, following film critic V.F Perkins, if there is too much attention to the apparatus and not enough to the performers, then everything falls out of balance. Or as Thomas himself describes it, "A television show is like a house of cards, and if you place one of those cards wrong, the show will collapse" (*Neptune Noir* 2). The way Logan looks at the belt in the cupboard is what makes this scene work, not the fact of the belt itself, and as such, it is testimony to the intensity which actor Jason Dohring brought to his role.

## Performing Father and Daughter

Referring to a scene in season two when Keith Mars tells Veronica he can no longer trust her, Rob Thomas writes that

> ... it wasn't until I was directing it, and I saw Enrico and Kristen perform it that I had a moment of clarity about the consequences. Frankly, it was so much more powerful when I heard it performed than when I heard it in my head that I thought to myself, "Oh shit. That's gonna really resonate..." [*Neptune Noir* 104].

The performance of Enrico Colantino as Veronica's father, and the way in which Kristen Bell performs Veronica when she is with him on screen, not only managed to take writer and director Thomas by surprise in the moment described above, but was clearly an on-going highlight of the show for many viewers. Bell and Colantino's performances were awarded an American Family Television Award in 2006 in the category of "Favorite Father and Daughter."[5] This was justly deserved since their double act requires them to transition from the register of melodrama to comedy and the narrative seriousness of the crime drama in the course of an episode and sometimes even in the course of a sequence of shots, as is the case in the very first episode.

The first scene in which we see Veronica and Keith together takes place in the downtown offices of Mars Investigations, where Veronica plays the part of after-school receptionist and side-kick to her father's private eye. As Veronica arrives, she sees the car of Celeste Kane parked outside. After a bit of banter between lawyer Cliff McCormack and Veronica which initiates another narrative thread, Celeste Kane emerges from the inner office escorted by Keith. At this point Keith and Veronica exchange a look. He returns to his office and shuts the door.

Cut to the next scene of father and daughter eating dinner together, side by side in a wide shot which encompasses the space of Veronica's desk, the window behind them and the open door to Keith's office. He wants to talk about school and her grades, she wants to know what Celeste Kane was up to. Keith tries to deflect Veronica by talking about powdered cheese, Veronica wants to know if Celeste thinks her husband is seeing someone else. During this latter interchange, the camera focuses on first one and then the other, before pulling back to frame them once again in the same wide shot as before as the phone rings. Veronica in her role as receptionist answers, handing the receiver to Keith, who starts to write down the details. Immediately, they are all business, and it's clear that this is a highly efficient team effort. Keith has to fly to Mexico right away to apprehend a bail jumper. Veronica promises to organize his ticket by the time he gets to the airport and to book him a car. During this interchange, Veronica is framed in the foreground, while Keith can be seen in his office bustling about and organizing his overnight bag. They bicker about the type of rental car he needs. Last time she booked him a Laser, he wants something cheaper this time. "Fine," she says in frustration, "I'll get you a Crown Vic. Once a cop...." Keith walks back into close up and kisses her; his final words are "And when you go after Jake Kane, take Back-up." "I always do," says Veronica.

It's a smart sequence, establishing as it does that Colantino and Bell can play off each other like a couple of seasoned performers in a screw-ball comedy or a television sitcom. The position of the camera, which is placed so as to capture them both in the frame at once, confirms Klevan's suggestions about the significance of perspective in comedy. Situating Veronica and Keith side by side as they talk at cross purposes focuses attention on the nature of their interaction in a shared space in ways that switching between two characters' points of view would not. The absence of this kind of cutting for most of this scene allows the performers to set their own comic rhythm, to perform for each other as well as for the audience as if they were on a stage. Significantly, when the camera goes in for a close-up, it's the melodramatic moment in the middle of the scene when they are discussing the Kane case.

The same wide framing is used again later in the episode when Keith returns from Mexico. As he walks into the apartment from the left of the screen, Veronica is in the foreground at her desk. Keith is framed behind her by an internal architrave as he announces his successful capture of the bail-jumper and produces the check with a comic flourish, announcing that there will be no dinners in a sack tonight. "Tonight," he quips, "we will eat like the lower middle class to which we aspire." Keith then does a little vaudeville dance to disappear to the right behind the architrave. There's a comic beat as Veronica grins with amusement at his silliness. Keith's head pops back into the frame, as if round the corner of a proscenium arch, to announce it's for real: "Steaks! Fire up the barbecue!" Veronica laughs.

While this scene is clearly played for laughs, its comic effect is enhanced by the positioning of the camera which frames Keith as if on a stage performing for Veronica; the scene which follows, however, switches from comedy to melodrama half way through. As Keith cheerfully bops to the diegetic music while barbecuing the steaks on the verandah of their apartment block, Veronica shows him a photograph of a car parked at the Camelot motel, the one which belonged to whomever Jake Kane was meeting for his extra-marital tryst. Keith's face darkens as he looks at it. His jaw sets, the mood immediately changes. The camera moves in for an intense close-up of his face as he warns Veronica off the case. Her back is to us, but as he walks away, she turns toward the camera, stunned and puzzled. The comedy is over, and Veronica is once again faced with the problem of discovering what is going on: the problem which is driving the thriller narrative. The close-up on her face confirms the seriousness of the moment.

## Ekphrasis, Why?

I initially posed a series of questions asking why anyone would engage in the practice of ekphratic criticism. In the process of trying to perform it with reference to just a few of the many memorable performances and moments to be found in this television series, I hope I may have produced some answers. Looking closely at *Veronica Mars* from the perspective of performance, using Klevan's categories of position, place, and plot as a set of clues to guide me, I've discovered that writing about what happens in the frame has helped me to understand how and why I continue to be engaged by the show. In Klevan's words, this type of analysis requires us as viewers to "slow down, stop or dwell" so that we might be better able to "savour the intensity of an interaction, an intonation or an expression," becoming more aware of the "reverberations" of a moment in order to reflect on the "resonance" it may contain (103). Undertaking this kind of close analysis has both enabled and enhanced my own understanding of how and why this show works for me.

I've also discovered how impossible it is to fully capture in words what is happening on screen and that like other forms of textual analysis, ekphratic criticism is not just about description but also and inevitably, interpretation. What I am offering here is therefore an interpretation of how some of the key performances in *Veronica Mars* conspire to convince me that this is a show which demonstrates the art of television, and the art of performance in the long-form television drama series at its best. What I hope my words on the page have managed to convey is something of the intensity of the experience of watching *Veronica Mars*, revealing the ways in which the performance of the actors on screen may come to move us, even as we watch in stillness.

## Notes

1. I'm thinking here of the French critics writing in *Cahiers Du Cinema* and the evolution of the concept of auteurism which, in claiming that a film had an author, established the basis for a film to be treated as a work of art.

2. See Jason Mittell's discussion of *Dragnet* in his book *Genre and Television* and the essay by Turnbull on *CSI* ("The Hook and the Look"), which also discusses Webb's legacy.

3. As revealed by Rob Thomas in his first interview with the Couch Baron on the fan website, Television Without Pity.

4. Commentator Zach Oat writes: "We Wish She'd Show Up on *Gossip Girl*. She's the voice of the title character, the blogger who narrates each episode and posts plot-stimulating factoids about the main characters online, but she's never been seen. Bell wants to do it, so why hasn't it been did?"

5. "8th Annual Family Television Awards."

## Works Cited

Couch Baron. "Sometimes Those Who Teach Can Also Do: The Rob Thomas Interview, Part I." *TelevisionwithoutPity.* Television without Pity, 2 Mar. 2005. Web. 20 Apr. 2007.

"8th Annual Family Television Awards: November 29, 2006 at the Beverly Hilton, Beverly Hills, California." ANA [Association of National Advertisers], 2007. Web. 21 Jan. 2010.

Klevan, Andrew. *Film Performance: From Achievement to Appreciation.* London: Wallflower, 2005. Print.

Mittell, Jason. *Genre and Television: From Cop Shows to Cartoons in American Culture.* New York: Routledge, 2004. Print.

Naremore, James. *Acting in the Cinema.* Berkley: University of California Press, 1988. Print.

Oat, Zach. "Kristen Bell: Our Unfulfilled Wishes for Her Career." *Televisionwithout Pity.* Television without Pity, n.d. Web. 21 Jan. 2010.

Roscoe, Jane. "Real entertainment: New Factual Hybrid Television." *Media International Australia* 100 (2001): 9–20. Print.

Stern, Lesley, and George Kouvaris. *Falling for You: Essays on Cinema and Performance.* Sydney: Power, 1999. Print.

Thomas, Rob, ed. *Neptune Noir: Unauthorized Investigations into* Veronica Mars. Dallas: BenBella, 2006. Print.

Turnbull, Sue. "The Hook and the Look: *CSI* and the Aesthetics of the Television Crime Series." *Reading CSI: Crime Television Under the Microscope.* Ed. Mike Allen. London: I.B. Tauris, 2007. 15–32. Print.

_____. "Moments of Inspiration: Performing Spike." *European Journal of Cultural Studies* 8.3 (2005): 367–373. Print.

Whedon, Joss. "Ace of Case." *EW.com.* Entertainment Weekly, Oct 14, 2005. Web. 21 Jan. 2010.

# 3

## So Cal Pietà

### *Veronica Mars, Logan Echolls, and the Search for the Mother*

#### RHONDA V. WILCOX

Early in season one, Veronica Mars says in voiceover, "The best way to dull the pain of your best friend's murder is to have your mother abandon you" ("You Think You Know Somebody," 1.5).[1] And in the next episode, her father Keith says to her, "I used to think that solving the [Lilly Kane murder] case was the key to our happiness. Solve the case, and my reputation is restored. Solve the case, and your mom comes home. Solve the case, and you go back to being a normal teenage girl" ("Return of the Kane," 1.6). Veronica Mars is not a normal teenage girl. She is the center of a series which *The Village Voice* called the first ever combination of *Heathers* and *Chinatown*—a description that series creator Rob Thomas happily embraces (Press; "Veronica Mars: Not Your Average"). This young detective is the hero of a show very publicly praised by both Stephen King and *Buffy* creator Joss Whedon; indeed, Whedon and company are such fans that *Buffy* alums Alyson Hannigan, Charisma Carpenter, and Whedon himself have acted on the series. Veronica Mars is one of a set of strong female television characters in the early twenty-first century—such as Xena Warrior Princess, *Alias*'s Sydney Bristow, *Witchblade*'s Sara Pezzini, La Femme Nikita (one character calls Ms. Mars La Femme Veronica ["Clash of the Tritons," 1.12]), and Buffy the Vampire Slayer.[2] Like Buffy before her, Veronica is a Campbellian hero, traveling through strange worlds and dying to her old self to be reborn a greater champion (Cf. Wilcox, Ch. 2–6, and see Zinder in this volume). Like Buffy—and, for that matter, Sam Spade—Veronica fights her battles with a quip in her heart. Like Buffy, Veronica inhabits a series that floats from genre to genre, freely recombining the elements. Certainly there are elements of the *noir* detective and of teen angst.[3] Perhaps most surprisingly, *Veronica Mars* also follows traditional melodramatic romance in the formula described by Janice Radway. All of these entwine in the search for the mother that Veronica must pursue, and the many shapes which that search takes. In particular, the series' ability to balance Veronica's roles as both hero and romance heroine is significant; and Rob Thomas's emblematic season-framing visual of the Pièta combines those hero and heroine roles with the search for the mother.

## The Damaged Hero

*Veronica Mars* begins with the traditional *noir* detective's voiceover, provided by actress Kristen Bell. It is a teenager speaking, but she is just as aware of social strata as Philip Marlowe or Sam Spade. "That's my school. If you go here, your parents are either millionaires or your parents work for millionaires. Neptune, California — a town without a middle class." Stephen King, despite his enthusiastic praise, also says that the series "bears little resemblance to life as I know it." Perhaps that is in part because, as Richard Gess points out, billionaires' kids would normally be in private school. But the series, with Neptune High, showcases an extreme version of the class warfare (and they do use that term) which can be found in any American high school ("Return of the Kane," 1.6). In her flashback life before the time in which the series is set, Veronica was an innocent girl, happily living in the top strata: her father was the sheriff, her best friend Lilly Kane was a software billionaire's daughter who dated a movie star's son, Logan Echolls; Veronica's boyfriend Duncan Kane was Lilly's smart, handsome, popular brother. When Lilly is mysteriously murdered, Veronica's father Keith Mars accuses Lilly's father Jake Kane of killing his own daughter. But Abel Koontz dishonestly confesses to the crime (Kane? Abel? Yes, like *Buffy*, *Veronica Mars* has fun with names).[4] Thus Veronica's father is disgraced and turned out of office; her mother sinks into alcoholism and abandons her impoverished family; Logan accuses her of disloyalty for siding with her father; Duncan has at this point already dropped her; and virtually the whole school turns against her. When she attends an A-lister party to show that they have not beaten her, she is drugged and raped. "You want to know how I lost my virginity? So do I," she says in the pilot. The innocent with her long blonde hair and white dress suffers the death of the maiden; she is, as she says, "no longer that girl." The Veronica we meet has cropped hair and carries a taser.

First in Radway's thirteen steps of the ideal romance is "the heroine's social identity is destroyed" (134). The latter part of this chapter will focus on Radway's romance heroine. To begin with, however, we will consider Veronica as hero. Radway herself notes that her analysis relates to the treatment of the hero in Vladimir Propp's *Morphology of the Folk Tale* (133), which in turn has many features in common with Campbell's monomyth. The order of the elements may vary. Certainly, however, the general elements of Departure / Initiation / Return can be seen: Veronica departs from her socioeconomic status (and innocence); she goes through a long road of trials (as Campbell calls it) in her initiation into the darker side of life; and she is returned to status with a wealthy boyfriend and, later, a new life in college. It may also help to establish that Veronica accomplishes heroic deeds: In episode after episode, she saves others through her courage and intelligence. The first season focuses on long mystery arcs — Lilly's murder, Veronica's rape, her mother's disappearance. But each episode has its own short mystery and a chance for Veronica to help someone. As Logan puts it, "Veronica Mars — saving the world one pointless act at a time" ("Blast from the Past," 2.5). In the first episode, she saves her friend Wallace from a biker gang; in the second episode, she saves the leader of that gang from a false criminal accusation ("Credit Where Credit's Due"). In the third episode, her detective work brings about the reconciliation of a transgendered parent and the son who thought the parent was dead ("Meet John Smith"). She finds missing dogs ("Hot Dogs," 1.19) and locates the school mascot ("Betty and Veronica," 1.16); she also reveals election fraud ("Return of the Kane," 1.6) and clears a student wrongly accused of planning to bomb the school ("Weapons of Class Destruction," 1.18). Most of the time she responds to requests from fellow high school students, requests which become more and more frequent as her reputation grows; but she is able to step outside her high school world as well, for instance when her work on a jury helps protect a young Latina whose claims against two privileged young white men are being discounted ("One Angry Veronica," 2.10).

In many ways, stepping outside her world is key for Veronica. Our hero dies to her old self and then goes to the different world which every hero must explore. The boundaries Veronica heroically crosses are not physical territories, but territories of social and economic class, race and ethnicity, sex and gender. She is propelled through them by her investigation of her best friend's death — the Kane murder, biblically named for the beginning of all murders, with all that this suggests about human participation in evil. A survey of some of the major characters may help to demonstrate Veronica's abilities to cross sociological boundaries most of us cannot. These characters are the hero's helpers, as Propp calls them; and in Veronica's case, they also represent the different worlds of this hero's journey.

## *The Hero's Helpers*

One of my favorite characters is Eli Navarro, a.k.a. Weevil. He is the head of the Hispanic motorcycle gang known as the PCHers (for the Pacific Coast Highway area they dominate). He rules the group and dispenses justice as needed. They steal cars, but he has always insisted that they not sell drugs. In the pilot, Veronica impresses him by helping to keep some of his gang members from being arrested; and in the second episode, Veronica prevents Eli himself from being unjustly jailed. As a result, they become friends or at least allies, though they do not always trust each other.[5] Eli is in fact, despite his difficulties with school, one of the smartest characters in a show filled with smart characters; and it is enjoyable to watch Veronica and Eli try to outsmart each other and then have the fun of explaining themselves to each other afterwards (see, e.g., "Ain't No Magic Mountain High Enough," 2.13). They often do favors for each other. One of the show's great pleasures is seeing petite blonde Veronica, threatened by a member of the upper class, suddenly being backed up by a revving motorcycle gang of, as they call themselves, Mexicans. This has happened so often that I must confess I started thinking of Eli as the deus ex Mexican. If she starts to slip into her earlier naive mindset, Eli is the most likely to call Veronica on it. In the third episode, before she proves his innocence once again, she lets slip that she has suspected him because of his reputation, and he answers: "My reputation? Then ... I guess what everybody says about you is true, too — that you like it a little freaky — that you spy on Duncan Kane — that you send him pictures of yourself. Be honest, Veronica. You think you're this big outsider — but push comes to shove, you're still one of them. You still *think* like one of them" ("Meet John Smith," 1.3). She rises to his challenge, however, and follows the unspoken *noir* hero detective's code of seeing the truth despite the shadows. She is also following the Campbellian hero's path of exploring a different world — Eli Navarro's world.

The "Duncan Kane" Eli mentions, Veronica's first love, the billionaire's son, has mysteriously and suddenly dropped her some time *before* his sister's murder. In the pilot, Veronica's loving dad uses his trademark phrase "Who's your daddy?" and soon after, we learn that the question is not merely rhetorical. Duncan has found out that Veronica may be his half-sister, that Jake Kane may be her biological father; and Duncan immediately stops dating her, understandably choosing not to explain his reasons. Shades of *Chinatown* indeed (and the *noir* touch of incest is also sometimes present in the more gothic of romances). So the hero Veronica has crossed another kind of dangerous line here, it seems. She only months later learns of this possibility — which, among other things, means that she may be the heir to millions of the

Kane billions. But, despite sending off for a DNA test, she decides not to look at the results. As she says, "When I had a chance to learn my paternity, I chose blissful ignorance with a side of gnawing doubt" ("The King of Bling," 1.13). The search for the father, as well as for the mother, is a part of the *Veronica Mars* story, as it is for many a hero (see Millman and Berner; see Leavitt and Leavitt in this volume). She later chooses to sign away her rights to the Kane fortune and only after she has done so learns that her father has also gotten a paternity test which, to their joy, shows that she is his. At the end of the first season, Duncan explains that he, extremely intoxicated, had made love with Veronica at the infamous party after they had broken up and she had been ostracized. (One of the flashbacks reveals that Duncan and Veronica had earlier confessed that they were both virgins, with resultant teasing from Logan and Lilly ["The Wrath of Con," 1.4].) After their lovemaking, Duncan had kept a tormented silence because of fears of possible incest. With the revelation that they are not siblings, Duncan once more becomes her boyfriend and provides Veronica investigative help of the kind only a billionaire's son can — including, for example, providing stationery from his father's company when the occasion calls for it.

Veronica's post–Lilly best friend is a very different sort of person from the Kanes, at first seeming just a simple, normal guy. Wallace Fennel is the sweet, innocent new African American kid on the block. Veronica finds him duct-taped to the school flagpole with a crowd of students standing around gawking at the word "SNITCH" written on his naked chest.[6] She is the only one with nerve enough to cut him down; the others know he has been placed there by the PCHers. This happens before Veronica and Eli become allies; in fact, it starts their relationship too. Wallace is so grateful for Veronica's action that they become fast friends, and despite her reputation as a bitchy slut, he learns that she, like him, is highly moral and loyal. She is also perfectly happy to take advantage of their friendship in the cause of her work. To quote a typical exchange, Veronica asks, "Can you do me a weird favor without asking any questions?" and Wallace replies, "Isn't that the bedrock on which our friendship is founded?" ("Betty and Veronica," 1.16). Wallace conveniently signs up to be an assistant in the school's administrative office, thus becoming a detective's dream source of student records and faculty backgrounds. Furthermore, Wallace, who is only a little taller than Veronica, later becomes a basketball hero, opening up other doors for Veronica's investigations in both high school and college, and enabling him to attend the same college as Veronica, his academic hotshot friend who can quote lines from Pope's *Essay on Man* on request. Like Veronica, Wallace struggles with issues of paternity: he is shocked to learn that the man who raised him is not his biological father, and Wallace leaves for a while to live with his newly discovered parent — and yet another detective — a Chicago cop.

Wallace, as Sue Turnbull notes, "provid[es] a moral compass at those moments when Veronica's desire for revenge blurs her vision" (319), and his approval is one of the reasons Veronica later becomes the girlfriend of Logan Echolls, whom she describes in the pilot as the school's "obligatory psychotic jackass"; Wallace starts to see more in Logan, and lets Veronica know. Veronica and Logan, as mentioned before, have stopped being friends because of Lilly Kane's murder and the subsequent investigation. If Veronica has an equal in slashing wit, it is Logan; and he slashes directly at her for much of the series. He is the promiscuous, racist, classist, drug-using bad boy; he is even accused of murder. Like Veronica and like Eli, however, he is a better person than his reputation would suggest, and that is in part because, like Veronica, he has suffered. In one of the series' most stunning sequences, we see Logan selecting from an array of beautiful belts; it seems the rich boy is adorning himself. But then we hear offscreen that Logan is being beaten by that belt, held in the hand of his movie star father ("Return of the Kane," 1.6). "Cigarette burns and broken noses"— Logan is abused ("Ruskie Business," 1.15). And his mother sits trembling by with a drink in her hand, using alcohol as Veronica's mother did. When Lynn Echolls apparently jumps off the Coronado Bridge, Logan believes that she is still alive and asks Veronica to find her for him. Veronica, who has spent months searching for her own mother, takes the job for free. Though Lynn Echolls cannot be found even by Veronica, the search brings her and Logan together. Veronica's choice not to charge Logan for her work (because, she says, Lynn was always nice to her, and because she knows the loss of a mother herself) is one of the reasons they are later able to cross the socioeconomic barrier and connect with each other. As Roz Kaveney says, "The relationship between Logan and Veronica is precisely what would not normally happen in a teen movie where he would almost always remain an unregenerate villain" (181).

Furthermore Logan, like Veronica's other friends, provides help in her many investigations. Although, like Duncan, he is wealthy, Logan more often provides direct physical aid. When, for example, Veronica is waylaid by a young man she fears is about to bomb the school, she conceals her cell phone so that Logan, with whom she has been acerbically conversing, hears where she is being taken. He shows up in time to punch the guy repeatedly in the face, and when they learn he is a federal agent, does not take kindly to a request that the agent be allowed to speak to Veronica alone: "Dream on, Jump Street," he responds. In the moments afterward, he and Veronica share their first kiss ("Weapons of Class Destruction," 1.18). On at least two other occasions Logan shows up at just the right moment to rescue Veronica with gun (unloaded) or fists, because he is sharp enough to realize when she needs him — a quality of attentiveness Radway attributes to the romance hero — along with promiscuousness (tamed by the heroine), tendencies to physical violence, and high social position, all of which Logan of course has (128–29, 134). Logan is also sharp enough to know his help is not usually needed by this young woman whom Keith Mars calls "my badass action figure daughter" (1.9).

The other of Veronica's main helpers is a young woman, Mac — another misfit, though in this case she is a misfit in her own family. They are, as she says, "Nachos and Nascar," while she is "falafels and Fellini" ("Silence of the Lamb," 1.11). Mac is, like Veronica, brilliant (as Wendy Wagner has pointed out, intelligence is probably Veronica's greatest power). A computer hacker extraordinaire, Mac, like Buffy's Willow, provides valuable help to the hero (she calls herself Q to Veronica's Bond.) Mac is also yet another of the teens with paternity problems: like Logan and Veronica, she is missing a mother, though in an even more twisted fashion: Mac and the snobbish, wealthy Madison Sinclair were switched at birth, as Veronica discovers in one of her investigations ("Silence of the Lamb," 1.11). Her story in particular explores a repeated theme of genetics versus nurture. Her world is the world of the intelligentsia — or rather, of technology, of computers.

So Veronica has a series of helpers, just as Vladimir Propp would expect the hero to do. As Martaus says, "Veronica learns to accept help and rely on friendships in a way no noir detective or adolescent male literary figure does" (78). But while in *Buffy* the Scooby Gang constitutes a family of friends — all of them in relationship to each other and all of them at one point or another virtually equal in importance — even superpower-less Xander saves the day on more than one occasion — here, in *Veronica Mars*, the helpers for the most part have individual relationships to the central character. There is not the happy family group (though before the Fall — before Lilly's death and Veronica's rape — Veronica, Lilly, Logan, and Duncan are in some senses such a group). The helpers here are very separate (with the partial exception of best friends Duncan and Logan). The Mexican biker, the billionaire's son, the African American basketball player, the abused movie star's kid, the misfit middle class computer whiz — all of these show the different worlds Veronica can walk through as she responds to request after request for her help, as more and more people learn of her power to solve mysteries (of course she herself starts simply as a helper for her father, who has become a private investigator). Veronica's helpers also, in a sense, constitute some of her powers — extensions of her own formidable abilities (as is appropriate to Propp's analysis). But they are all, in some senses, rulers in their own domains who pay fealty to Veronica, drawn to her by her intelligence, passion, and integrity, in spite of her Sam Spade shady reputation.

## Losing, Rejecting, and Regaining the Mother

Her passion and intelligence are most ferociously and loyally used in the search for Lilly Kane's murderer — and in the search for Veronica's own mother. The *Veronica Mars* series, in fact, is filled with lost women — as may already be apparent (see Mayer in this volume). Janice Radway argues that "the ideal [romance] heroine's journey toward female selfhood [is] a chronicle of her efforts to both reject and regain her mother" (124), and variations on that theme are numerous in this series. Radway, basing her work in part on Propp and in part on Chodorow's study of the reproduction of mothering, argues that the ideal romance fulfills both the "quest for motherly nurturance" (124) and the quest for a patriarchally powerful lover — both to be found in one extremely male, promiscuous, cruel-seeming, sometimes violent hero who "behind his protective exterior hides an affectionate and tender soul" (128, 134). Logan fills the bill, and many further instances of his nature could be cited; as will later be seen, he will in some senses fill the role of the missing mother as well as the passionate lover.

But to return to the more obvious: the first of the lost women is Logan's girlfriend Lilly Kane. Lilly is presented as psychologically older and wiser than the innocent Veronica; one might consider her a mentor and thus in some senses a mother figure. Lilly and Veronica are linked, paralleled by Lilly's murderer, who turns out to be Aaron Echolls, who, in a grossly Oedipal fashion, has made love with his son's girlfriend and then killed her. (Cf. Beeler in this volume.) In the second season's last episode, Aaron tells Veronica that neither she nor Lilly would shut up — and Radway points out that one of the main qualities of the Romance heroine is her refusal to have her voice silenced (124). The witty Veronica certainly does refuse to be silenced; but Lilly *begins* her story silenced, dead. Lilly is also described as "lov[ing] guys" ("Hot Dogs," 1.19); she has relationships (that we know of) with Logan, Eli, and Aaron Echolls. The young woman of active sexuality is safely dead; and she might be seen as a representation of a hidden part of the more innocent Veronica — a loss in more than one way. It is only after Lilly's death is resolved, after Veronica finds her murderer, that Veronica chooses to become sexually active.

Veronica searches for the murderer of the friend who in some ways represents her own sexual side at the same time as she searches for her mother, the source of nurturance. But she follows Radway's pattern precisely in that she both regains and rejects the mother in order to individuate. In flashbacks we see that this mother clearly loves her daughter; but the show uses alcoholism to represent her weakness. When Veronica finally does locate Lianne Mars, she convinces her mother to enter a 12-week rehab program for which Veronica pays by using all her hard-earned college savings. Near the end of the first season, Lianne unexpectedly returns. She is welcomed by Veronica and Keith. But Veronica discovers that her mother is still drinking. Having checked herself out early, she has wasted Veronica's college money; and having deceived the family, she cannot be trusted. At about the same point in the narrative when Veronica discovers Lilly's murderer and in effect lays her to rest, Veronica also sends her mother away. She has repudiated her mother's weakness and Lilly's wildness, but can now incorporate, in her own way, the nurturance and sexuality they represent. At the end of season one the Oedipal father (Aaron Echolls) has been imprisoned and the weak mother (Lianne Mars) has been sent away — one level of resolution for Veronica and Logan.

In addition to Lilly, Veronica is paralleled with another beautiful blonde young woman who ends up dead. While Veronica and Duncan are broken up, Duncan dates Meg, one of the few nice girls in the school, and a friend of Veronica's. Indeed, Veronica — during the time when she feared she might be Duncan's half-sister — has helped bring the two of them together. Meg is put into a coma as a result of the bus crash that starts the second season and constitutes its season-long mystery. Veronica, toting her sex-ed class plastic baby, finds in a hospital visit that her comatose friend is genuinely pregnant, the mother of Duncan's child. Both Duncan and Veronica dream of Meg asking for help; Duncan dreams of Veronica and Meg together, emphatically presenting them as foils. Meg dies — yet another lost mother; and Duncan, like Veronica's dad, takes care of his daughter, though he must leave his beloved Veronica behind to do so.

Even without direct parallels to Veronica, the other major characters face the issue of the missing mother as well. In Wallace's case, his own mother is firmly in charge in her household, and in fact becomes, for a while, the friend and lover of Veronica's dad while he is separated from her mom — a situation which of course is too happy to endure. For Veronica to have a solid nuclear family would undo the narrative engine. And while Wallace has his virtuous but flawed mother, he confronts the pattern of the lost mother in another way: The young woman he falls for, Jackie, leaves him after a season because she has left her own child back in New York. She has come in search of her father, and has spent some months with him, but realizes that she is perpetuating the pattern and chooses to break it. She returns to mother her own child. As for bad boy Eli Navarro (Weevil), he lives with his grandmother. One more character who is missing a mother, Eli does at least have a maternal figure in his grandmother — a woman who works as a domestic servant in the home of the wealthier families, accentuating the class differences, especially when she is wrongly accused of theft. Like all characters in *Veronica Mars*, she is flawed; she is at first willing to let the younger Eli take the rap for his 18-year-old cousin Ciardo because she knows an 18-year-old's punishment would be worse. But she cooperates with Veronica once she learns Ciardo's fraud was done to buy gifts for a girl (played by Paris Hilton) who, as Mrs. Navarro says, "doesn't like her ice cubes made with tap water" ("Credit Where Credit's Due," 1.2). Eli is determined to graduate from high school mainly because his grandmother so badly wants this mark of modest socioeconomic success for him. One of the most painful moments in the series occurs when the sheriff arrests Eli during the ceremony, in front of his grandmother (now seriously ill), just before he is to receive his diploma. The fact that he does have a mother-figure, if not a mother, may explain some of the virtues of his character, though she is unable to protect him from the harshness of class antagonism. Another relationship that highlights not only emotional but class issues is Mac's loss of her biological mother (as discussed earlier). And even Logan's stepsister Trina (portrayed by *Buffy* alum Alyson Hannigan) is discovered to be an adopted child with a biological mother from a very different social class: the movie star's adoptee is genetically the child of a Neptune High lunch lady.

As for Logan's own mother and her disappearance, it should be recalled that there are clear parallels with Veronica's own mother. Even their names — Lianne and Lynn — echo each other. Both are attracted to wealthy men: Lynn is of course married to a movie star, and Lianne has a long-running affair with her high school sweetheart prom partner, billionaire software magnate Jake Kane. Both women depend on alcohol. Neither is strong enough to help her only child; as noted, Lynn merely listens, clearly suffering, sipping a drink while Aaron beats Logan; Lianne wastes Veronica's hard-won money (earned by her part-time work and detective fees) by leaving her re-hab early. It is true that Lianne leaves town in part because she fears for Veronica's life, having been threatened by Jake Kane's wife; however, that concern for Veronica is inconsistent: when she deceives her family about a relapse into alcoholism and Veronica tells her to leave, she steals a $50,000 reward check that Keith plans to use for Veronica's college money. As for Lynn Echolls, she too, in effect, deserts her child after substance abuse. After a public exposé of Aaron's infidelity, she retaliates. When Aaron then verbally attacks her and threatens to ruin her, Logan angrily defends his mother with the kind of loyalty Veronica had earlier shown hers — though with more violent emotion. The scene takes place at Logan's school, where his parents need to support him at a disciplinary hearing, but his mother runs to her car and tosses pills down her throat, then drives off. Her car is found on the Coronado Bridge, and video that Veronica later discovers seems to show her body falling into the water. Neither mother is there for her child; of the lost women of the series, these — and Lilly — are the most prominent.

All three are marked sexually as well. Veronica's best friend and blonde foil Lilly, as noted, has consensual sex not only with Logan and his father but apparently also Eli (Weevil) Navarro. She thus crosses class lines (more than one person assumes she does so as part of her rebellion against her parents) and in some senses makes equivalent Logan and Weevil, from two different classes. (Weevil's grandmother does domestic work for the Echolls.) Both young men genuinely care for Lilly (as their reaction to her death demonstrates — not to mention Weevil's "Lilly" tattoo). The lily is a flower associated with death, appropriately enough; it is also connected to the idea of purity, which hardly seems appropriate for the joyous wild child Lilly Kane.

As for Lianne Mars, she is adulterous — and Veronica learns this in her detective work. In the pilot, Veronica notes that when her mother abandoned her (when she was still innocent and virginal), she left a note in a unicorn music box. Unicorns, often collected (as figurines) by young girls, are associated in medieval emblems with virgins — maidens who can capture unicorns. This is no medieval Camelot, though; the Camelot, in fact, is the name of the motel where Veronica, in her detective work, inadvertently learns that Lianne has trysts with Jake (Guinevere? Lancelot?). Veronica is forced to confront her mother's adulterous sexuality in the absence of her mother, while she herself has been given the reputation of a "slut" after her drug-dosed rape.

While Veronica confronts dangerous sexuality in the form of Lilly and Lianne (another set of echoing names), Logan confronts it in the form of Lilly and Lynn. As he says, "I loved Lilly, and Lilly loved guys" ("Hot Dogs," 1.19); he knows she was not monogamous, and late in season one learns of her relationship with his father. His mother's sexuality is of a different sort. She is never shown as anything but monogamous. A star herself, however, Lynn is notably presented as an object of sexual desire, especially in "An Echolls Family Christmas" (1.10). At a poker game for teenage boys at the Echolls,' the cry of "Hot chick poolside" reveals the hot chick to be Logan's mom, whom all the boys (even his best friend Duncan) ogle through the glass doors. Only Logan does not rush to the glass; he sits with a cigar in his mouth, a cigar earlier sexualized by double-entendres about "hand-rolling" with Weevil. This poolside / hot wife / ogling teen scene is reiterated in season two, with Logan visiting the home of Dick and Cassidy (Beaver) Casablancas, while their stepmother Kendall swims. Having suffered a bad break-up with Veronica, Logan enters a meaningless affair with Kendall. Or one should not say meaningless: it is uncaring (he once asks her, "Did I hurt your feeling?"— using the grammatical singular to cruel effect), but certainly has meaning: the superficial parallels between Kendall and Lynne suggest, on Logan's part, a sad sort of search for the mother ("Nobody Puts Baby in a Corner," 2.7). Both Veronica and Logan, then, lack the nurturing of a mother but have been forced to contemplate their mothers' sex lives in a way few of us would like to do.

Radway's analysis of the ideal romance hero/heroine relationship suggests that its story allows for a childlike union with another that recreates the early union of mother and child. The bliss of this union provides a feeling of nurturance as well as a sexual object. Veronica and Logan clearly are two damaged characters who deeply long for that union.[7] Though both desperately search for their mothers, Logan is the more damaged; while Veronica's relationship with her father is still strong, Logan's is ghastly to a gothic extent, with repeated physical abuse and overtones of the incestuous through Aaron's relationship with Lilly.

Both Veronica and Logan have other romantic relationships: Veronica's first love is Logan's friend Duncan, and she later becomes seriously involved with college boy Piz (she also dates Deputy Leo). Logan's first love is Lilly; and in addition to having an affair with Kendall, he has a brief relationship with a very young, very innocent blonde whom he targets because of her father's wrongdoing, but whom he comes to care for (and who can be seen as a Veronica-substitute). But Veronica and Logan's relationship in the show is clearly the predominant romance. When Veronica has any major romantic encounter, Logan is there. Not long after the bus crash that kills a group of her classmates, she chooses *carpe diem*— she chooses to have sex with her first love Duncan, whose wealthy parents have moved out of town and who now lives in a hotel for his senior year; when she emerges from the room after that momentous choice, she encounters Logan, who asks, "What's different about you?"— almost the same words her father says hours later ("Driver Ed," 2.2). The first night she kisses Piz, the elevator doors open to reveal Logan as unintended witness (and trying not to mind — and failing ["Un-American Graffiti," 3.16]). Even when she kisses Deputy Leo, Logan is nearby doing a drunken, pantsless *Risky Business* imitation — drunk because of his unhappy realization that his mother is indeed dead ("Ruskie Business," 1.15). The writers do not let Logan leave Veronica's mind (or ours) during her other romantic encounters. He is Radway's "ideal" sensitive bad boy upper-class lover — though he is shown to be something other, too.

## Visual Emblems

Again and again, emotional loss is entangled with the pain that results from the separation of the classes. After all, traditional romance is, in part, a fantasy of overcoming class differences: the young woman marries a wealthy man, whether it is Cinderella and Prince Charming, Jane Eyre and Mr. Rochester, or *Twilight*'s Bella and Edward. But the psychological is just as important as the sociological in the pattern. And Veronica's own strength makes her a hero, not just a heroine. In fact, she even can be seen as both a mother, caring for those in need, and a Christ figure, suffering for the wickedness of this world. She can be *seen* as such in a very literal, visual fashion.

*Veronica Mars* is a visually conscious series. To mention just one example from season one, let me ask you to recall the famous scene in *Citizen Kane* of the long table separating the emotionally distant wealthy husband and wife, Mr. and Mrs. Charles Foster Kane. In the *Veronica Mars* series we have, of course, another wealthy family of Kanes; but this time, there is a child, a teenager, at the table halfway between the feuding parents — Duncan, between Jake and Celeste. The Kane husband and wife are just as distant, and now there is a son placed emotionally between them ("Meet John Smith," 1.3). Certainly the intertextual allusion is plain here.

But there is an even more striking example of an intertextual and intratextual[8] moment which deserves to be recognized for what Matthew Pateman calls the aesthetics of involution (referring both forward and back in the series, as well as simultaneously making reference to other texts). The shot I refer to recognizably recreates Michelangelo's Pietà, the statue in which, after the crucified Christ has been removed from the cross, his wounded body is held by Mother Mary. Veronica is positioned as a Christ figure — and of course at the beginning of the series, she has symbolically died, and then has gone on to save character after character. Thus this visual places her within the Campbellian hero pattern. But also, of course, Logan is taking the role of the mother, fulfilling Radway's requirement that the ideal romance hero be the powerful aggressive male who will nonetheless provide motherly nurturance ("Not Pictured," 2.22). Logan is in part successful in connecting to Veronica because, despite his protestations and raillery, he is genuinely attentive to her; he offers her "whatever you need" (1.21). (His mercurial changes in this regard also fit the romance hero pattern.) We might further note that, of course, there is gender-switching going on here. Yet the whole image tilts farther when the viewer knows that at the beginning of the season this same Pietà image was shot with Veronica in the role of the mother and bad boy Logan in the place of Christ ("Normal Is the Watchword," 2.1).[9]

So at the beginning of the season we see Veronica as the mother figure providing support and nurturance to the very damaged Logan — damaged physically and emotionally. Logan is in the position of the suffering Christ. Though in most ways he is hardly Christ-like, he certainly has suffered unjustly, has been wounded and almost killed for sins he did not commit. The first Pietà scene occurs, in terms of the story, right after Logan, drunk, has stood on the edge of the bridge apparently about to suicide like his mother; it seems that in his search for the mother he is about to follow his mother's path into death. He is there because Veronica herself has brought to light evidence that implicates him in Lilly's murder; and Eli has overheard her suspicions. Eli's gang accosts him, even though he is suicidally standing on the edge of that bridge. Logan knocks Eli unconscious, but the rest of the gang beats him brutally, and one of them, Felix, is knifed to death. Hearing that Aaron (thanks to Veronica and her dad) is now arrested for Lilly's murder, Logan shows up at Veronica's doorstep, and she takes him in. The crossing of the threshold (which can be seen as sexually symbolic) is highlighted because at the end of season one we see Veronica's face framed in the door, saying, "I was hoping it was you," but the audience does not know whom she is letting in; that revelation comes after the broadcast hiatus of the summer months in the first episode of season two. An early scene of the second-season opener is the point at which the first Pièta visual is presented, as well.

Joyce Millman also notes the two Pietà scenes; however, she discusses them in the context of the idea of Veronica's search for a father substitute. Certainly that is an important part of the story. I would also argue, though, that these images very much focus on the mother — the missing mother. Veronica tenderly holds Logan in dim light — far from the harshness we often see in her — a necessary, believable harshness that only makes this tenderness more important. The visual is of Veronica in the place of the Virgin Mother. This delicate, emotionally and visually poignant moment might be troubling if it did not have that wonderful parallel scene framing the second season, wherein Logan takes the position of the mother (2.22). In the first season, there are many episodic mysteries and a pair of season-long mystery arcs, the death of Lilly Kane and the rape of Veronica Mars. During the second season, there are once again many episodic mysteries for Veronica to work on, and one season-long arc: the crash over a cliff of that high school field trip bus, on which Veronica should have been. The resolution of this mystery revises the first season mystery of Veronica's rape; and the revision is surely no romance-novel rape.[10] At the end of season one, it seems a drugged Veronica (who had been given another girl's GHB-laced drink) had, after all, consensual sex — that there was no rape; Duncan's fear that she was his half-sister led to his silence about their intercourse. At the end of season two, Veronica learns that some Neptune boys were abused by their pedophile baseball coach (now the mayor), and that to keep them from going public with the shameful truth, one of them — Cassidy "Beaver" Casablancas — arranged their deaths with a bomb on the bus — killing all the passengers. And the year before, it was Cassidy who raped the unconscious Veronica on the same night that she had sex with Duncan. (In this class-conscious series, the story would have been very different had Veronica's rapist been lower-class; indeed, much of the story is about symbolic rape by the upper class.) She learns the truth, and when Cassidy lures her to the hotel rooftop during a party and threatens her, she tells him she has shared the information with her dad. But the brilliant, twisted Cassidy remotely detonates the plane on which his former coach is being returned to custody — after telling her that he will be killing her father at the same time, on the same plane. Veronica manages to text-message Logan; the two of them together fight off a gun-wielding Cassidy, who chooses to leap to his death rather than face infamy. It is after this devastation that, back at Veronica's apartment on the same couch where Veronica held Logan, we now see Veronica in the position of the Christ-figure, held by Logan.

So now Logan replaces the missing mother, gently cradling Veronica. The Pietà is compelling in part because we recall the Virgin Mother holding the baby Jesus in thousands of other images, while Michelangelo simultaneously makes us see very clearly that she now cradles the form of a man — someone she can no longer protect from the wounds of the world. Now Veronica is that wounded one, and Logan tries to cradle her in the dim light that echoes precisely the image of her earlier attempt to comfort him. At the opening of the episode, Veronica in voiceover says, "So this is how it is: The innocent suffer; the guilty go free; and truth and fiction are pretty much interchangeable." It is the episode in which Aaron Echolls' jury pronounces him not guilty of the murder he did commit — the murder of Lilly Kane. It is also the episode of Veronica's high school graduation. She dreams that her mother and father and she are together — and Lilly is still alive. She is awakened by the smell of bacon; her mother is gone, but her father still nurtures her. Near the end of the episode, after the rooftop scene, she dreams of her father again, and is awakened again by the smell of bacon: Now Logan is cooking for her, mothering her, just as her father has done. The dreadful moment when she realizes it is not her father — that Cassidy's actions were not a dream — is immediately followed by the shock of relief: Keith enters the kitchen to explain that he was not on the plane Cassidy exploded. Logan slips away, but both his cooking and motherly embrace in the Pietà scene show that he has filled the hole left by Veronica's mother, just as she has done for him.

Radway does indeed make the case for the ideal romance as expressing that longing for blissful union lost with the mother to whom we are no longer joined, and in *Veronica Mars*, both the events of the narrative and the visual image discover the mother for us. I think we should remember, however, that Rob Thomas chose to show us a mirror set of images — at the season's beginning and end — with both Veronica and Logan mothering each other. In terms of the balance of gender, this visual (not to mention the nature of Veronica's character) is significant. This romance heroine seems to be a third-wave feminist, as well.

Furthermore, the Pietà image does recall the hero. One of the great examples of Campbell's hero story — the hero who suffers, descends, and is reborn — is Jesus. Like Logan, Veronica is hardly a full-fledged Christ-figure. But she is someone who suffers while trying to do right in a world of evil; and the Pietà image calls that to mind, as well as the idea of the sorrowing mother. I find myself enjoying the fact that, in these paired images, Veronica begins as the mother and ends as the hero.

Rob Thomas thus demonstrates a master's use of television's opportunity for temporally extended visual patterns to heighten narrative and character. In the last season of *Veronica Mars*, the narrative moves into more emphasis on the *noir*; that fine balance between the elements of the hero-story and the ideal romance is lost. But the vividness of Rob Thomas and company's So Cal Pietà is an emblem of the complex beauty of this series. And it may tell us that in Veronica Mars, we have both a heroine and a hero.

# Notes

1. "So Cal Pietà: Veronica Mars, Logan Echolls, and the Search for the Mother" was presented in an earlier form at the Popular Culture in the South Conference, Savannah, Georgia, 5–7 October 2006.

2. For discussion of this group of characters, see Early and Kennedy's collection *Athena's Daughters: Television's New Women Warriors.*

3. On the combination of *noir* and adolescent narrative in the series, see Alaine Martaus.

4. See the chapter titled "'I Think I Can Name Myself': Naming and Identity in *Buffy the Vampire Slayer*" in my *Why Buffy Matters*; and see Beeler and Mayer, this volume, on Veronica's own name.

5. Martaus notes that Veronica's partnerships with Eli and Wallace "cross lines of gender and race" (82).

6. Lynne Edwards notes that the spelling is actually "SNICH," and she terms the scene "lynching, Neptune-style" (75).

7. Chodorow's study is based on the idea that females reproduce patterns based on the relationship with the same-sex parent, the mother. Radway focuses on the union

with the ideal romance male as substituting for the female's childhood union with the mother. It is therefore all the more interesting to see Rob Thomas's paralleling of Logan's search for his mother with Veronica's search for hers. Though Logan's search might simply be seen as Oedipal, it is complicated by the parallel.

8. I use the term *intratextual* to refer to allusions made not to other texts (intertextual) or to the world outside the text (extratextual) but to another moment within a long text such as a television series; see *Why Buffy Matters* 193.

9. Both episodes (2.1 and 2.22) are written by Rob Thomas and directed by John Kretchmer (who also directed for *Buffy the Vampire Slayer*); for the second, the story is by Thomas with the teleplay co-written by John Enbom.

10. On some of the issues of romance-novel rape, see Radway 141–44. On representations of rape see also Whitney and Mayer in this volume.

## Works Cited

Berner, Amy. "Daddy Dualities." Thomas 58–70. Print.

Campbell, Joseph. *The Hero with a Thousand Faces*. 2d ed. Princeton: Princeton University Press, 1968. Print.

Chodorow, Nancy. *The Reproduction of Mothering: Psychoanalysis and the Sociology of Gender*. Berkeley: University of California Press, 1978. Print.

Early, Frances, and Kathleen Kennedy, eds. *Athena's Daughters: Television's New Women Warriors*. Syracuse: Syracuse University Press, 2003. Print.

Edwards, Lynne. "On the Down-Low: How a *Buffy* Fan Fell in Love with *Veronica Mars*." Thomas 72–80. Print.

Gess, Richard. Conversation with the author. September 9, 2006.

Kaveney, Roz. *Teen Dreams: Reading Teen Film and Television from* Heathers *to* Veronica Mars. London: I.B. Tauris, 2006. Print.

King, Stephen. "Confessions of a TV Slut." *Entertainment Weekly* 31 Mar. 2006: 72. Print.

Martaus, Alaine. "'You Get Tough. You Get Even': Rape, Anger, Cynicism, and the Vigilante Girl Detective in *Veronica Mars*." *Clues: A Journal of Detection* 27.1 (Spring 2009): 74–86. Print.

Millman, Joyce. "Daddy's Girl." Thomas 46–57. Print.

Pateman, Matthew. *The Aesthetics of Culture in* Buffy the Vampire Slayer. Jefferson, NC: McFarland, 2006. Print.

Press, Joy. "The Teen Beat: Regarding the Geekiness of High Schoolers." *VillageVoice. com*. The Village Voice, 30 Aug. 2004. Web. 29 Mar. 2010.

Propp, Vladimir. *Morphology of the Folk Tale*. Trans. Laurence Scott. 2d ed. American Folklore Society Bibliographical and Special Series 9; Indiana University Research Center in Anthropology, Folklore, and Linguistics Publication 10. Austin: University of Texas Press, 1968. Print.

Radway, Janice. *Reading the Romance: Women, Patriarchy, and Popular Literature*. Chapel Hill: University of North Carolina Press, 1984. Print.

Thomas, Rob, ed. *Neptune Noir: Unauthorized Investigations into* Veronica Mars. Dallas: BenBella, 2006. Print.

Turnbull, Sue. "*Veronica Mars*." *The Essential Cult TV Reader*. Ed. David Lavery. Lexington: University Press of Kentucky, 2010. 314–21. Print.

"Veronica Mars: Not Your Average Teen Detective." DVD Feature. *Veronica Mars: The Complete Second Season.* Warner Brothers, 2006. DVD.

Wagner, Wendy. "'I'll Destroy You Worse': Veronica Mars as Post-Buffy Feminist Heroine." Popular Culture in the South Conference / American Culture in the South Conference: Jacksonville, FL, 6–8 Oct. 2005.

Whedon, Joss. "*Buffy*'s Creator Gazes into the Future of TV." *TV Guide* 26 Dec. 2005: 26. Print.

Wilcox, Rhonda V. *Why Buffy Matters: The Art of* Buffy the Vampire Slayer. London: I.B. Tauris, 2005. Print.

# 4

# "Who's Your Daddy?"
## *Issues of Fatherhood*
### SARAH A. LEAVITT AND LEWIS A. LEAVITT

"Who's your daddy?" Keith Mars jovially calls to Veronica as he is carried away on a stretcher at the end of Season 1 of *Veronica Mars*. The juxtaposition of his medical condition — severe — and his banter is made more poignant because his paternity had been in question for much of the previous year. Perhaps Veronica's only moment of unfiltered joy of the entire three-season series was a result of finding out that Keith was, indeed, her father; and her moment of deepest pain was the moment she thought he was dead. In presenting a complex yet integral father-daughter relationship, the show breaks new ground in teenage broadcast media with Keith and Veronica Mars. But what does fatherhood mean on *Veronica Mars*? How is Keith and Veronica's relationship tested? Have the writers, yearning to depict a new kind of father, paid a high cost — the loss of a stable mother figure? How does the Veronica-Keith dyad compare with other parenting relationships on the program, and how does it push the high school drama genre's tolerance for strong parents? Perhaps most importantly, how does Keith and Veronica's relationship challenge the *noir* genre by giving each a stable partner, while simultaneously fulfilling the *noir* need for tragic couplings?

The relationship between Veronica and Keith is one of the more unusual and delightful parts of this complex show, and merits discussion and exploration. The strength that Veronica gains from her father's devotion arguably accounts for the tempering of her desire to avenge both her own family and her various clients. Her frequent deviation from his rules only serves to elucidate both his moral grounding and her inner struggles. *Veronica Mars* pushes the familiar against the subversive and constantly treats Keith and Veronica — rather than any romantic entanglement — as the central relationship in the show. In a key theme throughout the first season, the very issue of paternity is interrogated. What is paternity? Is it love, protection, stability ... or biology? At one point Veronica declares, as she shreds the DNA test results sight unseen, that behavior trumps biology: Keith is her father no matter the outcome. As she says to him, "The hero is the one [the parent] who stays" ("Meet John Smith," 1.3).

Veronica and Keith's relationship can usefully be compared to the troubling relationships that the other children of Neptune have with their parents (Berner). Here again the confrontation between nature and nurture evokes the teenage fantasy of a search for the true parent. The fairytale trope of hidden "noble" birth is transformed into a more plebeian reality for both Veronica — when she discovers she is not, after all, Jake Kane's daughter and therefore not an heiress — and her friend Mac. Cindy "Mac" Mackenzie, in fact, was switched at birth with '09er (wealthy) Madison Sinclair, and both Mac and Madison live with parents who misunderstand them. When Mac makes the decision to stay with her non-biological parents, she wistfully admits that they have done the work of raising her, even when she does not fit in with the rest of the family ("Silence of the Lamb," 1.11). Veronica respects Mac's painful decision and is forced to think about the meaning of parenting.

The curse of bad parenting permeates the show: while many teenager-focused shows emphasize only the cluelessness and social clumsiness of parents, *Veronica Mars* exposes the brutal destructiveness of parental misconduct. In a misguided effort to protect his son, for instance, Jake Kane bungles his daughter Lilly's murder case. By the end of the series, son Duncan has long ago fled the country and Jake is a crushed man who has been unable to leave behind his demons. Duncan himself has left town with his baby daughter to prevent his ex-girlfriend's abusive parents from raising the baby. The Casablancas brothers, Dick and Cassidy, have been morally and socially crippled by the actions of their father, who squandered the family's money and fled the country, leaving them with Kendall, an unlikely — and non-nurturing — stepmother. Jackie Cook's father Terrance, though a wealthy ex-athlete, was a murder suspect who made his daughter's life at school miserable and encouraged her to leave town and return to her mother. Logan Echolls' father Aaron — a celebrity beloved by fans but violent at home — provided him with a lifetime of verbal and physical abuse. Aaron's treachery with both of Logan's girlfriends was but one feature of a long, troubled relationship. Even the fathers of relatively minor characters — Hannah Griffith's cocaine-addicted liar of a father, for example — did not fare much better.

With the stand-out exception of Wallace's mother Alicia Fennel, Neptune's matriarchs are a cohort of incompetent, flawed, desperate, drug-and-alcohol-riddled individuals. *Veronica Mars* thus reads against the history of television dramas where the mother is usually the source of stability and common sense. In their examination of the angst and turmoil of family relationships, the writers have offered us instead the pathology of the flawed mother. Even Eli "Weevil" Navarro's grandmother, ostensibly having provided a safe home for her family, knowingly lets Weevil go to jail for a crime he did not commit ("Credit Where Credit's Due," 1.2). In the context of the class warfare that is Neptune, it is of interest that it is "parents who work for millionaires," all of them single parents, who provide empathy and protective love. Indeed, we learn late in Season 2 that it is Jackie's waitress mother (and not her wealthy father) who has provided her with the most protection, in caring for Jackie's son. Rob Thomas's story captures our attention by focusing on core issues of teenagers and young adults in the maelstrom of class conflict. The story subverts the teenage dream of wealth, celebrity and power by exposing the rot of family dysfunction as a characteristic of Neptune's ruling class. Veronica and Keith, a family living on the fringes of '09er culture, valorize single fatherhood while simultaneously exposing the fault lines in Neptune's — and America's — more traditional family structures.

As a father and a daughter watching this program, we were encouraged by the complex portrayal of the Veronica-Keith relationship and convinced of its significance in the history of teen relationships on television. The father-daughter relationship is central to the plotting of both mysteries-of-the-week and the arc mysteries of the series: indeed, Veronica and Keith are the only two characters who appear in every episode. The relationship is shown on the show in many ways, including: protection, power struggles, and domesticity. As we have seen, Keith and Veronica must protect each other, both literally saving each other's lives ("Leave It to Beaver," 1.22; "Nevermind the Buttocks," 2.19). The power struggles emphasize how Veronica sometimes uses Keith's lessons inappropriately. But there is a positive context: The domestic scenes often revolve around food, in which the story is told through glimpses of an altered — yet precious — normalcy.

## Teen Dramas

In most television teen dramas, the parents are peripheral at best. Before, or after, *Veronica Mars*, few explored the father-daughter bond in any kind of depth. It is a truism of teen dramas that, though there is one central character with two parents, most teens do not live with both parents. In the past few decades significant two-parent families on teen dramas have included the Walshes of *Beverly Hills, 90210* (1990–2000) and the Wilsons of *90210* (2008– ), the Cohens of *The O.C.* (2003–07), the Chases on *My So-Called Life* (1994–95), and the Weirs on *Freaks and Geeks* (1999–2000).[1] In each case, the parents are portrayed as out of touch to the point of being a comic foil to the "real" players in the show. The "bad parents"—Ryan Atwood's on *The O.C.*, Rayanne Graff's on *My So-Called Life*, and Kim Kelley's on *Freaks and Geeks*, provide backstories for their teens' bad behavior. The "good parents" are there at the end of the day to give lectures and hugs, but their storylines are not influenced by those of their children. A prominent counter-example of a healthy two-parent family are Tami and Eric Taylor of *Friday Night Lights* (2006– ), which is considered more of a community drama than a teen-centered story.

On *Dawson's Creek* (1998–2003), Dawson Leery is the only one with a stable family life: Joey Potter's mother has died and her father is in prison and Jen Lindley's parents have abandoned her. Dawson's parents fail him miserably, however, in the first season and, though they are rehabilitated—and even remarried—they are never able to offer him anything more than the occasional inspirational talk. His parents represent stability and comfort, but they do not factor into most of his storylines. On *One Tree Hill* (2003– ), Nathan Scott files for minor independence from his domineering father and drug-addicted mother, while Peyton, Brooke, and Rachel's surviving parents all live out of town and Hayley's are off-screen. The short-lived *Hidden Palms* (2000) started off the pilot with Johnny Miller's father's suicide. On *Gossip Girl* (2007– ), all of the main characters live with only one parent by the end of the first season. *Friday Night Lights*, notable for the strong relationships in the Taylor family, otherwise fits in with the teen drama's penchant for troubled child-father relationships. Of the main characters, Tyra, Tim, Smash, Matt, and Lyla, most have absent fathers from the start or soon thereafter. Matt Saracen has one of the more difficult relationships with his father, a soldier living overseas in Iraq. Matt is left behind to care for his ailing grandmother, without a father figure other than his football coach. On *Vampire Diaries* (2009– ), like the long-running *Party of Five* (1994–2000), the main characters' parents die off-screen before the first episode. Elena and her brother Jeremy live with an aunt whose parenting skills are minimal at best.

Single parents on teen dramas have tended to be single mothers. Three of these can serve as examples: Buffy's mother Joyce Summers on *Buffy the Vampire Slayer* (1997–2003), Rory's mother Lorelai Gilmore on *Gilmore Girls* (2000–07), and Lucas's mother Karen Roe on *One Tree Hill*. Buffy's mother spends two seasons in complete ignorance that her daughter is a violent vampire slayer, leaving her training to father-figure Rupert Giles (Wilcox 26). Buffy's mother doesn't live to see the end of the series and indeed her death emphasizes the important stabilizing role she had in her daughter's life, as Buffy becomes unhinged afterwards and almost unable to go forward. Buffy's relationship with her mother is based on the idea that she knows about the world (and the underworld) whereas Joyce is ignorant of the evil that surrounds her and cannot help her slayer daughter navigate the Hellmouth and its demons (Williams).

Lorelai and Rory on *Gilmore Girls* have a complex, two-sided relationship — complete with a "break-up" in Season 6. For the most part throughout the series, however, the two are shown more as best friends than mother-daughter, talking frequently on the phone when Rory is away at school and eating most of their meals at a local diner when both are in town. Much of their relationship, in fact, is based on the idea that Lorelai is not a traditional mother: she does not cook, for example. But in the end, she has taught her daughter the important values of forgiveness, relentless pursuit of goals, and loyalty. Rory memorably says to her mother at the end of the series: "You've given me all I need." On *One Tree Hill*, Karen began the show having made a singular choice: to keep her son Lucas away from his real father, even when he could have offered financial security. Though she became a peripheral character, the entire premise of the show was based on her decisions and Lucas always showed her fierce loyalty.

Two-parent families, dysfunctional families, and strong single mothers, then, have much recent precedent on network television dramas. For in-depth, nuanced treatment of single fathers, however, television has been more remiss. Certainly, comedies have showcased single fathers, from 1960s-era shows such as *My Three Sons* (1960–72), in which widower Steve Douglas raises his children, the short-lived sitcom *Gidget* (1965–66), and *The Courtship of Eddie's Father* (1969–72), in which Tom Corbett, with much help, raises his son Eddie, to 1980s shows such as *Full House* (1987–95) and *My Two Dads* (1987–90). There are certainly many portrayals of single fatherhood in children's literature, notably in *Nancy Drew*, and in movies, from *To Kill a Mockingbird* (1962) to *Pretty in Pink* (1986) to Eddie Murphy's *Imagine That* (2009). In recent teen dramas, perhaps Rufus Humphrey on *Gossip Girl*, single father to Jenny and Dan, is a signal example. But Rufus is not presented as being particularly effective in interceding in a positive way in his children's lives, other than to make his signature waffles. Rarely, if ever, has the father-daughter relationship *itself* been so central to the plot of a teen-centered television show as on *Veronica Mars*.

Veronica's most important relationship is with her father; she has no clique to fall back on. Though she builds a cadre of devoted friends, they rarely interact in friendly ways with one another. As she says in the pilot, even when Keith has hidden information from her, he's the one person she can love and trust completely. Her father trusts her in complicated ways: he knows she lies to him about small things frequently — "I don't belieeeeeeve you," he memorably says when she pretends to need the camera for a school project ("Look Who's Stalking," 2.20) — but he believes *in* her enough to know that she always has a bigger, better purpose in mind. Furthermore, he sees her not just as strong but also as capable and takes her seriously as an adult without condescension, giving her real responsibility in the office well before she earns her private investigator license. Their relationship is more than an aside on this television show: indeed, it forms the backbone without which the series could not stand.

Critical discussions of teen television series, most notably *Buffy the Vampire Slayer*, commonly note the absent biological father and concentrate on the psychological dimensions of father substitutes and mothers' roles (Battis). It is in *Veronica Mars* that we encounter an unusually strong father-daughter bond and significant elements of daughter-father identification. The internal and external struggles of this relationship, emblematic of teenagers' developmental struggle on their path to adulthood (Steinberg), is explored with unusual nuance in *Veronica Mars*. This struggle is notable for its centrality in such a series and part of why *Veronica Mars* matters for adolescents. The valence of this potentially stormy bond has a long history in literature, echoing Shakespeare's examination of and insight into the reciprocity of domination and defiance between fathers and daughters (Dreher 11; 41). The power of this struggle's trajectory is found in both its dynamic arc, as Keith and Veronica both strive to define their bond even as outside influences work to force its re-interpretation, and in its poignant depiction when its strength is tested.

## Protection

As Keith and Veronica navigate their new life without wife-and-mother Lianne, they spend much time protecting each other, or trying to, from perceived psychological and physical danger. From the beginning, we realize that Veronica has given up a lot to protect her father, enduring constant attacks at school. She made the choice to believe in him, defend him, and protect him from detractors when he risked (and lost) his career for accusing Jake Kane of his daughter Lilly's murder. However, for most of the series, it is

Keith who tries to protect his daughter while she resists and finds ways to get around his barriers.

In the pilot, Keith tries to hide from Veronica the fact that Lianne is back in town and conducting some sort of business — sordid or otherwise — with her former flame Jake Kane. Veronica, who does not yet realize the extent of her mother's relationship with her ex-boyfriend's father, accepts that Keith is trying to protect her, but vows nonetheless to get to the bottom of the mystery. In fact, Keith has hidden much of his research on the Lilly Kane murder from his daughter in a locked safe. When Veronica shows him the license plate of the car that she observed meeting Jake at the Camelot Motel, he forbids her from looking further into the case. Veronica, of course, ignores the request and ends up tracking her mother to Arizona. Thus, early in the series, we see an extended story of Veronica evading the protective wall Keith has tried to build around her. It ends with her trying to crawl back in, realizing that she needs Keith even as she resists his rules.

Veronica spends a great deal of time in Season 1 generally thinking and worrying about her mother. Lianne Mars is a complex entity for the father-daughter dyad: she threatens their bond. Instead of the mother being the glue that holds the family together, she eats away at it in the first season, with her previous affair with her high school sweetheart Jake literally coming back to cast doubt over Keith's paternity. The discovery of Jake and Lianne's affair is what broke up Veronica with her first love, Jake's son Duncan (who, if Veronica's father was Jake, would be her half-brother), but more crucially it threatened to nullify the relationship she had with the most important person in her life, her father.

The lengths that both Veronica and Keith go to in order to protect each other from Lianne demonstrate their reluctance to deal openly with the threat she caused. When Veronica throws away the results of the paternity test, she demonstrates her faith in the sanctity of her relationship with Keith, whether or not he is her biological father; she also silently forgives Lianne for making her doubt the relationship, which she now realizes is stronger than blood. This is shown by her renewed confidence and her putting aside biological probing of their relationship while she continues to test the psychological and social bond (Kaveney 179). That Keith goes through with the test shows not his denial of its importance but his need for his bond to be verified, an act that proved important to Veronica as well. Her delight at learning he really is her father indicates that certainly biology is an important factor. She is relieved to have proved that she descended from a person she believes in rather than the shady Jake Kane.

Despite their trust, much of Veronica and Keith's relationship consists of hiding things from each other (Ramos 104). In fact, Veronica hides some of the most significant and frightening moments of her life from her father, preventing him, in effect, from protecting her from the things of which she is most afraid. She never tells him she was raped at a party while in high school, an event which has driven much of her anger and resentment toward the '09ers. This is information known by Keith's biggest professional rival, Sheriff Lamb, of which Keith himself is unaware. The fact that Logan Echolls knows the whole truth about the night of Shelly's party means that he necessarily has responsibility to understand the significance of that secret she has never shared even with her father. Therefore, when Logan breaks that trust in Season 3 by sleeping with Madison Sinclair, Veronica cannot forgive him. Her grief over that incident seems out of proportion only if one ignores the significance of Logan's knowing what Keith did not: that Madison was the person who gave Veronica the drugged drink at the party, leading to her rape. Logan thus demonstrated to her that he was no longer a proper caretaker of her most painful secret, leaving her to bear it alone.

Veronica's personal experience fuels her need in the third season to find the Hearst Rapist. Veronica's own encounter of having her head partially shaved as a warning by part of the team of rapists ("Of Vice and Men," 3.7) is another secret she kept from her father and another thing that — though she is comforted after the fact by both Logan and Keith — she shares only with Logan. In fact, Keith — though he certainly warns her away from that case, worries about her, and comforts her — does not know the extent of her involvement in the case, and therefore cannot ultimately protect her from the sexual vulnerability and violence she encounters as a young woman. This perhaps emphasizes the limits of the father-daughter relationship, as there are limits to what can be discussed. Keith promises that he's only a phone call away at any given time, but, in fact, he is not always there to help her, as her experience on the roof of the Neptune Grand when Cassidy Casablancas tries to kill her ("Not Pictured," 2.22) and when she fears for her life while hiding in Moe's closet ("Spit & Eggs," 3.9) make clear. When Mac's roommate Parker Lee shows up with the rape whistle at the end of "Spit and Eggs," it is a triumph for Parker personally. But it is also a purposeful departure (as was the finale of Season 2, for different reasons) from the origin myth of the show, which included Keith's heroic rescue of his daughter during her final battle with Aaron Echolls. The first season arc established Keith as Veronica's appropriate rescuer and therefore his absence was felt more acutely both on the Neptune Grand roof and in the corridors of Hearst College's Bennis Hall (Millman 58).

## Power Struggle

When we meet the Mars family in Season 1, they have just undergone a major transformation in their community status: Keith no longer represents the law: he has lost the position of sheriff and has become a private investigator. This creates a way for Veronica to have more leeway in how she pursues her cases. By the end of the series, Keith has come full circle and is reinstated in the sheriff's office, if temporarily, moving Veronica's less-than-legal actions into the spotlight. Indeed, throughout the series, Keith sticks fairly close to the law. Though he often falsely impersonates people — even federal agents — there are lines he will not cross. Conversely, Veronica tests fairly significant boundaries of legality when she works on her cases. Her willingness to deceive involves several actions of which Keith disapproves: getting friends in trouble; breaking federal law; and manufacturing fake ID cards for underage drinkers. Sometimes Keith knows about these breeches and looks the other way, and other times he is deeply disappointed in her for her actions.

In the first season, as Veronica gains experience in private investigating through helping fellow Neptune High students locate missing parents, find missing money, and get even with ex-boyfriends, her law-breaking habits are relatively minimal. She does, however, run afoul of her father when she bugs a potted plant and has Wallace bring it to his mother's office at Kane Software. Keith is angry, not only because Veronica has threatened his relationship with Alicia but also because she has selfishly put both of their friends in jeopardy. The incident is only one of many where Keith questions Veronica's tactics. Among her most significant violation of Keith's moral code is in the planning and execution of Duncan's escape to Mexico ("Donut Run," 2.11). Though Keith, of course, protects her from the FBI and lies for her, he is furious that she has "played" him and done such significant damage to his trust of her judgment. His realization that his tutelage in the techniques of the private investigator has directly led to her deception is perhaps at the bottom of his despair. However, even after this serious rift between them, Keith does not offer consequences or punishment to his daughter. Their relationship continues to be one in which Veronica tests the boundaries and refuses to be stopped by Keith's disapproval. In this way their relationship is somewhat lopsided, as Veronica is unable and unwilling to temper her own actions to humor — or honor — her father.

Keith's becoming acting sheriff again in Season 3 after the death of Sheriff Lamb marks an important moment in the story of Keith and Veronica's relationship. His square footing on one side of the law stands in strong contrast to her continuation of business as usual. When he discovers that somebody has been making fake ID cards for underage drinkers in Neptune, and that one of these boys has drunkenly wandered into a fatal car accident, he is horrified to discover that his daughter has had an indirect role in the incident (though she did not provide an ID for this boy). She has always seen fake IDs as a carrot to lure her friends and even acquaintances into helping her solve crimes. Indeed, even before her mystery-solving days, she and Lilly obtained fake drivers' licenses. She sees the IDs as part of a game she is winning against Sheriff Lamb, not as a tool of teenage destruction. When Keith confronts Veronica it is obvious that not only is he disappointed in her actions but that he is disappointed in himself for his lack of ability to protect Neptune from his daughter's deception. Though he is somewhat impressed with her for making the best fake IDs in town, he is nonetheless upset at her lack of remorse. At the end of the series, when Veronica's actions again threaten to get her in serious trouble, Keith goes outside his own ethical comfort zone and purposefully destroys the evidence of her climbing the fence at Jake Kane's mansion. He does so without wavering. He may still be disappointed in her for rushing into cases without proper protection, but he is also proud that she solved her mystery. That he is less angry at this major transgression than he was at her manufacture of fake ID cards indicates that he recognizes and is in awe — if not fear — of her power, and understands that she intends to use that power for good, at least as she sees it.

Of course, Veronica is not the only one to transgress. Keith has his own imagined moral boundary lines and is unafraid to intimidate his foes, whether Alicia's destructive tenant or Jake Kane himself, whom Keith tried to browbeat into confessing to Lilly's murder, a crime for which Kane was not directly guilty. Keith's choices ultimately destroy his chances of winning the sheriff's position in season two and, presumably, again in season three. Veronica stands by him through all of these morally questionable moves, though she draws her own line when he begins to date a married woman, something she has seen so many men do in her line of work, and something she simply cannot condone.

Ultimately, Keith has taught Veronica the techniques she needs to not only solve crimes but also break the law; he has taught her how to trick authorities but also how to exact vengeance. She has used his methods, but not always in ways of which he might approve. Indeed, the greatest compliment she can give him — taking the private investigator exam, wanting to follow at least partly in his career path — is mitigated by her actions at the end of the series. Prioritizing vengeance over anything else, she is responsible for her own downfall. She can never be an FBI agent because she does not have enough respect for the law, and her father will never be elected sheriff because he cannot stop her, cannot reject her, and will always cover up her crimes. The two of them end the series where they started — outcasts from the careers they ultimately want, outsiders in a society to which they cannot conform. Veronica's futile vote for Keith in the final scene of the series demonstrates that even as she has ruined his career, she remains her father's biggest supporter: "You know I love you, right?" she asks in the finale ("The Bitch Is Back," 3.20). She recognizes her part in his fall, even if they both know that, despite everything, she would do the same thing again. Veronica and her father share the role of tragic heroes. They seek justice but break the law. They help others but hurt themselves.

## Domesticity: Home and Food

The setting of Veronica Mars in Neptune, California, is sunny and bright but the atmosphere of moral ambiguity and transgression has the taste of film *noir* (Horsley). The bright sun of Neptune is often filtered through dark colored glass, leaving shadows and tempering the light. In the *noir* world that *Veronica Mars* inhabits, most families are unhappy at home, and most unhappiness is linked directly with home life. The happy home life of the Mars family is set in contrast to the experiences of the '09ers in their fancy mansions. Logan's father rigged the pool house to make illicit sex tapes with his son's girlfriend, and the home is threatened by violence both when Aaron beats up his daughter Trina's boyfriend and in a scene that shows Aaron about to use a belt on his son. The house is eventually burned to the ground. The Kane house, portrayed as a somber, sterile place, carries the ghost of Lilly, killed near the swimming pool. When Veronica visits Gia Goodman's house ("Nobody Puts Baby in a Corner," 2.7) the obsessive organization of the guests' belongings speaks to her of underlying family dysfunction. Meg Manning's family problems are also given an architectural component when Veronica discovers Meg's little sister being forced to hide in a closet.

Veronica and Keith's domestic realm is seen in contrast to these sorrowful places. The Mars apartment is the site of healing, especially for Veronica and Logan, who comfort each other in their Pietà-framed couch poses ("Normal Is the Watchword," 2.1; "Not Pictured," 2.22; see Wilcox, this volume), but also for Veronica and Keith as they are reunited at the end of Season 2 and continue to share the domestic space in Season 3. It is during Season 2, when Veronica breaches the domestic space by finding a passageway between their apartment and a hideout for Duncan, that the norm of inviolability of the Mars apartment becomes most evident ("Donut Run," 2.11). Her fierce desire to protect Duncan's daughter from being raised by Meg's abusive parents — in other words, to protect the single father and his daughter to the detriment of her own relationship with Duncan — drives her here. By passing baby Lilly's diapers through the cupboard, Veronica has literally cut into the fabric of the apartment. Keith's fury at uncovering her secret is magnified by this particular deception. The Mars apartment is a place where Veronica must feel safe: when she is angry with her father for dating a married woman, she shows her distress by physically leaving the house, the sacred space she shares with the most important person in her life. To her, Keith has not only been responsible for broken marriage vows, but has relinquished the moral high ground he had in his relationship with the adulterous Lianne and in his dealings with hundreds of infidelity cases at work. Though Keith at first sets aside her moralistic rants about his lover Harmony, he must struggle with that relationship, ultimately, by himself. Surely her rejection of not only him but his house makes a significant impact.

Mealtimes are an important way for *Veronica Mars* to tweak the ideal of domesticity. Consistently, the Mars family is shown with eating habits that speak to speed and convenience, rather than nutrition and traditional home cooking, beginning in the pilot, when Keith extols the virtues of orange powder on macaroni and cheese. Food helps tell the father-daughter story: they share celebratory meals at important times in their lives. When Keith finds a bond-jumper in the same episode, he gleefully prepares steak on the hibachi, proclaiming "no sack dinners tonight. Tonight, we eat like the lower-middle class to which we aspire!" as he celebrates success through food with his only family.

Food becomes an important marker of how others relate to the Mars duo. When Keith dates Veronica's guidance counselor in the first season, Rebecca's attempts to make dinner for the Mars family are futile. The family bond is restored only when Veronica and her father sit alone together with a lopsided birthday cake, intruders and their nutritious meals having been shut out of the picture. When Keith, Logan, and Veronica sit down to a meal together ("Charlie Don't Surf," 3.4), apparently the first time during the winding course of the relationship that this has occurred, Keith makes an effort to offer a complete dinner to Logan. This family meal — though deeply uncomfortable in many ways for Veronica, ever worried about her unpredictable boyfriend — actually serves to allow viewers to see the Mars relationship from the point of view of another character, in this case one whose relationship with his father is unredeemable. Within the dinner conversation banter, Logan sees a true family relationship, and the writers have used the domestic setting to show us how others see Veronica and Keith as a stable, positive dyad.

In scenes, both real and imagined, with her mother, Veronica enacts her specific fantasies about domesticity. Veronica and her mother enjoyed an evening of theme-night cooking, reminding Veronica wistfully of how it might be if her parents got back together ("Leave It to Beaver," 1.22). The domestic bliss is shattered when Veronica discovers that her alcoholic mother has been drinking, but the appreciative gaze that Keith gives his wife and daughter as they prepare food shows the yearning that both father and daughter have for this "typical" family relationship. Similarly, in Veronica's nostalgia-tinged fantasy at the end of Season 2 of how life would have been different if Lilly had not died, she imagines eating breakfast with both of her parents congenially in the kitchen, the picture of domestic tranquility. In the season 2 finale, Veronica wakes up to the sound of bacon sizzling and mistakenly assumes it is her father in the kitchen — her profound grief when she sees that he is not there highlights her strong association of Keith with the domestic sphere as her father stands in for *home*.

## Conclusion

To say that Keith serves as Veronica's moral foil is to perhaps misunderstand his role in her life: clearly Veronica's compass is often unhinged and Keith has in fact failed in many respects to instill in her a basic set of ethics, but he compromises himself many times as well. Keith is consistently shown to have a powerful sense of right — which he violates by hiding and destroying evidence, lying to the FBI, and dating a married woman — whereas Veronica's moral compass itself is often rather erratic. She often prioritizes vengeance over neutrality and suspects her closest friends of heinous crimes. She uses Wallace over and over again to serve her various causes. She ruins Keith's romantic relationships. She rarely takes the high road — favoring a fake "outing" of a client's ex-boyfriend for spite in Season 1; ripping Lilly's pendant off the neck of a young girl in Season 3. Deciding not to broadcast the evidence of Jackie's father's crimes at the school dance was a rare display of loyalty to others — in this case, Wallace. She is continually unable, until the very last episode, for example, to truly forgive Logan, one of the great loves of her life, for his transgressions. She accuses him of murder in the first season; breaks up with him over his arsonist act in the second season; and is furious that he left people in a burning hotel in Mexico and slept with Madison in the last season.

The series ends with Veronica realizing that Logan's violence and revenge tactics are actually appealing to her; that he truly understands her despite, or even because of, his obvious moral failings; that he is in fact akin to her in many ways. The realization is all the more striking in that it occurs, finally, at the same time as Keith comes to terms with his daughter's need for vengeance. This resolution parallels a resolution to the developmental process of adolescence. Both parents and children must transcend their preadolescent relationship and re-evaluate the way they understand themselves. That this resolution is not always successful or satisfying in real life is the saga of much psychic pain (Steinberg 117; Colton and Gore 24–26) and indeed commonly part of the core pathology giving rise to the story arc in film *noir* (Leibman 178–184). The pain of growing up is a canonical component of teen-oriented dramas and is evident in recent series which examine the stormy lives of even strong girls who have special powers (Jowett 188–190).

In the series finale Veronica betrays Keith for the last time and, presumably, ruins his chances to get re-elected as sheriff, which has been his dream since the beginning of the series. That his career failure is directly caused by Veronica's actions is difficult to stomach, both for viewers and for Veronica herself, since Keith is the only person she unconditionally loves. At the end of the series, the show's writers force Veronica to directly face the vengeance in her own character by realizing simultaneously what she finds attractive (and unattractive) in a boyfriend and by owning up to her role in Keith's election debacle. Significantly, Keith too must face her true character — and embrace it.

While Veronica has benefited from her stable, protective father, in fact, the very center of her existence is an obsessive and unfulfilled search — for answers, for her mother, for revenge. In the first season, she gave up everything for Keith, believing that he must have been right about Jake Kane. In the last season, he gave up everything for her, believing that she must have had her own reasons for going after the same man. Keith has offered his daughter nothing but protection, security, and a place to call home. In the *noir* world of Neptune, the greatest love leads not to success but to personal and professional destruction. As the *noir* heroine, Veronica leaves despair in her path. But Keith greets his daughter with a homemade dinner at the end of the series, even knowing of her treachery. With everything at stake, and with his eyes wide open, he takes her side.

## Note

1. One might also consider the Girardis of *Joan of Arcadia* (2003–05), though whether the series can be considered a teen drama is debatable.

# Works Cited

Battis, Jes. *Blood Relations: Chosen Families in* Buffy the Vampire Slayer *and* Angel. Jefferson, NC: McFarland, 2005. Print.

Berner, Amy. "Daddy Dualities." Thomas 58–70. Print.

Dreher, Diane Elizabeth. *Domination and Defiance: Fathers and Daughters in Shakespeare.* Lexington: University Press of Kentucky, 1986. Print.

Horsley, Lee. *The Noir Thriller.* Basingstoke, UK: Palgrave, 2001. Print.

Kaveney, Roz. *Teen Dreams: Reading Teen Film and Television from* Heathers *to* Veronica Mars. London: I.B. Tauris, 2006. Print.

Larson, Reed, and Linda Asmusssen. "Anger, Worry and Hurt in Early Adolescence." *Adolescent Stress: Causes and Consequences.* Ed. Mary Ellen Colten and Susan Gore. New York: Aldine de Gruyter, 1991. 21–41. Print.

Leibman, Nina C. "The Family Spree of Film Noir." *Journal of Popular Film and Television* 16.4 (1989): 168–184. Print.

Millman, Joyce. "Daddy's Girl." Thomas 46–57. Print.

Jowett, Lorna. *Sex and the Slayer: A Gender Studies Primer for the* Buffy *Fan.* Middletown, CT: Wesleyan University Press, 2005. Print.

Ramos, John. "I Cannot Tell a Lie." Thomas 104–114. Print.

Steinberg, Laurence. *Adolescence.* Boston: McGraw-Hill Higher Education, 1996. Print.

Thomas, Rob, ed. *Neptune Noir: Unauthorized Investigations into* Veronica Mars. Dallas: BenBella, 2006. Print.

Wilcox, Rhonda. *Why Buffy Matters: The Art of* Buffy the Vampire Slayer. London: I.B. Tauris, 2005. Print.

Williams, J.P. "Choosing Your Own Mother: Witchcraft and Female Power in Buffy the Vampire Slayer." *Fighting the Forces: What's at Stake in* Buffy the Vampire Slayer. Ed. Rhonda V. Wilcox and David Lavery. Lanham, MD: Rowman & Littlefield, 2002. 61–72. Print.

# 5

## Family Matters
### *Antigone, Veronica, and the Classical Greek Paradigm*
STAN BEELER

> Reversal of the situation is a change by which the action veers round
> to its opposite, subject always to our rule of probability or necessity....
> Recognition, as the name indicates, is a change from ignorance to
> knowledge, producing love or hate between the persons destined by
> the poet for good or bad fortune. The best form of recognition is
> coincident with a reversal of the situation, as in the *Oedipus.*
> —Aristotle, *Poetics* XI

Aristotle's summary of the best practices for the plot of the ancient Greek
tragedy is based upon his observation of dramatic form in his own time. Yet
despite the intervening two and one-half millennia and the concomitant
changes in form, intended audience, and perhaps also, the intent of drama,
the best contemporary dramas often pivot around a reversal of fortunes (peripateia) that hinges upon the discovery (anagnorisis) of familial relationships.
Rob Thomas, the creator of the hip, youth-oriented television drama *Veronica
Mars*, has embraced the spirit of Aristotle's comments on Athenian tragedy
and applied them to contemporary American television drama in a fashion
that never loses sight of the radically altered aesthetic, economic, and social
imperatives of contemporary television drama.

The plot arc of season one of *Veronica Mars* is ostensibly focused upon
Veronica's (Kristen Bell) attempts to discover the real murderer of her best
friend Lilly Kane (Amanda Seyfried). This relatively straightforward goal
would appear, at first blush, to have nothing to do with the plot imperatives

of ancient Greek tragedy as outlined above, but on closer inspection we see that there are a number of clear similarities. In keeping with this acknowledgement of traditional form, the series is rife with allusions to classical literature. For example the protagonist's name is composed of classical references that describe her character. Veronica's first name calls up images of the mercy of St. Veronica who wiped Christ's brow on his way to Golgotha; and her last, Mars, the Roman god of war. (See also Mayer, in this volume, on Veronica's name.) Her tough yet compassionate character is effectively described to the discerning audience who simply hears her name. Veronica is motivated in her search not only by compassion and a need for justice for her friend, but also an intense desire to exonerate her father and restore her own position in the community of Neptune Beach. She is torn between loyalty to her family and acceptance of the general wisdom and legal establishment of her community. Veronica, in terms poignantly clear to anyone who has ever attended a North American high school, loses everything by choosing loyalty to her father rather than siding with her friends. The creators of *Veronica Mars* have proven that although the incidental details of modern existence in a technologically-determined environment have changed, the powerful imperatives of family loyalty, self-knowledge, and betrayal are still as important in the development of drama as they were over two thousand years ago.

## Serial Drama Structure

Despite the similarities in theme and plot mentioned above, one cannot deny that contemporary serial television drama is quite a different beast than ancient Greek theatre, although I would argue that it serves a similar social function. Because the ancient Greeks developed their theatre from a religious ritual, it was, therefore, mandatory for free citizens of Athens to attend the theatre: the dramatic subjects of history and theology were considered a part of the citizen's education, and comedy provided a certain necessary social release. Drama was a form of social glue important to the unity of the Greek city-state. Despite the fact that television is not legally mandated in contemporary western society (yet), it does provide an underlying social consensus that allows certain basic ethical, historical and emotional concepts to be shared.[1] Of course, overtly didactic television is deprecated in all but a few specific genres — after-school specials, for example; nonetheless, television effectively conveys social norms as well as ethical concerns to its audience. This is usually done in an oblique fashion, through example, rather than by a direct moral "lesson." Maureen Ryan terms this effect "TV disguise." She points out that "*Battlestar Galactica* ... is a meditation on governing, power, the tension between the military and civilians, and an exploration of what human beings will do to each other — and for each other — when the 'normal' restrictions of human society are taken away, [and] *House* is really a weekly ethics seminar." Although the thematic structure of *Veronica Mars* differs from *House* and *Battlestar Galactica*, it is, without question, an example of television representing strong ethical principles which will be discussed later in this chapter.

Despite the similarities in social function of ancient Greek theatre and contemporary television drama, the form in which these messages are conveyed has undergone radical alterations. Greek drama was presented to its audience in a public assembly only a few times a year, while television is a nightly ritual in the homes of most of its audience. The Greek tragedies were submitted as a group of three for a public competition while contemporary television shows have strong economic incentives to become a part of the more private ritual viewing. For this reason contemporary television shows have developed a number of innovative narrative strategies to maintain their position in the lives of their audience. Television in its earliest form often deserved the appellation "great wasteland," but as the medium has evolved and audiences have become more sophisticated, some television has developed clear indications of artistic quality that make it worthy of its role as a forum for complex discussions of social norms. As Jason Mittell indicates, *Veronica Mars* is an example of

> a new form of entertainment television [which] has emerged over the last two decades to both critical and popular acclaim. This model of television storytelling is distinct for its use of narrative complexity as an alternative to the conventional episodic and serial forms that have typified most American television since its inception. We can see such innovative narrative form in popular hits ... as well as critically beloved but ratings challenged shows like *Arrested Development*, *Veronica Mars*, *Boomtown* and *Firefly* [29].

Mittell believes that narrative complexity of the sort he describes in his article is intrinsically related to the serial structure — as opposed to episodic narrative — of this sort of television. In fact, serial television makes a substantial break from the historically established narrative formats of live drama and film. Television series allow writers and producers more time to develop characters and plots providing options for narrative complexity that heretofore were only available to novelists. (Fiske and Hartley see television as a contemporary agent of defamiliarization that matches or even exceeds the narrative power of novelists like Joyce and Kafka; 6). After all, a successful contemporary serial drama can have the attention of its audience for between twenty-two and twenty-four one-hour sessions — excluding, of course, commercial interruptions in broadcast television — over the course of a season. If one compares this with the one to four hours available to traditional dramatic forms, the necessity of certain alterations in narrative structure becomes obvious. (See Ellis, Caughie, Fiske and Hartley, and Newcomb for more detailed discussions of the aesthetics of television's narrative formats.)

The radical difference in time available to the writers of serial dramas for development has resulted in some paradigmatic transformations in the structure of contemporary narratively complex television serials. For example, ancient Greek tragedy, as practiced by Sophocles and described by Aristotle, was founded on three dramatic unities — the unity of time, unity of place and unity of action — which have been a focal point of critical theory of drama ever since. The unity of time suggests that the diegetic reality of the narrative should not exceed more than a single day, unity of place means that the events represented in a play should be more or less confined to a single location, and unity of action indicates that a play should have a single plot. The reasons for these principles are partially historical, but may also be attributed to the natural limitations of the medium. Contemporary television drama violates all three of these rules as a matter of course, although one might argue that this has been true to some extent since Shakespeare's time. (Shakespeare himself, of course, often did not adhere to the unities.) *Veronica Mars*, as an example of complex television narrative, has developed innovations that take full advantage of the extended time while accommodating certain other limitations of the television medium.

Broadcast television series, although they have a longer overall contact with the audience, are limited to between forty-five minutes to one hour for each individual episode. These episodes have about four acts, each of which has a small narrative climax to keep the audience interested in the plot during the commercial break. For this reason, the narrative structure of *Veronica Mars* is far removed from the principle of unity of action, as it was traditionally defined. The writers must maintain the attention of the audience through all of these commercial distractions as well as encouraging them to tune in again in a week, or in the case of renewal, after a hiatus of several months. Given these parameters, multiple plots lines are the rule, rather than the exception. Michael Z. Newman explains that

> each serial episode resolves some questions but leaves many others dangling; serials tend to focus on ensembles [of actors], with each episode interweaving several strands of narrative in alternation scene by scene; a season has approximately twenty four episodes,[3] begins in fall and ends in spring, and offers sweeps periods every November, February and May [16].

Newman points out that these techniques have been developed to maintain audience interest over a sustained period of time. Although he does not explicitly mention it, sweeps are significant elements in plot structures, as they tend to artificially mandate a multiple-episode climax in the narrative to assure that audience levels are at their maximum while statistical snapshots of audiences are taken. In the third season of *Veronica Mars*, the February sweeps period incorporates a two episode sub-plot concerning the murder of Coach Berry ("Postgame Mortem," 3.13 and "Mars, Bars," 3.14). Moreover, the death of Sheriff Lamb in "Mars, Bars," although not directly related to the Berry murder, resolves of one of the series' long-standing narrative threads. Keith Mars is returned to his former status as sheriff and justice is restored to its natural order.

*Veronica Mars* is an excellent example of the narratively complex television series designed to take into account the practical narrative and economic realities of its form. Each episode is made up of plot elements that contain both a self-standing mystery that is resolved by the end of the allotted hour and elements of the long-term plot arcs, which can last up to an entire season.

In the pilot episode of the series the short-term plot goal that is presented in the teaser[4] is the resolution of the conflict between Wallace (Percy Daggs III) and the Pacific Coast Highway bike gang. An early shot shows Wallace duct-taped to a pole in his high-school courtyard. Veronica frees him from this immediate dilemma, and over the course of the rest of the episode, resolves the difficulty that resulted in his predicament. Wallace has earned the enmity of the PCH bike gang through his duties as a clerk in a convenience store. This plot line serves two primary purposes: the first is to establish Veronica's friendship with Wallace, which is central to the series, and the second is to demonstrate her methodologies and ethical position. Veronica's ethics, which are shaped, rather than destroyed, by her recent experience of tragedy and betrayal, are an important point of comparison between this series and ancient Greek drama. In a classroom situation Veronica sums up her ethical stance of hope in the face of adversity by paraphrasing the following lines from Alexander Pope's *An Essay on Man. Epistle I*: "Hope springs eternal in the human breast; / Man never is, but always to be blest: / The soul, uneasy and confined from home, / Rests and expatiates in a life to come" (8) as "Life's a bitch until you die." Despite this somewhat fatalistic attitude, Veronica does all she can to alleviate the suffering of her friends and clients.

The "free Wallace" plot line, although much shorter in duration, runs in parallel with the two other teleological imperatives that determine the first season: the search for Lilly Kane's real murderer and the enigma of Lianne Mars' (Corinne Bohrer) departure. These longer-running plot structures are the true innovation of narratively complex television and, perhaps, the most contrary to Aristotle's "unities of action and time." Each week Veronica solves a short term "case," but like Wallace's conflict, these cases add to the overarching structure of the long-term plots through the introduction of characters — in this case Wallace and PCH motorcycle gang leader, Weevil (Francis Capra) — or establishing underlying information that serves to further illuminate the grand quest.

In the second season, the "grand quest" is the search for the high school bus bomber, and during the course of the season each episode-long sub-plot adds information or character development to the longer plot. One might usefully compare this narrative structure to a skeleton, with the longer plot arc serving as a backbone for the series while each individual episode serves as a rib, connected to the backbone, but not as important to the well-being of the entity. For example, in "Like a Virgin" (1.8) computer expert Cindy "Mac" Mackenzie (Tina Majorino) is introduced and serves as a friend and ally through the next two seasons. In "Silence of the Lamb," (1.11) Mac's character is given further depth when Veronica discovers that Mac was "switched at birth" and she has never known her real parents. Veronica reveals that Mac's real parents are the Sinclairs, and Madison, one of the series antagonists, is the real daughter of the family who raised Mac ("Silence of the Lamb" 1.11).

In "Green Eyed Monster" (2.4), Wallace discovers that he too does not know his true father. Narrative complexity is served through the measured revelations about characters, and in the world of *Veronica Mars* these revelations tend to reflect the principle of peripateia. Primary characters in the series, Veronica, Wallace and Mac all have revelations concerning their true parentage that bring about a major transformation in their situations. In Veronica's case the revelation is false, but the knowledge of its possibility irrevocably alters her relationship with her mother while deepening her respect for her father. In Mac's case, her bitter attitude toward her socio-economic status is deepened by the knowledge that she has been betrayed by her parents. Wallace's relationship with his mother is radically altered by the knowledge that she lied to him about his father's death. As Veronica's two closest friends share her uncertainty about heritage, this strongly influences the underlying ethical principles and character relationships that determine the action in the series.

## Plot and Ethical Positions

Perhaps the best way to highlight the use of plot structure to develop clear ethical positions in *Veronica Mars* is to compare it to G.W.F. Hegel's understanding of ancient Greek tragedy. G.W.F. Hegel, a leading light of nineteenth-century German philosophy and, perhaps, one of the most influential interpreters of Greek tragedy since Aristotle's contemporary insights into the art form, considered Sophocles' play *Antigone* to be nearly perfect in its structure. To Hegel, Greek drama's primary purpose was to demonstrate the basic incompatibility of individual happiness in the face of the universal ethical and social principles embodied in the ancient Greek pantheon (Hegel 331–2). He believed that the Greek hero does not fail because of moral weakness (tragic flaw), but because he or she cannot possibly follow all of the conflicting ethical principles represented by the gods:

> Bei allen diesen tragischen Konflikten nun aber müssen wir vornehmlich die falsche Vorstellung von *Schuld* oder *Unschuld* beiseite lassen. Die tragischen Heroen sind ebenso schuldig als unschuldig.

> In the first place we must give up the false notions of *guilt* and *innocence* in all of these tragic conflicts. The tragic heroes are just as guilty as they are innocent. [my translation] [Hegel 331].

The Greek term often translated as "tragic flaw" is actually *hamartia*, and it literally means "missing the mark," as when an archer misses the target. Hegel saw that tragedy occurred when a character was unable to reconcile conflicting duties to more than one god or ethical principle. Therefore, he considered Sophocles' *Antigone* to be a paradigmatic example of the Greek tragedy, as it clearly represented tragedy as the resolution of mutually exclusive yet equally valid ethical principles.

At this point a brief summary of the plot of *Antigone* may be in order. The title character is the product of the incestuous relationship between Oedipus and his mother / wife Jocasta. This background serves to strengthen her relationship to the sacred principles of family, as she is doubly related to every member of her family. She also owes natural allegiance to the ruling family of the city-state Thebes, as she is a member of the royal family. This situation does not seem to be a problem until her two natural allegiances come into conflict when her two brothers, Eteocles and Polyneices, kill each other in a battle for the throne of Thebes. Creon, the king of Thebes, declares that Polyneices should not be given the honor of a burial since he brought an army of foreigners against the city. Antigone, following her natural tendency to put family first, defies the order and buries her brother. Creon is outraged at this offence to the city and has Antigone walled up in a cave to die of starvation. Carol Jacobs summarizes Hegel's interpretation of the play as follows:

> The story he [Hegel] tells is that of the ethical order — an ethical world divided between two kinds of law, the human and the divine, between the law of the community, government, or nation on the one hand, and the law of the gods

that governs the family on the other. It is a world to be divided as well between man and woman [891].

Antigone is asked to balance her duty to family with her duty to the community of the city-state; she chooses family, and the city-state has her executed for disloyalty. Both elements are positive forces in the lives of individuals, but in this situation they are in conflict, and Antigone's death is the only way to resolve the conflict.

The predicament faced by Veronica Mars in the first season story arc is remarkably accessible to the same sort of Hegelian analysis as *Antigone*, with a few significant differences that hinge upon the changing role of women in contemporary society. Like *Antigone*, Veronica is a young woman who has a natural allegiance to her family, especially her father. Unlike Antigone, this allegiance is based upon similarity of character and interests. This sort of intellectual and professional affinity would not be possible in the firmly patriarchal society of *Antigone*. In Hegel's opinion, the Greek heroes are incapable of deviating from their natural affinities, while in the contemporary ethical structure of *Veronica Mars*, our hero chooses her allegiances through the exercise of her free will. In "Drinking the Kool-Aid" (1.8), Veronica emphasizes her freely chosen affinity for her father by shredding the results of a paternity test without actually looking at them. In the beginning of the story, Keith Mars (Enrico Colantoni) is a representative of the state and political order as well as the central pillar of Veronica's family life. He is the chief of police for the community of Neptune, California. When the plot begins, however, Keith has lost his job and become a private investigator. (In this discussion, the term *story* refers to the events that make up Veronica Mars' life, and *plot* is the arrangement of those events as they appear in the episode of the series.) For Veronica as for Antigone, the unity of loyalty to family and loyalty to the official mechanisms of society has been broken; her natural state of harmony has been disrupted by outside forces. Veronica, a loyal daughter, like Antigone, has chosen to partake in her father's change of status. (Sophocles' Antigone is transformed from princess to caretaker for her blind and disgraced father in a peripateia generated by her *father's* recognition of his own true identity.) Before the radical upset of her situation initiated by her friend's murder and her father's obstreperous accusations, Veronica, like most teenagers, had begun to develop a life of her own through friends and romantic attachments; she was dating the brother of her best friend Lilly. Duncan (Teddy Dunn) and Lilly Kane are children of one of the most wealthy and influential men in the town of Neptune, and Veronica's social sphere has been transformed from the solid middle-class of her father to the elite group of plutocrats who are designated by their postal code as '09ers. When her friend Lilly is murdered,

Keith Mars precipitates the conflict between Veronica's two allegiances by accusing the Kane family of involvement in the murder. Veronica opts to declare her allegiance to her natural family rather than the social group she shares with her romantic partner, Duncan Kane. This is parallel to Antigone's decision to choose loyalty to her brother over Creon, the father of her fiancée Haemon. Creon, like Jake, is in a position of great power in his community and his son, Haemon, like Duncan, has the equivalent accoutrements of influence and social status. Although contemporary American society does not have hereditary rulers, it is still obvious that wealth and its concomitant political influence are still closely connected to family. As a result of her decision, Veronica becomes *persona non grata* among the popular circle of friends she has developed at high-school. This loss of status is further complicated by a loss of honor; when attempting to maintain her social circle by attending an 09er party, she is drugged and raped.

## Veronica as a Fury

The combination of events that leads Veronica away from her previous social situation also results in a transformation in her ethical stance. The above backstory of *Veronica Mars* is essentially an anagnorsis combined with peripateia. Veronica recognizes that her powerful social group was dependent upon her boyfriend and his family, and she can no longer depend upon her old "friends" for support. This recognition is combined with a complete reversal of her social status. Moreover, her formal relationship with the legal establishment has been disrupted. Natural justice and the legal system are no longer in harmony in Neptune. Keith Mars has lost his job as sheriff because he insisted on doing it ethically, thus proving that the money and power of the Kane family can override due process of the law. Veronica's rape, although reported to the police, is derided by the official mechanisms of justice as a feeble attempt at vengeance through false accusations. Once she has realized that she has no recourse through the official justice system, Veronica chooses to accomplish justice as a personal commitment rather than the responsibility of professionals; she chooses to become a Fury. The three Furies were deities of ancient Greek Mythology dedicated to vengeance. In some sense Veronica embodies all three Furies: She is Alecto, whose name means Unceasing in Anger, in her resentment of her treatment at the hands of her former friends; Tisephone, Avenger of Murder, in her relentless pursuit of Lilly's killer; and in some ways Megaera, Jealous, as she is especially concerned with bringing the wealthy low. Veronica's struggles against the inequities of the legal system embody Aristotle's definition of natural justice: rules of law that are absolute and not affected by the conventions and rules of society. For example, in "You Think You Know Somebody" (1.5), Veronica manages to foil a complex drug smuggling plot without recourse to the legal authorities. In fact, in the course of most of her investigations she actually breaks laws. (She is notorious for her ability to create false identity cards and for using illegal electronic surveillance techniques.) This disjunction between ethical behavior and strict adherence to the legal system highlights the similarity of Veronica and Antigone's situation.

## The Family Knot

Although, as indicated above, there are a host of ethical parallels between Antigone and Veronica Mars, in the matter of family, Veronica is closer to Oedipus than his daughter. Soon after Keith loses his job, Veronica's mother Lianne disappears, and one of the primary elements of the first season plot arc is Veronica's search for the missing mother. (See Wilcox in this volume.) This quest is entirely consistent with Veronica's role as champion of the family as a social entity, but in a particularly interesting plot development we slowly discover that Lianne is not necessarily worthy of Veronica's filial respect. In "Like a Virgin," Abel Koontz (Christian Clemenson), the man who is willingly framed for Lilly Kane's murder, reveals that Lianne had an ongoing affair with Jake Kane (Kyle Secor), and it is quite possible that Veronica is actually Jake's daughter rather than Keith's. When Koontz suggests that her mother used to visit Jake Kane in his office, Veronica is outraged. She refuses to believe him until he points out that her physical appearance would suggest that she is not Keith Mars' daughter ("Like a Virgin" 1.8). For Veronica, this is an anagnorsis combined with a major peripateia in the best Aristotelian tradition. Through a revelation of a previously unknown relationship, the dynamics of her entire family have been altered. Although her father is eventually revealed to be her genetic parent in "Leave It to Beaver" (1.22), her mother is revealed as untrustworthy. The fact that the revelation of Jake as her "true" father is a false anagnorsis is entirely consistent with the general principles of knowledge as developed in *Veronica Mars*; for although the plot depends heavily upon the tragic precedents of Greek drama, the epistemological foundations are firmly anchored in our contemporary society. In the world of *Veronica Mars*, nothing is ever as simple as it seems, and all information is suspect. In episode after episode, Veronica discovers that she has befriended the wrong person or she has defended a guilty party.

Veronica's sense of disillusionment is appropriate to a twenty-first-century hero and serves to point out another element of the dramatic provenance of the series; that is, film *noir*. Veronica, like most film *noir* heroes, is cynical, tends to operate outside of the traditional framework of the law, and is often disillusioned by those in whom she places her trust. (See Rob Thomas' collection, *Neptune Noir*, for a more detailed explication of this connection; and see Alaine Martaus.)

## Conclusion

From this brief analysis of the major plot structures of *Veronica Mars* it is clear that even television aimed at a youth market can maintain the highest artistic standards — standards that call to mind the timeless values of Greek tragedy. In the three short seasons of its existence, *Veronica Mars* presented its audience with a complex narrative that engaged with many of the fundamental questions of human existence consistent with the traditions of classical theatre. This is not to say, however, that the series ever gave up its contemporary modes and methodologies. Individual episodes of *Veronica Mars* are far more dependant upon one another than even the most tightly integrated of the Greek trilogies. Each episode of this carefully crafted series delivered a story that engaged the audience for a full forty-some minutes. It had mini-climaxes that matched perfectly with commercial breaks and sweeps episodes which were designed to enhance the experience of the non-fan audience segment that dropped in from time to time. Multiple plot lines spun a skein of complex narrative webs that involved the loyal fans in an experience that closely emulated the experience of reading a serialized novel. Yet, in the end, *Veronica Mars* was cancelled before the narrative had run its course. Fans who watched the series from beginning to the inconclusive end are left with an experience similar to that of the scholar of ancient Greek tragedy who knows that many of the greatest plays of the trilogies will never be found.

## Notes

1. Despite the fact that television provides a relatively homogeneous view of what is good and what is evil, there are a few differences in national viewpoints that pop up from time to time. Serra Tinic points this out in a discussion of the differences between Canadian and American style: "Although the above comments appear to indicate primarily the stylistic differences between Canadian and American programming, they actually speak to the divergent sensibilities, as referred to by producers

throughout the course of this study and the negotiation of the sensibilities in television programs" (117).

2. This is not to say that the unities were completely discarded after Shakespeare. For example, the Aristotelian unities were an important point of discussion for French neo-classical drama.

3. Newman is referring to standard broadcast television practices in the United States. In other countries television series may have fewer episodes and no commercial breaks. Alternate formats are also developing in the U.S. to accommodate (for example) summer replacement series, cable network paradigms, and changes in broadcast schedules that insert a hiatus in what used to be mid-season.

4. "The teaser" is the term used by television writers to designate the scene that appears before the credits for each episode roll. It sets up the episode's primary plot: "In television writing today one of the 'musts' is to let the audience know exactly what the episode is about by page three. That's right, by the end of the teaser. When you're designing the opening sequence it not only has to pique the interest of the audience, it has to set up the rest of your story" (Brody 147).

# Works Cited

Aristotle. *Poetics*. Trans. S.H. Butcher. *Critical Theory Since Plato*. Hazard Adams, ed. New York: Harcourt Brace Jovanovich, 1992. 50–66. Print.

Brody, Larry. *Television Writing from the Inside Out: Your Channel to Success*. New York: Applause, 2003. Print.

Caughie, John. "Telephilia and Distraction: Terms of Engagement." *Journal of British Cinema & Television* 3.1 (2006): 5–18. Print.

Ellis, John. *Visible Fictions: Cinema, Television, Video*. 2d ed. London and New York: Routledge, 1992. Print.

Fiske, John, and John Hartley. *Reading Television*. London: Methuen, 1980. Print.

Hegel, Georg Wilhelm Friedrich. *Vorlesungen über die Ästhetik: Dritter Teil, Die Poesie*. Rüdiger Bubner, ed. Stuttgart: Reclam, 1971. Print.

Ierulli, Molly. "The Politics of Pathos: Electra and Antigone in the Polis." *The South Atlantic Quarterly* 98.3 (1999): 477–500. Print.

Jacobs, Carol. "Dusting Antigone." *MLN: Comparative Literature Issue* 111.5 (1996): 889–917. Print.

Martaus, Alaine. "'You Get Tough. You Get Even': Rape, Anger, Cynicism, and the Vigilante Girl Detective in *Veronica Mars*." *Clues: A Journal of Detection* 27.1 (Spring 2009): 74–86. Print.

Mittell, Jason. "Narrative Complexity in Contemporary American Television." *The Velvet Light Trap* 58 (2006): 29–40. Print.

Newman, Michael Z. "From Beats to Arcs: Toward a Poetic of Television Narrative." *The Velvet Light Trap* 58 (2006): 16–28. Print.

Newcomb, Horace, ed. *Television: The Critical View*. 7th ed. New York: Oxford University Press, 2006. Print.

Ouellette, Laurie, and Justin Lewis. "Moving Beyond the 'Vast Wasteland': Cultural Policy and Television in the United States." *The Television Studies Reader*. Ed. Robert C. Allen and Annette Hill. London and New York: Routledge. 2004. 52–65. Print.

Pope, Alexander, and Daniel Clark. *An Essay on Man*. London: W. & H. Merriam, 1844. Print.

Ryan, Maureen. "Plot Is the Candy Coating: Scratch the Surface on a TV Show, You Can Find a Hero's Journey or a Treatise on Government." *Chicago Tribune* 18 Aug. 2007. *Los Angeles Times Article Collections*. Web. 28 June 2010.

Thomas, Rob, ed. *Neptune Noir: Unauthorized Investigations into* Veronica Mars. Dallas: BenBella, 2006. Print.

Tinic, Serra. *On Location: Canada's Television Industry in a Global Market*. Toronto: University of Toronto Press, 2005. Print.

# 6

## Rethinking "The Getting Even Part"

### *Feminist Anger and Vigilante Justice in a Post-9/11 America*

TAMY BURNETT AND MELISSA TOWNSEND

> There's the part of me that thinks Veronica should grow and evolve.
> She should get past her pettiness. She should learn how to forgive....
> The other part of me wants to keep her complicated. Difficult. Testy.
> I don't want her to soften into angelic heroine who consistently does
> the "right thing." Like America, Veronica and I are at a crossroads.
> — Rob Thomas, creator of *Veronica Mars* (148)

When a classmate asks Veronica Mars how she deals with sustained exclusion and mistreatment by her peers, the teen responds, "Here's what you do. You get tough. You get even" ("Like a Virgin," 1.8). Indeed, throughout *Veronica Mars*' run, Veronica's raison d'être seems to continually shift back and forth between justice and vengeance. Even when searching for justice — for her murdered best friend, for her classmates who are victims of a bombed school bus, for young women raped on her college campus, or for her own sexual assault — Veronica is quick to formulate plans designed to extract petty vengeance from those who have wronged her. Later in the same episode, the classmate, Meg, suggests Veronica modify her response by saying, "Getting tough? Yeah, that was good advice. And I needed that. The getting even part? You might want to rethink that one." Meg's suggestion here represents an ongoing struggle for Veronica's character: where should she draw the line between justice and vengeance?

The series' pilot makes plain the wealth of injustices and harms Veronica

95

has already suffered before the series even begins: abandonment by her mother, murder of her best friend, loss of social status when her father is fired from his job as sheriff (and subsequent loss of socio-economic status), rejection in the form of an inexplicable and unexpected break-up with her boyfriend, rape after being drugged at a classmate's party, and humiliation when the new sheriff mocks her attempt to report the crime. These various factors — especially the rape, which serves as a tipping point — irrevocably alter Veronica's view of justice and her own safety in her world; because of this shift, *Veronica Mars* begins with its heroine a sarcastic, cynical young woman whose penchant for vengeance is easily understood. However, as the series progresses, Veronica remains hardened to a degree, unable to fully return to the carefree girl pictured in pre-series flashbacks. Indeed, repeatedly Veronica finds herself at a crossroads, having to choose between holding onto her anger, sense of violation, and loss of faith in the social systems that should have protected and advocated for her — in short, all the factors which contribute to her desire for vengeance — and letting go of her suspicions and fear, forgiving those who have harmed her, and trusting again in social systems and authorities for her safety and well being. Both because of the time frame in which the series originally aired (2004–2007) and because of this preoccupation with questions of justice versus vengeance, *Veronica Mars* offers insight into the American psyche at a time when the nation was still eager to define itself as "post–9/11." In addition to helping understand the U.S as a nation at war in response the terrorist attacks of September 11, 2001,[1] the ongoing tension between justice and vengeance helps illuminate *Veronica Mars'* construction of a strong feminist protagonist.

While *Veronica Mars* provides useful commentary on American attitudes in reaction to 9/11, we cannot overlook historical precedent for the nation's response to conflict. In December 1941, the Japanese bombing of Pearl Harbor led to such national change that America joined a world war from which it had previously worked hard to remain apart, a choice that served to reinvigorate a floundering national economy and resulted in the enactment of more social welfare policy than any other period in the nation's history. While these positive outcomes are among the first (American) history textbooks delineate, America's response to the attack on Pearl Harbor also resulted in numerous outcomes of a less positive nature. For example, a nation which defines itself through the rhetoric of freedom and opportunity for all nonetheless imprisoned Japanese Americans all along its west coast (the coast closest geographically to Japan and with the heaviest population of Asian immigrants) in internment camps for the duration of the war while simultaneously winning the race to create a weapon so powerful and destructive it ended the war and created a sustained sense of hostility between east and west for decades to come. In addition, Americans in the post–World War II Cold War–era witnessed systemic persecution of political minorities and other social "deviants" like homosexuals,[2] as well as cultural reinforcement of rigid gender roles and ideals of family, all of which ultimately created a nation that lived and thrived on the politics of fear for much of the next thirty years.

There is no doubt that America has been changed yet again since 9/11. The complexity of Americans' collective response to the attacks stems from the fact that there were, and still are, multiple reactions occurring simultaneously: grief over the loss of life; fear, resulting in a newly understood sense of vulnerability; anger channeled into the "War on Terror," which later included war in Iraq; patriotic pride and worry (simultaneous) in response to the passage of the Patriot Act, giving the government leave to impinge upon previously inviolable individual rights; and righteousness and horror (also simultaneous) in response to reports of torture of political detainees. However, the most notable change within the U.S. collective psyche in the direct aftermath of September 11 was an overwhelming sense of unity. As a part of this rise in national unity, Virginia A. Chanley argues that trust in the government by U.S. citizens nearly doubled in the immediate aftermath of the terrorist attacks, with a correlating decrease in cynicism regarding government/military action and spending.

That level of unity was unsustainable, however; as early as 2003, when the U.S. marched to war in Iraq, Dale Krane shows that not only were members of America's two major political parties, Republicans and Democrats, arguing and divided, but divisiveness was also growing between individual states and the federal government. Deborah J. Schildkraut found that although there was an increase in unity rhetoric by political elites, the masses were far from united, division occurring most often along lines of culture and race. For example, by 2004, hate-motivated violence toward Arabs, Muslims, and South Asians was on the rise and was understood by the American public as "a regrettable, but expected, response to the terrorist attacks" (Ahmad 1262). Parallel to American experience with World War II, the U.S. response to the terrorist attacks of 9/11 manifested as a complex web of reactions, experiences, and motivations, as America struggled to balance its thirst for vengeance with a national identity that prides itself on justice. These two historical examples are significant for their impact on America's sense of self as well as for the pattern they represent: Americans' understandings of justice are impacted dramatically when citizens find themselves in the position of being vulnerable. The lesson here is clear: when Americans feel personally and individually victimized, the country feels equally empowered to take significant action, but

Americans are also subject to the whims of fear and anger. Veronica Mars, as a character, is no different.

Veronica's personal "9/11" is the rape she experiences. While other events leave her vulnerable, or shake her faith in social authority like the judicial system, her rape and the sheriff's crude, sneering response to her attempt to report the assault mark a critical moment of change in Veronica's psyche and approach to the world around her. While Veronica understands the rape as a culmination of her status as a social outcast (after all, she was drugged and raped at a party full of her peers and no one cared enough to step in and keep her safe), it is also the point at which she realizes that her world is filled with injustice and no one is going to advocate for her other than herself— a realization symbolized in the shift from long-haired pastel-colored clothes-wearing Veronica of pre-series flashback to the short haired young woman who routinely wears long sleeved shirts and layers in Southern California (her wardrobe change depicting a classic response to sexual assault wherein the victim takes to wearing more concealing clothing). Further, flashback Veronica is carefree and happy, whereas present Veronica is cynical and angry, quick to act vengeful and constantly working to ensure she is not again victimized by others or the social authority that should work to protect her.

In considering this parallel between *Veronica Mars* and America's post–9/11 cultural consciousness, we wish to particularly engage with Deanna Carlyle's essay "The United States of America: Teen Noir as America's New Zeitgeist." Carlyle writes that "9/11 was the defining event for America's current sense of violation" (152), arguing, as we do here, that Veronica's sense of victimization positions Veronica parallel to the American public. She expands her claim by pointing to the fact that "in season one, Veronica exacted revenge for offenses committed against her and those she loved, much in the way the U.S. bombed the Taliban out of power in Afghanistan after 9/11, hunting down and killing al-Qaeda members throughout the world" (153). However, Carlyle's analysis ultimately offers a blueprint for recovery from the state of violation and abandonment she identifies in *Veronica Mars*, suggesting that true power lies in responding to these violations through forgiveness, accepting one's own vulnerability and pain, and acting to protect innocence in one's self and others — rather than seeking revenge. This is the point at which we disagree with Carlyle's essay; while the path Carlyle posits is appealing for the resolution it offers and is, undoubtedly, the more emotionally healthy course of action, we are disturbed and troubled by what such a path would mean for Veronica, especially in terms of her construction as a feminist figure. Further, while the analogy of Veronica's experiences to 9/11 is valid, it can only extend so far. In examining the limits of the analogy, we offer new insight into both America's response to 9/11 and Veronica's development as a strong female character.

A key component in understanding this negotiation lies in understanding the genre choices of *Veronica Mars* and how those choices frame ideas of justice and the individual. The series' engagement with and revision of the noir genre is at the heart of its negotiations of justice. Lani Diane Rich suggests that the noir element in *Veronica Mars*, which she defines as a way "to describe story-telling with a dark edge, expressed visually by shadowy lighting and the classic Venetian blind stripes on any wall that'll have 'em," (9–10) is successful due to its pairing with the use of camp, a style of "over-the-top storytelling with a hint of kitsch that's not even trying for reality" (10); because the two genres temper each other, the series offers a more engaging narrative that resists the danger of becoming too dark or too silly. Similarly, Chris McCubbin argues that *Veronica Mars'* connection to the noir genre is captivating because the series calls upon more that just that one genre: "*Veronica Mars* blends hard-boiled detective fiction and film noir, where everything is corrupt and fundamentally hopeless, with the family drama/coming-of-age story, which is wholesome and intrinsically hopeful" (140; see also Alaine Martaus on the combination of noir and coming-of-age). And, of course, we cannot ignore the obvious and much-cited comparison of *Veronica Mars* to the genre-exploding *Buffy the Vampire Slayer* (1997–2003), most often in terms of the empowered female teenage hero genre. All of these comparisons exemplify the ways in which *Veronica Mars* conforms to, challenges, or rewrites genre rules, all of which affect the narrative in significant ways. However, the comparisons also inevitably come back to the base component of noir, reinforcing the impor-tance of that genre's influence. Indeed, given how central questions of justice/corruption are to the noir genre and to *Veronica Mars*, an analysis of the series' construction of Veronica as agent of justice must engage with the rich history of this genre.

Veronica's acts in the name of justice position her as a vigilante, a role traditionally constructed as a (masculine) agent working outside the law, seek-ing justice when socially sanctioned institutions fail in their duty to provide justice. Alafair Burke's description of Veronica's hometown as "lawless" (116) posits that that the failure of these social institutions is exactly what gives Veronica authority to act. She writes, "In Neptune, the criminal justice system is consistently either indifferent or incapacitated" (116), ultimately suggesting that "the law, ... [in Neptune] is an impediment — not a vehicle — to justice" (123). Although legal and governmental authorities are presented as uniformly corrupt, Veronica's brand of justice in response to them is not uncomplicated or unproblematic. Veronica's commitment to seeking justice for justice's sake is often undermined when she accepts (or demands) monetary compensation when helping someone with whom she has no personal relationship. Similarly, Veronica frequently skirts or outright breaks the law in her pursuit of justice, and she lies frequently when doing so advances her cause. Veronica seems to operate from the slippery moral slope of an "ends justify the means" perspective, but as John Ramon points out, viewers are willing to forgive Veronica these actions because her dishonesties occur within an already corrupt system, allowing for the moral rule that "lies told in pursuit of the truth are acceptable" (107). As Kristin Kidder remarks, what is most important in understanding Veronica's construction as a vigilante figure and the appeal of that construction is the truth that "as long as the vigilante's notions of justice remain in line with those of mainstream America, the term is not likely to be used as a pejorative" (127). During the show's original run of programming, one possible draw for some American viewers may have been that Veronica's vigilantism embodied a parallel cultural desire to take action in response to the feelings of helplessness and violation that impacted American cultural consciousness following 9/11.

The extent and severity of Veronica's vigilante action follows a trajectory wherein her confidence in her actions and their scope in a specific situation are inversely proportional to the size of the failure/transgression the social authority in question has committed against her. The scope of that past failure is always present in the backstory provided in the pilot episode, and viewers are continuously reminded of this through the repeated use of flashbacks during the first season. However, the ongoing extent of that failure is elaborated upon throughout all three seasons with repeated betrayal by various modes of social authority. Veronica's brand of justice is driven by her sense of entitlement to pursue her justice on her terms, entitlement she demands upon realizing that the institutions that should help her will not. Carlyle argues that, at some point, Veronica must get past the wrongs done to her in the setup of the series in order to find peace and move on as a person. Indeed, such a path may be the only course of action open to America as a sustainable, long-term means of dealing with the cultural and governmental response to 9/11. But where Veronica differs from the American people post–9/11, and from Carlyle's assessment, is in the continual nature of her victimization by figures of authority. Veronica's vigilantism and vengeance-tinged justice is not only legitimized in the pilot episode and first season as a response to the collective events that shape our first impressions of Veronica. Rather, this attitude is also legitimized on a weekly basis as Veronica is continually victimized in various ways.

The three tiers of social authority which operate in Veronica's life serve to illustrate the relationship between her continual victimization and her continual pursuit of her own brand of justice. The first level is the conventional authority of law enforcement and the criminal justice system, which plays the largest role in establishing and demonstrating her vigilante justice. This entity is the most corrupt, with the most serious consequences for Veronica, and it is the one she cares the least about hurting in her pursuit of true justice. The second tier is the political/governmental authority in Neptune. This form of authority also exerts significant impact on justice in Neptune and for Veronica, and it is important because of Veronica's desire to believe in the system, even as she is repeatedly failed by it. The third tier is found in Veronica's primary social environment — school. This tier has two layers: the first is composed of school officials who shift between traditional authority figures who fail Veronica and individuals who turn to Veronica as a peer, requesting her assistance; and the second is made up by other students who are Veronica's peers and who also shift between making Veronica a victim and enlisting her aid when they are in turn victimized by an unfailingly unjust social structure.

The first tier of social authority is the one that has most obviously and egregiously failed Veronica: the law enforcement in Neptune, as embodied by Sheriff Lamb, the man who took Keith Mars' position as sheriff after Keith was recalled from office during the Lilly Kane murder investigation.[3] Although Lamb is obviously insecure in his position, belittling Keith and harassing Veronica when he can, his response to Veronica's report of her sexual assault — suggesting she was filing a false report while simultaneously insinuating that she should be stronger by suggesting she "go see the wizard [and] ask for a little backbone" (Pilot) — clearly shows viewers why Veronica's anger and perception of him as a corrupt, ineffectual authority figure (and by extension, the rest of the sheriff's office) is accurate and justified. While Veronica happily takes advantage of any opportunity to expose corruption and inefficacy in the sheriff's office, the depths of law enforcement's failure of her — and everyone else in Neptune — is displayed by her actions in "Donut Run" (2.11). Veronica crafts a plan to help her first love Duncan escape the country with his infant daughter, in order to prevent the child's abusive maternal grandparents from gaining custody, and the lynch-pin of her plan relies on Lamb's arrogance and propensity for grandstanding. Because of her absolute faith that Lamb will act in a manner designed to advance his career, even — especially — at the cost of true justice, Veronica manipulates him into unwittingly smuggling Duncan over the border into Mexico (Lamb does so not realizing Duncan has stowed away in the trunk of his patrol car). Not only does Veronica thumb her nose at Lamb and the law enforcement authority he represents through her actions here, she also makes Lamb an accomplice in enacting the justice Neptune's corrupt system is incapable of providing.

The series makes clear, however, that it is not just law enforcement but also the legal judiciary system that fails Veronica. The most obvious example here is the acquittal of Aaron Echolls when charged with Lilly Kane's murder ("Happy Go Lucky," 2.21); although his celebrity and community status undoubtedly contribute to the verdict, the prosecution's case begins to deteriorate during Veronica's testimony when the defense lawyer forces her to admit to having been diagnosed with a sexually transmitted disease, attacking her credibility through the old, underhanded, gendered victim-blaming tactic so often employed by rapists, domestic abusers and, apparently, movie stars who lock young women in refrigerators and set them on fire (i.e., a sexually active, single woman's integrity cannot be trusted). The defense lawyer then uses suggestions of Veronica's "promiscuity" to provoke her father into displaying anger while on the stand, further damaging the prosecution's case. Although using victims' past sexual history to discredit them is a violation of the Model Rules of Professional Conduct of the American Bar Association and often disallowed by judges in reality (and the defense lawyer's obtainment of Veronica's medical records is a direct violation of HIPPA laws), the *Veronica Mars'* writing team's choice to use this tactic reinforces how corrupt the legal system in Neptune is; what is reprehensible and often inadmissible in the real-life U.S. judicial system secures a murderer's freedom in Neptune.

In contrast, "One Angry Veronica" (2.10) shows Veronica working the judicial system and succeeding in directing it towards justice. In the episode, Veronica is called for jury duty and her co-jurors appoint her the jury forewoman as a "chance for her to learn about civic responsibility in the justice system." The irony, of course, is that it is Veronica who delivers a lesson in civic responsibility and justice when she convinces the other jurors to look past their prejudices that favor the rich, white defendants over their poor, Latina victim, as well as to resist the desire to complete their service quickly and simply (and at the expense of true justice). Aaron Echolls' acquittal and Veronica's success as jury forewoman seem to present contradictory messages about Neptune's legal system; in fact, the underlying reality in Neptune is that while the system may still be viable — and Veronica never fully loses her faith in its potential — the men and women who run the system are the source of its pervasive corruption. And when those in charge fail Veronica, and they do so spectacularly time and again, she feels no compunction in subverting them in an equally spectacular manner.

The second tier of authority is political/governmental. In the larger context of the setup of the show, political authority is held by the voters of Neptune and Balboa County (in which the unincorporated Neptune exists). While early episodes do not feature politicians, viewers know from Veronica's backstory that it was the voters that removed Keith from office in a special recall election when they did not like the direction of his investigation into Lilly Kane's murder, a decision that irrevocably altered the lives of members of the Mars family. His lower income means the Mars family must sell their house; the added financial strain contributes significantly to the dissolution of Keith's marriage to Veronica's mother and results in Lianne Mars' abandonment of her husband and daughter; subsequently, Keith's absence from the sheriff's office compounds the issue of Veronica seeking legal justice for her rape. Had his constituents not voted Keith out of office, Veronica would have been able to continue living in her house, her nuclear family would have been more likely to stay together, and she would not have found herself in the position to be victimized either by her rapist[4] or by Sheriff Lamb while attempting to report her rape.

However, once specific political figures are introduced into the series, they offer Veronica no more access to justice than the voters did. For example, one major figure who embodies political authority in Veronica's world is the ironically-named Woody Goodman, the mayor of Neptune. Although he provides many reasons throughout the course of the second season of the show for the audience to dislike him, there is one instance in particular in which Goodman's abuses of his authority result in injustice that directly impacts Veronica. In order to save his own political skin in "Look Who's Stalking" (2.20), Goodman intentionally smears Keith's name to create a political scandal that will prevent a ballot measure Goodman initiated from passing — an action Goodman is blackmailed into undertaking to prevent exposure for past crimes. While Goodman's action in response to the assistance Keith provides is a personal betrayal, the twisted cause-and-effect chain of events that leads to his blackmail and subsequent manipulation of the public demonstrates how far-reaching the corruption of the political system is. From this moment on, hurting Woody Goodman is of no consequence to Veronica. If he gets caught in the crossfire of her pursuit of justice for herself or her paying clientele, viewers understand that he had it coming.

In addition to this direct impact on Veronica, the conclusion to the second season's mystery of the bombed school bus reveals a complex web of corruption and injustice that again connects Goodman to Veronica. The mystery of Veronica's rape takes several twists in the first two seasons. Veronica's initial categorization of the event as rape occurs because she wakes up in a torn dress, missing her underwear, feeling the physical aftermath of experiencing sexual intercourse for the first time, and with no memory of the night before (Pilot).

Subsequently she learns that she slept (voluntarily) with her ex-boyfriend Duncan (who did not know she was drugged), and she redefines this pivotal event as consensual sex even though she never regains memory of the night ("A Trip to the Dentist," 1.21). Finally, though, she learns, through the diagnosis of the sexually transmitted disease, that she was exposed sexually to someone other than Duncan, someone who did in fact rape her while she was unconscious. The twist, however, is that her rapists' actions were not the result of malicious targeting of her specifically, as she first believes. Instead, her rapist is Cassidy "Beaver" Casablancas, a young man whose actions are motivated by his desire to prove his masculinity in the face of two factors: his older brother's taunts and past sexual abuse by his little league coach — who is, of course, none other than Woody Goodman ("Not Pictured," 2.22). Goodman's sexual abuse of the prepubescent baseball players in his care instigated a cycle that led to an abused young man attempting to overcome his shame and psychological trauma through sexually assaulting someone else. That Goodman could get away with his actions for so many years is a gross miscarriage of justice; further, that he could go on to be a much-loved town leader reflects the inherent corruption of Neptune. In such an environment, where injustices are perpetuated and corruption is seemingly rewarded, Veronica's continued commitment to vigilante justice is justifiable and even desirable.

The third tier of authority that victimizes Veronica exists in her primary social world(s): her school settings. The traditional authority figures in her school life are Vice Principal Clemmons (high school) and Dean O'Dell (college). Both of these men initially react to Veronica in the same manner as other social authority figures; while they do not treat her with the same contempt as Sheriff Lamb or engage in as corrupt behaviors as Mayor Goodman, both Clemmons and O'Dell first experience adversarial relationships with Veronica. For example, the pilot episode shows then–Vice Principal Clemmons targeting Veronica's locker during a "random" locker search (it is made clear that this search is neither random nor infrequent), suggesting, at a minimum, that his opinion of Veronica has been colored by her family's very public fall from grace. Likewise, O'Dell's first meeting with Veronica follows this pattern when he threatens to expel Veronica unless she reveals a confidential source for a story she wrote for the college newspaper ("Wichita Linebacker," 3.03).

However, both men come to realize that Veronica's unorthodox methods get results; this realization causes them to call upon Veronica for assistance. While each man's interactions with Veronica might suggest they are creating an alliance with Veronica and therefore representing a social authority interested in true justice, the truth is that neither man fully escapes the corruption that permeates the larger social authorities of Neptune. Clemmons, especially, continually manipulates Veronica to help him, with a clear understanding on the part of all involved that, should their cover be blown, neither would admit to having been working with the other. Clemmons sometimes engages Veronica's investigative services by appealing to her better nature, but he also threatens her at times, with punishments ranging from suspension to the loss of her college scholarship. Typically, she gains nothing from these interactions, not even the monetary benefit her classmates are willing to give her. Dean O'Dell seems to be on a more promising trajectory than Clemmons, and his interactions with Veronica — after she makes clear what she has to offer by helping him — more closely approach the level of mutually beneficial allies. However, O'Dell's murder in "Spit and Eggs" (3.09) removes him from Veronica's world before he has the chance to fully reject the model of corrupt social authority in which he exists, perhaps suggesting that Neptune has no place for authority figures who may evolve out of corruption.

Outside of the traditional authority figures of Clemmons and O'Dell exists another layer of social authority in Veronica's school environments. Rather than specific individuals, this social authority is comprised of the peers and peer groups that represent authority in Veronica's world. In the world of Neptune High School, Veronica was once a part of the "09er" social group (comprised of students who reside in the wealthy zip code 90909), best friend to Lilly Kane and girlfriend to Duncan Kane — children of one of the wealthiest and most revered families in town. Lilly and Duncan's approval helped ease Veronica's entry into this social circle, despite her family's working-class status. Veronica is expelled from that heightened social status when Duncan dumps her shortly before his sister's death. The examples of how her social peers wrong Veronica after the pilot episode are systemic and numerous and are such a staple of the show that, in many cases, the individuals responsible aren't specifically named, although viewers understand that the actions are perpetrated by some portion of the 09er group. For instance, in "Like a Virgin" (1.8), 09er girls stuff Veronica's clothing into the toilet while she is showering after gym class, leaving the naked Veronica with no choice but to borrow Meg's cheerleading uniform. While the image of Veronica as a cheerleader is comical to viewers because it contradicts what we have come to expect of the character so far, as exemplified by her non-designer, non-conforming (seemingly non-expensive) preferences in clothing,[5] the girls' actions constitute a serious assault on Veronica's physical person and on her refusal to engage with their vision of "school spirit." Another example is found in the episode "Clash of the Tritons" (1.12), where two 09er boys who get in trouble for underage drinking blame Veronica for the fake IDs they made themselves; they are banking on

Veronica's lack of social standing and continual position as a victim to make her an easy target in the larger corrupt levels of social authority in Neptune.

Although the third season educational setting of Hearst College does not yield social ostracization for Veronica in the same manner of (petty) personal attacks, her forceful personality and commitment to seeking justice alternatively endear her to various social groups and make her suspect in her peers' eyes, ranging from the college equivalent of the 09er clique, the Greek system, to individuals. One of the most overt attacks by an individual peer is found in "Hi, Infidelity" (3.06), when the student teaching assistant for her introductory criminology course accuses her of plagiarism and falsifies the "proof" backing up his accusation. The other student, Timothy, is motivated by jealousy over Veronica's status as favored student by the course professor (a position Timothy previously had held), and his jealousy manifests in the childish personal attack reminiscent of Veronica's high school experiences with her peers. Given the continual assaults on Veronica's scholastic and social standing in both high school and college, the groups of students and her school administrators consistently position Veronica in the role of the victim. Because of this corruption and sustained victimization of Veronica, she maintains her commitment to justice and her acts of vengeance throughout the series.

Veronica's continual victimization at the hands of various tiers of social authority — the law, government/political institutions, school authority figures, and peer groups — means that she is continually in the position of victim. Her actions make small gains towards justice, but the system remains corrupt and injustices flourish. This is the significant point of divergence in the *Veronica Mars*/post–9/11 analogy. The attack that so altered American cultural consciousness was a singular event with multiple, complex actions taken in response. For Veronica, her rape is only a tipping point, an event significant enough to alter her understanding of the world and her role in an unjust society. In 2006, between *Veronica Mars*' second and third seasons and as support for the war and the then-current administration began to drop off, series' creator Rob Thomas wrote, "Like America, Veronica and I are at a crossroads" (148). What the third season clearly demonstrates is that Thomas recognized the necessity of Veronica maintaining her quest for justice, even — perhaps especially — when that quest is characterized by Veronica's desire to "get even." While Veronica's approach to life is far from uncomplicated and does come with significant cost at times (especially to her personal life, as witnessed by the implosion of her relationship with Logan in the third season, fueled in large part by her sustained cynicism and suspicion), we contend that *Veronica Mars* would have failed its feminist roots had Veronica's character developed in any other way. To give up on her anger, to cease to fight back or exercise every talent available to her in order to protect herself and others from injustice, would perhaps make Veronica "nicer" as a softer, more traditionally feminine woman. But doing so would also undermine the strength of Veronica Mars, both the character and the series.

This is a message only reinforced in the episode that turned out to be the series' finale. The concluding episode, "The Bitch Is Back" (3.20), makes clear that Veronica's battle is far from over. Keith is once again running for the position of County Sheriff, but his name has been once more damaged by corrupt social power, appropriately and ironically in the person of Jake Kane, as Keith's investigation into Jake Kane specifically following Lilly's murder led to his recall from office. The series' final images show Veronica exiting a polling station on Election Day; Veronica's voting is one last attempt to normalize her world, to have her faith in the system restored. However, the closing shot is an image of disillusionment and disappointment reinforced by the title line of the song "It Never Rains in Southern California" playing as viewers see Veronica walking away into a gray, rainy day. The dismal image, in contrast with the lyrics proclaiming that what viewers see is something that "never" happens, makes clear Keith will not win the election. While Veronica can get tough and attempt to get even, the sad truth is that her ongoing victimization means she can never truly become "even"; the system and her society are too corrupt.

In the context, then, of Meg's suggestion that Veronica "rethink" her "get even" attitude and Carlyle's argument that *Veronica Mars* offers a model for healing by releasing one's anger, we suggest that the series makes clear that not only does Veronica maintain her defining characteristic but also that her character can develop in no other way. A Veronica who gives up her anger and thirst for justice, regardless of how tinged with vengeance that justice may be, is one who would be nothing more than an agency-less victim because she lives in a world wherein she is continually victimized. And Veronica Mars is anything but a passive victim. The choice of noir as the base genre for the series demands social corruption to some degree, and Veronica presents an attractive option for responding to such corruption. Like many of her small screen teen heroine peers, Veronica is witty and regularly overcomes much more powerful opponents, but she is also angry and vengeful — characteristics that are not traditionally feminine. In embracing and sustaining them, *Veronica Mars* offers a needed alternative model of feminist agency. Indeed, "the bitch is back" in the series finale because the system is still corrupt, and only by remaining vigilant in her efforts on behalf of justice will Veronica remain true to herself.

## Notes

1. It is perhaps too simplistic to suggest that the events of September 11 are the sole cause of the United States' military actions in Iraq and Afghanistan following 2001; however, we contend that one of the direct results of 9/11 is a cultural desire for retributive action, and, without that desire, Americans as a whole would not have been as willing to pursue sustained foreign military action, especially in Iraq. Thus, for the purposes of this essay, we posit a causative link between 9/11 and subsequent military action as a means of attempting to "get even."

2. For more on the persecution of homosexuals during the McCarthy era, see David K. Johnson's *The Lavender Scare: The Cold War Persecution of Gays and Lesbians in the Federal Government* (University of Chicago Press, 2004).

3. In *Neptune Noir*, Rob Thomas suggests that more than simply coveting the sheriff's office prior to his appointment, Lamb actively helped exacerbate the high tensions in Neptune in an effort to discredit Keith and accelerate his own career advancement: "I've always believed that Lamb actually leaked information to the press during the original Lilly Kane investigation. The one thing Lamb has ever done successfully he did as deputy, and that was stab Keith in the back" (114).

4. This is the initial implication of the backstory and Veronica's understanding of it; viewers familiar with the true sequence of events the night of Veronica's rape later know the situation's complexities ultimately preclude this simple reading (the sequence of plot twists is detailed later in this essay). What is important for understanding her characterization when the series begins, however, is her understanding of the rape at that point; as Martaus argues, "It is from her [Veronica's] belief in the rape that her anger and cynicism emerge" (76).

5. Jennifer Gillan points out that certain viewers realize that some of Veronica's wardrobe is more expensive than it might seem.

## Works Cited

Ahmad, Muneer I. "A Rage Shared by Law: Post–September 11 Racial Violence as Crimes of Passion." *California Law Review* 92.5 (2004): 1259–1330. *JSTOR.* Web. 22 Oct. 2009.

Burke, Alafair. "Lawless Neptune." Thomas 115–23. Print.

Carlyle, Deanna. "The United States of Veronica: Teen Noir as America's New Zeitgeist." Thomas 149–59. Print.

Chanley, Virginia A. "Trust in Government in the Aftermath of 9/11: Determinants and Consequences." *9/11 and Its Aftermath: Perspectives from Political Psychology.* Spec. *Political Psychology* 23.3 (2002): 469–83. *JSTOR.* Web. 22 Oct. 2009.

Gillan, Jennifer. "Fashion Sleuths and Aerie Girls: *Veronica Mars*' Fan Forums and Network Strategies of Fan Address." *Teen Television: Essays on Programming and Fandom.* Eds. Sharon Marie Ross and Louisa Ellen Stein. Jefferson, NC: McFarland, 2008. 185–206. Print.

Johnson, David K. *The Lavender Scare: The Cold War Persecution of Gays and Lesbians in the Federal Government.* Chicago: University of Chicago Press, 2004. Print.

Kidder, Kristin. "The New Normal: Breaking the Boundaries of Vigilantism in *Veronica Mars*." Thomas 125–33. Print.

Krane, Dale. "The State of American Federalism, 2002–2003: Division Replaces Unity." *Publius* 33.3 (2003): 1–44. *JSTOR.* Web. 22 Oct. 2009.

Martaus, Alaine. "'You Get Tough. You Get Even': Rape, Anger, Cynicism, and the Vigilante Girl Detective in *Veronica Mars.*" *Clues: A Journal of Detection* 27.1 (2009): 74–86. Print.

McCubbin, Chris. "The Duck and the Detective." Thomas 135–47. Print.

Ramos, John. "'I Cannot Tell a Lie. And if You Believe That....'" Thomas 104–112. Print.

Rich, Lani Diana. "Welcome to Camp Noir." Thomas 9–19. Print.

Schildkraut, Deborah J. "The More Things Change ... American Identity and Mass and Elite Responses to 9/11." *9/11 and Its Aftermath: Perspectives from Political Psychology. Political Psychology* 23.3 (2002): 511–35. *JSTOR.* Web. 22 Oct. 2009.

Thomas, Rob, ed. *Neptune Noir: Unauthorized Investigations into* Veronica Mars. Dallas: BenBella, 2006. Print.

# 7

## "Get My Revenge On"
### *The Anti-Hero's Journey*

PAUL ZINDER

The relationships in Veronica Mars's life shape her into a character who thrives on adversity, particularly when a threat befalls someone she loves (or has loved). Veronica's confidence in her ability to solve the problems of others is driven by her own intelligence, which she trusts to solve puzzles laid in front of her. A reading of the narrative structure of select episodes from the three seasons of *Veronica Mars*, however, reveals a protagonist who battles the main players in her immediate domain, including those closest to her, as often as she does traditional "villains," exposing the truth of a weary existence. By the end of the series, her approach to such challenges makes her a tragic archetype, a figure whose actions never satisfy her own psychological needs. While her quests in the series' stand-alone mysteries are often undertaken for weaker individuals, they are not always altruistic. Frequently, self-involvement rules her choices, each mission formulated to draw her closer to the life she seeks, one with a caring mother and a moral community, one that can never exist. The final episode of *Veronica Mars*, in fact, leaves her defeated and defined by a selfish decision to earn personal retribution for the tattering of her reputation at the expense of the person she loves the most, her father Keith Mars ("The Bitch Is Back," 3.20). This irrevocable act individualizes Veronica Mars as a specific kind of character.

Joseph Campbell defines the hero as one with "strength, cleverness, and wisdom" and an "extraordinary capacity ... to face and survive [each] experience" (*The Hero* 327). Although she manifests numerous characteristics of the archetypical hero, Veronica's isolation from her peer group tags her an outcast and her overt rebellion against the social hierarchy defines her reality, which marks her more appropriately an anti-hero (Vogler 42). She does not

110

necessarily, however, deflect audience sympathies during her quest. The following close-reading of *Veronica Mars* reveals that many of its protagonist's decisions classify her teenage journey as that of a postmodern anti-hero. Veronica Mars is fallible, relatable, and human, which leaves the audience wanting more as she recedes from the camera in the rain and her image fades to black for the final time in the series (3.20).

As the female teenager of a single dad, *Veronica Mars'* titular character does not abide by Joseph Campbell's frequent relegation of a woman to the role of the "mother" and "protectress of the hero" (*The Hero's Journey* 93).[1] In fact, Veronica's function and achievements in many of the jobs undertaken by Mars Investigations equal those of her father. Major narrative arcs in the series define her hero's journey. Using Campbell's terminology, the first season of the series represents Veronica's "Departure," the second her "Initiation," and the third her "Return." As a postmodern anti-hero, however, her Return does not prove triumphant.

## Departure *of a Former 09er: Veronica's Quest*

"If you're like me, you just keep chasing the storm."
— Veronica Mars in "Meet John Smith" (1.3)

In season one of *Veronica Mars*, the murder of Veronica's best friend Lilly Kane obsesses her and catalyzes her initial call to adventure (Pilot). As the homicide occurred months before the narrative present of the series' pilot, Veronica's character has already experienced a seismic shift in her societal station when the show launches. Her former self, a happy and proud member of the "09ers," the most popular of Neptune High School's in-crowd, was fortunate enough to be the daughter of the local sheriff, Keith Mars, and the girlfriend of Duncan Kane, the son of one of the wealthiest and most respected of the town's citizens (Pilot). Lilly's murder, the arrest of a questionable suspect, Duncan's rejection, and Veronica's father's very public downfall from his position of authority make her an outsider in her own peer group, a prerequisite in the development of an anti-hero (Vogler 41).

Joseph Campbell notes that a hero's removal from her "center of gravity ... to a zone unknown" signals a "call to adventure" (*The Hero* 58). Veronica's new persona, one of a cynical, unpopular teenager who doesn't "know what's true anymore" ("Credit Where Credit's Due," 1.2), is partially rooted in feelings of betrayal due to her mother's disappearance shortly after Keith's removal from office. As Veronica says, "the best way to dull the pain of your best friend's murder is to have your mother abandon you as soon as possible" ("You Think You Know Somebody," 1.5). Had these personal tragedies not occurred, the series offers no reason to conclude that Veronica wouldn't have remained an average teen content to "talk on the phone and paint [her] nails like the other girls" ("Normal Is the Watchword," 2.1). Instead, Veronica takes it upon herself to "bring this family back together" (Pilot), by choosing to depart on a personal journey of discovery (*The Hero* 58), leading to the crushing disappointment of Lianne Mars' repeated lapse into alcoholism and duplicity ("Leave It to Beaver," 1.22).

As with most heroes, Veronica's subconscious accosts her as she undertakes her initial journey (*The Hero* 55). The narrative composition of *Veronica Mars'* first season utilizes both flashback and dream sequences as equally important indicators of Veronica's unconscious thought and of the challenges that lie before her. In the series pilot, scenes that catalyze Veronica's stubborn pursuit of the truth are introduced in a heavily-filtered (mind-altered) visual style pronouncing each moment a facet of Veronica's larger memory. Duncan's unceremonious (and unexplained) rejection of Veronica occurs near the Neptune High lockers, filmed through a dark blue filter as overexposed backlight shines in the far distance, as though Veronica's happiness sits just out of her reach. The hue covering the flash of Lilly's pronouncement that "I've got a secret, a good one" is a softer blue, and accentuates the golden highlights in Lilly and Veronica's hair, making them angelic spirits of the past. When Veronica awakens in flashback to find herself a victim of sexual assault, a counterintuitive high-contrast cheerful yellow light mocks her despair, as she weeps quietly in the morning sun. The harsh blue filter returns when Sheriff Lamb dismisses her reported rape in his office, in images whose clarity confirms his infuriating incompetence (1.1). A unique visual strategy transfigures each of Veronica's retrospections, separating the scenes from her current reality, which lends them an otherworldly (unconscious) significance.

Veronica's discovery of her mother's relationship with Jake Kane makes her wonder if she has engaged in incest with ex-boyfriend Duncan Kane ("The Girl Next Door," 1.7), which denotes a situation that Campbell might label "the herald" that "sound[s] the call to some high historical undertaking" (*The Hero* 51). Later in the first season, the audience is informed of the whereabouts of Lilly's parents on the night of her murder through Veronica's scattered memories of a conversation with her drunken mother in a roadside bar ("Betty and Veronica," 1.16). In these scenes, which are framed by a stand-alone mystery involving Neptune High's stolen mascot, Veronica's vocal quality evokes both a young child ("You should have seen me last night…. We had an '80s dance at school") and her mother's superior ("I know about you and Jake

Kane"). Whether Veronica sits across from Lianne in the grimy pub's booth or stands next to her against an oppressively lit wall as her mother smokes, images from the conversation continue to interrupt Veronica's daily activity, as though they need further review (1.16). These individual flashbacks demonstrate the potency of the hero's subconscious (*The Hero* 72), ultimately completing the whole of Veronica's latest discovery: that accused murderer Abel Koontz has a daughter that he may be trying to save (1.16).

The complex story design of "A Trip to the Dentist" encompasses flashbacks that imbue Veronica's visual mind with several points-of-view, as multiple characters afford her with differing eyewitness accounts of the events leading to her alleged sexual assault at Shelly Pomeroy's party the previous year (1.21). Campbell notes that during the hero's Departure, "regions of the unknown ... are free fields for the projection of unconscious content [including] incestuous *libido*" (*The Hero* 79). As Veronica was drugged during this encounter, her experience "forgotten," the personal ramifications tied to the truth (including whether or not she was raped and whether she slept with Duncan, who she fears may be her half-brother) depend solely on her ability to tie pieces of the disparate tales together in her mind's eye, her "detective work ... a method of regaining control of her environment" (Martaus 77). Ultimately, the revelation that Duncan and she had consensual sex offers little immediate comfort, though this investigation eventually impacts significant psychological revelations, most notably the welcome proof that Keith is her biological father, final substantiation that she hasn't engaged in an incestuous relationship ("Leave It to Beaver," 1.22).

Dream also plays a role in Veronica's Departure. The specter of Lilly hangs over the entire first season, appearing in flashback form in several episodes (including: "Credit Where Credit's Due" [1.2], "The Wrath of Con" [1.4], "The Girl Next Door" [1.7], etc.). Her ghostly presence also appears in Veronica's dreams, as the hero's "guide" (*The Hero* 55) in "Kanes and Abel's," when she (correctly) informs Veronica that her parents aren't murderers (1.17), and as a "protecting power" (*The Hero* 71) when she warns Veronica of future suffering by insisting, "you know how things are going to be, don't you" ("Leave It to Beaver," 1.22)?[2]

*Veronica Mars'* first season finale provides its protagonist with obstacles that challenge her known experience. Veronica's discovery of videotapes that implicate Aaron Echols as the lover of Lilly Kane forces her to brave conventional boundaries (*The Hero* 82), as his status of fame and power make him too influential an entity to be taken lightly as a suspect in Lilly's murder. The danger inherent in her climactic physical confrontation with Aaron is visualized in the violent sequence in which he traps Veronica in a refrigerator and sets the area aflame ("Leave It to Beaver" 1.22). According to Campbell, the hero, at this stage in her Departure, "instead of conquering or conciliating the power ... is swallowed into the unknown, and would appear to have died" (*The Hero* 90). Keith's arrival to save his daughter implies the truth of her limited strength (she is a teenager, after all) and becomes a harbinger of future events ("Leave It to Beaver," 1.22). By the end of the first season, Veronica is shaken and weakened by her adventure, and unknowingly prepared to be victimized.

## *Neptune High* Initiation: *Kidnapping, Rape, and Murder*

> "I was wondering where we were drawing the ethical line this year."
> — Wallace Fennel in "Normal Is the Watchword" (2.1)

*Veronica Mars* contains several major narrative arcs that Campbell might have described as events "where [the hero] must survive a succession of trials" (*The Hero* 97). During the show's second season, the mystery surrounding the bus accident ("Normal Is the Watchword," 2.1), the disclosure (and eventual impact) of Duncan's impending fatherhood ("My Mother, the Fiend," 2.9), and the confirmation that Cassidy Casablancas is a rapist and murderer ("Not Pictured," 2.22), form part of Veronica's Initiation period as a hero. Her responses to certain challenges complicate her heroic character, however, and test audience sympathies. As an anti-hero, Veronica does not experience her "perilous journey into the darkness" (*The Hero* 101) without fiddling with her moral compass.

Although one could argue that Lianne Mars's desertion of her family denotes personality flaws that bestowed upon her daughter the cynicism of an anti-hero (Vogler 41), Veronica's private inquiry regarding her mother's high school suspension in "My Mother, the Fiend" (2.9) generates an unexpected outcome. One of the hero's goals during her Initiation phase is to find "the 'bad' mother ... the absent, unattainable mother" (*The Hero* 111). In fact, Veronica insists to Keith that she just needs "a little proof that my mom was a good person" ("My Mother, the Fiend" 2.9). Although Veronica discovers that Lianne's suspension was due to her defense of Mary Mooney, the deaf lunch-lady who as a student became pregnant with the child of the Vice Principal at Neptune High, her behavior during this pursuit remains instructive. Veronica's health class assignment in "My Mother, the Fiend" makes her the "mother" of an animatronic baby, and her frequent disregard for her own "progeny" throughout the episode echoes that of her mother for her (2.9).[3]

Veronica's risky embrace of anti-hero territory in "Donut Run" (2.11) also relates to a baby's welfare. After Meg Manning dies from injuries sustained in the bus accident, leaving Duncan the single-father of the baby dubbed "Faith" by Meg's fundamentalist parents, Veronica assists Duncan in the kidnapping of his own child (2.11). Veronica's wide experience in skirting rules usually serves as an indicator of her high intelligence as well as her remarkable (and often admirable) ability to conquer societal barriers. The emotional power of the narrative construction of "Donut Run," however, reminds the audience that Veronica remains at times a selfish teenager, one who is willing to hurt others by inviting risks she believes worthwhile.

An anti-hero dismisses directives by the governors of the social order (Vogler 42). Veronica misinforms the civil agencies (including the sheriff's department and the FBI) of her knowledge of Duncan's whereabouts. Her disregard for her own father throughout "Donut Run" (2.11), however, specifies an important moment in her (anti)hero's Initiation. Campbell notes that conflict between father and offspring is crucial in the Initiation phase of a hero's journey, as the knowledge attained during this experience serves the child in moving to a place of authority (*The Hero* 136). Veronica's contempt for certain power figures in the status quo, however, defines her anti-hero status (Vogler 42) and informs her everyday activity (as seen in her counterattacks on the Kanes' security chief Clarence Wiedman in "Silence of the Lamb" [1.11] and "Betty and Veronica" [1.16], in the bugging and duping of Sheriff Lamb in "Blast from the Past" [2.5] and "Donut Run" [2.11], etc.). Her compulsion to save Duncan and his baby places Keith under this umbrella of disdain. Veronica covertly coerces him into two unfamiliar roles — as an investigator who loses the truth, and as the father of a daughter willing to hurt him ("Donut Run," 2.11).

Keith believes that Veronica suffers early in "Donut Run" due to her breakup with Duncan and reminds her that "anything you need, honey, I'm here."[4] But after Veronica dismisses her arrest and Sheriff Lamb with a snarky comment, Keith slams his hand onto the interrogation table and insists, "this is not a joke.... What Duncan has done is wrong and if you've helped him in any way you're going to prison. Now shape up!" By employing his parental authority, Keith places the serious accusations leveled against Veronica into proper perspective. After he finds that she "played" him, his voice quivers as he declares, "it's not just your life you're gambling with, Veronica. I would not survive without you." Keith's childlike assertion acknowledges Veronica's diminishing of his patriarchal command (2.11). In fact, Campbell might label this scene "a radical readjustment of [her] emotional relationship to the parental images" (*The Hero* 137), another common attribute of a hero's phase of Initiation.

Veronica has, however, neglected the "great care on the part of the [hero's] father" (*The Hero* 133). Her contention that she "had to" betray Keith in "Donut Run" dismisses his claims to the contrary. When Veronica lies to Keith in the interrogation room, she claims that she sold Celeste Kane's jewelry so that Duncan could hire a lawyer and begin proceedings to adopt his baby, a viable, legal option. Her distrust of both parental facility (Meg Manning's parents, the baby's grandparents, are proven abusers ["Nobody Puts Baby in a Corner," 2.7]) and societal jurisdiction (Neptune's courts operate as part of "a corrupt justice system" [Martaus 82]) leads her to choose criminal abduction over proper procedure (2.11). Veronica's perspective on the kidnapping of Duncan's baby positions her as an archetypical postmodern anti-hero, one who characterizes morality in shades of gray (McWilliams 71; and see Edwards 76). Her actions in "Donut Run" are never again queried in the series, validating her questionable treatment of Keith.

Although Keith's declaration that he may never trust Veronica again after her deceit is "forgotten by the next episode" (Ramos 109), the emotional impression of the aforementioned father/daughter scene in "Donut Run" (2.11) would surface again in "Not Pictured" (2.22), the second season finale of *Veronica Mars*. The mystery surrounding the school bus accident serves as the season-long plot-arc equivalent to the search for Lilly's murderer in season one. Keith's physical absence from the site of Veronica's climactic rooftop brawl with the rapist/murderer Cassidy "Beaver" Casablancas in "Not Pictured" (2.22) prevents him from assuming a protective role for her as he had in his physical battle with Aaron Echolls the year before ("Leave It to Beaver" 1.22), and serves as an integral component of her Initiation, as she must finally "face the world of specialized adult action" without parental aid (*The Hero* 136). Keith's "abandonment" of Veronica (Millman 57) in "Not Pictured" actually facilitates her advancement as a hero (2.22).

Veronica's horror upon believing that Beaver had detonated a bomb aboard Keith's plane strikes the very heart of her emotional being. As she points a shaking gun at Beaver, Veronica reminds Logan Echolls and the audience of what's at stake. "He killed my father, he killed everyone on the bus, he raped me!" While Logan's proclamation that "you're not a killer, Veronica!" proves accurate, her experience on that rooftop provides her character with imperatives necessary to continue the anti-hero's journey ("Not Pictured," 2.22).

Early in "Not Pictured," Veronica experiences a utopian dream. Lianne stands in the kitchen enjoying a happy breakfast with her husband and daughter. As the sequence continues, Keith appears in his sheriff's uniform, Veronica meets Wallace for the first time in Neptune High's hallway (instead of at the flag pole in the series "Pilot"), and Veronica sees Lilly frolicking in front of the Lilly Kane Memorial fountain, all of which validate the sequence as pure fantasy (2.22). This vision elucidates the meaning of Veronica's second dream in the episode, which emerges as she grieves the loss of her father.

The morning after the horrifying events on the roof of the Neptune Grand Hotel, images again pervade Veronica's subconscious, appropriate markers for the completion of her Initiation (*The Hero* 121). As she sleeps on Logan's lap in a classic Pietà position,[5] Veronica dreams of a happy childhood puppet show performed by Keith. Sitting on a blanket giggling, little girl Veronica listens to her father make goofy noises, a sock-puppet on each of his hands. Bright morning sun saturates the scene, representative of both a new beginning and a long-ago past ("Not Pictured," 2.22). The absence of Lianne in Veronica's latest vision is instructive, as the consideration that her father may have died remains shockingly real, implying her own potential "orphaning." The significance of the dream relates to one of Keith's comments in "Donut Run" (2.11), but reverses the figures in power. Can Veronica live without her father? When Keith appears moments later in their apartment in the narrative present and recites dialogue reminiscent of her dream ("Is that breakfast I smell?"), Veronica's catharsis overcomes her ("Not Pictured," 2.22).

The anguish Veronica experiences throughout her Initiation phase evinces her continuing development as a hero-figure (*The Hero* 190). However, her refusal to learn from her mistakes, to harness her less desirable qualities, will trigger her final punishment as an anti-hero in the third season of the series.

# Return *of the Anti-Hero: Defeatist Adolescent Fury*

> "You don't care now but holy crap are you going to care when I start to get my revenge on."
> — Veronica Mars in "The Bitch Is Back" (3.20)

Season three of *Veronica Mars* deconstructs traits of the archetypical hero's journey. After her escape from potential defeat at the hands of Cassidy Casablancas and realization that her father avoided the doomed plane bound for Neptune ("Not Pictured," 2.22), her Return to her teen existence disallows her from experiencing Campbell's "magic flight" to a society improved by her actions (*The Hero* 197). Christopher Vogler defines this stage in the journey as a time when a "story's energy" increases again, as a hero's Return offers the protagonist fresh hardship (193). Veronica's new daily habitat, Hearst College, simply replaces Neptune High as the crime-ridden center of her universe.

Structurally, *Veronica Mars* changes in season three. Veronica's major investigations into the murder of Lilly Kane and the bombing of the school bus full of students took the entirety of each of the first two respective seasons to conclude. The serialized nature of the show intertwines individual long-term mysteries with several subplots, making the first and second season finales series pinnacles ("Leave It to Beaver," 1.22 and "Not Pictured," 2.22). Two major subplots steer Veronica's main activities in the third season of the program: the search for the Heart College rapist ("My Big Fat Greek Rush Week," 3.2) and for the person who shot Dean O'Dell ("Spit & Eggs," 3.9), which dilutes the narrative substance and impact of each. The closing curtain, "The Bitch Is Back" (3.20), the open-ended series finale, punishes Veronica for embracing her anti-hero vocation.

Campbell writes that under normal circumstances, a hero's Return may be delayed by her questioning of self and refusal to re-engage with the local populace (*The Hero* 193). The hero may decide to retreat from the life she knew before her adventures, allowing her fellow humans to fend for themselves (*The Hero* 218). Veronica abides by an alternate approach, taking inspiration in the demise of another character (*The Hero* 238). Veronica seems remarkably stable after her own near-death experience and the suicide of Beaver Casablancas, and welcomes a return to her informal occupation when tendered her first task at Hearst College.

In "Welcome Wagon" (3.1), Veronica braves the flimsiest season premiere mystery in the history of *Veronica Mars*. Wallace's new roommate, Piz Piznarski, finds that all of his possessions have been stolen out of his car by a group calling themselves the "Hearst College Welcome Wagon Committee." The comical nature of the circumstances epitomizes a common trait of the Return phase of hero-narratives (*The Hero* 197), as the culprit proves to be a college student mentor to three prepubescent thieves (3.1).

Rape again dominates a seasonal subplot, as the Hearst College assailant becomes Veronica's significant foe ("Spit & Eggs," 3.9). Her discovery that she was in the same room when her friend Mac's roommate Parker Lee was attacked prompts Veronica's mission to stop the rapist, as she stands accused of failing to act ("My Big Fat Greek Rush Week," 3.2). Guilt evidently motivates Veronica's determination to identify the campus rapist, as she shows little interest in the horrifying events when she witnesses an anti-rape rally in "Welcome Wagon" (3.1). Her renewed devotion to the journey (Vogler 195) dominates the first half of *Veronica Mars'* third season.

"Spit & Eggs" (3.09) utilizes a chase sequence as a framing device to place the bloodied Veronica in the shadow of the rapist at both the opening and closing moments of the episode. Christopher Vogler contends that chases are common ingredients in a hero's period of Return, and Veronica's situation recalls her experience at Shelly Pomeroy's party three years earlier, which ramps up the tension of the pursuit (197). After she escapes from the rapist Mercer Hayes (by stabbing him with a symbolic phallus, a model unicorn) and finds comfort in Moe's dorm room, Veronica realizes that the tea he's given her has been laced with a date-rape drug, which weakens her for another sexual predator.[6] The drug proves only a "delaying obstacle" (*The Hero* 201), however, as Veronica's rape whistle alerts Parker and fellow students to her aid (3.9). She has, this time, escaped the horror of sexual violation.

Thankfully, the appeal and sway of romance does not abandon Veronica at any point during her journey. Her on-and-off relationship with Logan Echolls continues in the third season of the series, providing the proceedings with ample passion at opportune moments. As Rhonda Wilcox observes in this volume, Logan exhibits qualities often attributed to the romantic hero, which only adds an intriguing suitability to their match. Both characters seem to recognize, however, that Veronica's "Crossing of the Return Threshold" requires the push and pull of her heart (*The Hero* 228). If their relationship progressed smoothly and without dramatic interruption, Veronica's development as a hero would conclude.

The couple sits on a campus bench trading barbs about the Clint Eastwood marathon they recently enjoyed ("Welcome Wagon," 3.1), Veronica places a tracking device on Logan's cell phone when feeling insecure and alone ("Wichita Linebacker," 3.3), she actively (and angrily) avoids him when Logan admits to running from the scene after Mercer set fire to a motel in Tijuana ("Of Vice and Men," 3.7), and they break up twice (in "Spit & Eggs" 3.9 and in "There's Got to Be a Morning After Pill" 3.12) only to remain intimately connected as Logan beats the stuffing out of students he believes to have disrespected Veronica in the series finale ("The Bitch Is Back," 3.20). As Campbell notes, the "encounter and separation, for all its wildness, is typical of the sufferings of love" (*The Hero* 228).

In his analysis of fictional paradigms, Frank Kermode argues that a text "imposes ... development, character, a past which matters and a future ... determined by the project of the author rather than that of the characters. They have their choices, but the novel has its end" (140). As the final episode of *Veronica Mars*, the narrative design of "The Bitch Is Back" (3.20) shoulders definitive responsibility for the concluding impact of its protagonist's televised existence, thereby retaining significant meaning that may have been lessened had the series not been untimely canceled with questions left unanswered.

Joseph Campbell theorizes that "the conclusion of the childhood cycle is the return" when the hero's "true character is revealed" (*The Hero* 328). As an absolute text, *Veronica Mars* completed its run (and evolution) in its third season finale, so the episode's content leaves a lasting impression of Veronica's moral fiber. "The Bitch Is Back" (3.20) characterizes Veronica Mars as an immature, self-involved, and ultimately destructive anti-hero.

When a secret Hearst society distributes an intimate videotape of Veronica and Piz to the entire campus ("Weevils Wobble but They Don't Go Down," 3.19), Veronica's final case will lead her to betray Keith one last time. Veronica breaks into the Kane mansion, steals Jake Kane's hard drive, pressures Cindy "Mac" MacKenzie to crack the drive and retrieve information regarding the members of the clandestine group, "The Castle," all while her father (currently Acting Sheriff and campaigning to be officially elected to the position) fends off Kane and Clarence Wiedman, whose witness confirms that someone who fits Veronica's description scaled the fence to enter the Kane estate. Pop culture anti-heroes have a compulsion to "be heard at all costs" (Bostic 55). Veronica's refusal to return her father's calls (disguised pleas) and his realization that his daughter has once again broken the law compels Keith to erase the security video that connects her to the theft in an effort to protect her. This actionable offense (Keith faces indictment for destroying evidence at the end of the series) will likely result in his defeat in the election for sheriff, costing him the fulfill-ment he deserves ("The Bitch Is Back," 3.20).

Considering Veronica's progression as an anti-hero, her knowing betrayal of her father (with impunity) in "Donut Run" (2.11) actually prepares her to disregard the consequences of her actions in "The Bitch Is Back" (3.20). While she believes that personal retribution in this latest quest represents an appro-priate response to unethical behavior by others (she hands a list of the members of The Castle to a reporter from the school newspaper), her insistence that Jake Kane spare her dad from reprisal comes "a little too late" (3.20). Veronica's conceit matches that of many heroes during the Return stage, as her "self-righteousness leads to a misunderstanding, not only of oneself but of the nature of both man and the cosmos" (*The Hero* 238). Her behavior also cor-roborates Keith's doubt in "Donut Run" about whether he should ever trust Veronica again (2.11).

Veronica, unable to surrender her ego to protect her own father, ensures them both of unhappiness. Jean Paul Sartre notes that when a character "com-mits himself to anything, fully realizing that he is not only choosing what he will be, but is thereby ... a legislator deciding for the whole of mankind — in such a moment he cannot escape from the sense of profound and complete responsibility" (qtd. in Kermode 143). Veronica's inability to see past her own thirst for revenge in "The Bitch Is Back" (3.20) leaves the audience of *Veronica Mars* with a lasting image of stormy despair, one of our teenage detective wandering into the distance after again failing to find comfort in a world without justice. Serves an anti-hero right.

## Notes

1. Many feminist scholars have problematized Joseph Campbell's definitions of mythological archetypes, particularly his tendency to gender the hero's journey as male. The immense bibliography of notable work is too formidable to list here, but see Judith Butler's *Gender Trouble*, Jane Gallop's *The Daughter's Seduction: Feminism and Psychoanalysis*, Estelle Lauter's *Feminist Archetypal Theory: A Revision of Jungian Thought*, Pam Morris's *Literature and Feminism*, Carol Pearson and Katherine Pope's *Female Hero in British and American Literature*, and Annis Pratt's *Archetypal Patterns in Women's Poetry* for important examinations of gender construction in art and literature.

2. Lilly also serves as a protecting power in *Veronica Mars'* second season premiere, when her specter beckons Veronica at the gas station, prompting her to miss the school bus that would plunge off the edge of a cliff minutes later ("Normal Is the Watchword," 2.1).

3. In this volume, Rhonda V. Wilcox's "So Cal Pietà: Veronica Mars, Logan Echolls and the Search for the Mother" includes an extensive discussion regarding the impact of Lianne Mars as Veronica's absent mother.

4. See Mayer in this volume.

5. As Wilcox writes in this volume, the choice to include the Pietà image in this scene harkens back to the beginning of the second season, when the roles were reversed and Veronica assumed the "mother" role for Logan in the mise-en-scène ("Normal Is the Watchword," 2.1).

6. Veronica's lack of caution in this scene is rather curious, as she had previously been drugged and prepared for assault two episodes earlier only to be saved by Logan in "Of Vice and Men" (3.07).

## Works Cited

Bostic, Jeff Q., et al. "From Alice Cooper to Marilyn Manson: The Significance of Adolescent Antiheroes." *Academic Psychiatry* 27 (2003): 54–62. Web. 15 April 2010.

Campbell, Joseph. *The Hero with a Thousand Faces.* 1949. London: Fontana Press, 1993. Print.

_____. *The Hero's Journey: Joseph Campbell on His Life and Work.* Novato: New World Library, 1990. Print.

Edwards, Lynne. "On the Down-Low: How a *Buffy* Fan Fell in Love with *Veronica Mars.*" Thomas 73–80. Print.

Kermode, Frank. *The Sense of an Ending: Studies in the Theory of Fiction with a New Epilogue.* New York: Oxford University Press, 2000. Print.

Martaus, Alaine. "'You Get Tough. You Get Even': Rape, Anger, Cynicism, and the Vigilante Girl Detective in *Veronica Mars*." *CLUES: A Journal of Detection* 27.1 (2006): 74–86. Print.

McWilliams, Ora. *"Hey Batman, What Are Your Parents Getting You for Christmas?": The Orphan Narrative and Non-Traditional Families in American SuperHero Publications*. Diss. Bowling Green State University, 2006. Print.

Millman, Joyce. "Daddy's Girl." Thomas 46–56. Print.

Ramos, John. "I Cannot Tell a Lie. And if You Believe That...." Thomas 104–112. Print.

Thomas, Rob, ed. *Neptune Noir: Unauthorized Investigations into* Veronica Mars. Dallas: BenBella, 2006. Print.

Vogler, Christopher. *The Writer's Journey: Mythic Structure for Storytellers and Screenwriters*. London: Pan Books, 1999. Print.

# 8

## This Teen Sleuth's Tricks Aren't Just for Kids
### *Connecting with an Intergenerational Audience*

LISA EMMERTON

The "teen television" genre has its roots in the 1950s and 1960s when the Baby Boomer generation came of age and an unprecedented number of teenagers with disposable income caught the notice of eager marketers; indeed, Bill Osgerby states that the "rise of 'teen' programming in American TV schedules was indebted, at least in part, to market economics. TV series appealing to teenage audiences and depicting the exploits of jaunty teens were a bankable proposition because young people had come to represent a powerful economic force after World War II" (72). He goes on to mention that the "range of products geared to the young was literally boundless, consumer industries interacting with and reinforcing one another in their efforts to woo the lucrative youth market" (73). This cross-promotional marketing strategy is still in use, and it has intensified as the postmodern media landscape has created a plethora of opportunities to separate teens from their allowance money.[1]

Rob Thomas, a frustrated television writer who often wondered "how clearly god-awful programming made it on the air" (1), made an important intervention into this teen TV tradition with one of the most intelligent youth series to be broadcast on network television in recent years. At first glance, *Veronica Mars* (2004–2007) appears to be a show for teenagers. The series contains a number of traits that viewers have come to associate with the "teen genre"; teen characters and themes feature prominently throughout all three seasons. Furthermore, the series was broadcast on networks that target a youth audience (the series started out on UPN, and later moved to CW when UPN merged with The WB). Series creator Rob Thomas openly states that he developed _Veronica Mars_ with intent to produce a quality teen drama:

> With my high school teaching background as well as my start in young adult fiction, I'd long wanted to do a teen drama. The trouble was, my favorite teen drama ever, _Freaks and Geeks_ [1999–2000], was already on the air, and it was failing. There weren't many networks clamoring to put another teen drama in primetime — unless it was a soap opera about sexy kids doing sexy things [5].

Thomas's frustration with network television, particularly with network executives and their reluctance to experiment with fresh, edgy material, played a major role in developing _Veronica Mars_, a series that presents a number of challenges to our understanding of television genres and their target audiences. In a market already oversaturated with images of "sexy kids doing sexy things," _Veronica Mars_ took the all-too-familiar scenario in which privileged "So Cal" kids revel in the anguish produced by their glamorous lifestyle and turned it on its head. _Veronica Mars_ simultaneously points to the inadequacies of many _contemporary_ youth dramas and provides a demonstration that it is possible to produce quality series that deal with teen issues.

We would expect a show that features teenage characters in a Southern California high school setting to attract a teenage audience. Yet _Veronica Mars_ attracted a viewership that contained a surprising number of adults. Before the series was cancelled, BenBella books released a volume titled _Neptune Noir: Unauthorized Investigations into Veronica Mars_ as part of its Smart Pop series. Edited by Rob Thomas, the book contains a collection of essays written by academics, journalists, media critics, and fiction writers, all of them adults professing their love for a show that is supposed to be for teenagers. What is it about this show that allows it to extend its reach beyond its intended teen audience? The obvious answer is that it is extremely well-written, and it follows in the footsteps of Joss Whedon's _Buffy the Vampire Slayer_ (1997–2003), reinventing the "Valley Girl" trope by turning the petite, athletic blonde into a delightfully witty, incisive heroine who vanquishes her enemies. Lynne Edwards feels as though her love for _Veronica Mars_ somehow constitutes "cheating" on Buffy:

> I am on the down-low with Veronica Mars. I still love Buffy, the mythical slayer who battled vampires while looking for love and who empowered her posse, the Scoobies, to do the same. As a virtual Scooby, I reveled in our weekly triumphs, our loves and our losses — and our unrivaled kill-ratio. Yet, here I am, tiptoeing behind Buffy's back every week for some Neptune nookie. How did I let this happen? [73].

The similarities between Buffy and Veronica are well known; many press descriptions and reviews of _Veronica Mars_ make comparisons between the two: *The Seattle Times* called Veronica "a tougher Buffy for the 21st century" (McFadden). Both series have a strong academic following. Scholars are drawn to *Veronica Mars* because, much like *Buffy*, Thomas's series contains clever writing, complex narratives, highly developed characters and unique experiments with genre. However, adults from various walks of life can appreciate a series like *Veronica Mars*, because the series employs a number of strategies that allow it speak to multiple audiences at once. Though its characters and themes seem to target Generation Y (individuals born in the 1980s and 1990s — typically defined as the children of the Baby Boomers), there are a number of aesthetic and narrative elements that indicate an attempt to appeal to Boomers and members of Gen X as well.

## Bridging the Generation Gap

In *Teen TV: Genre, Consumption and Identity*, Glyn Davis and Kay Dickinson assert that the popular teen drama *Dawson's Creek* (1998–2003) exemplifies many of the characteristics that have come to define the teen television genre in the late twentieth and early twenty-first centuries: "a use of language which is too sophisticated for the ages of the characters; frequent intertextual references; recourse to a sense of community based on generation; a blunt, somewhat melodramatic use of emotion and aphoristic psychological reasoning; and a prominent pop music soundtrack" (1). Following on the heels of *Dawson's Creek*, *Veronica Mars* possesses all of these traits. Veronica (Kristen Bell) does not speak like a typical teenager; rather, her words, particularly her terse and telling voiceovers, demonstrate eloquence and wisdom beyond her years. For example, in "Meet John Smith," Veronica describes her life after the fallout of the Lilly Kane murder: "Tragedy blows through your life like a tornado, uprooting everything, creating chaos. You wait for the dust to settle, and then you choose. You can live in the wreckage and pretend it's still the mansion you remember. Or you can crawl from the rubble and slowly rebuild. Because after disaster strikes, the important thing is that you move on. But if you're like me, you just keep chasing the storm" (1.3). This piece of voiceover narration is but one example of Veronica's articulate and very mature self-reflexivity. Intertextual references are a common occurrence; many facets of the show, from plot and dialogue to visual imagery and episode titles, are riddled with allusions to well-known works of high art and popular culture (note, for example, the episode titles mentioned later in this chapter). The melodramatic use of emotion, aphoristic psychological reasoning, and a prominent pop music soundtrack are also key features of *Veronica Mars*. It is generally accepted that these features are necessary to successfully prompt teens to spend their disposable income on a range of products manufactured just for them. Today's postmodern youth culture is, after all, market driven and dominated by self-perpetuating media images.

It is, however, more difficult to determine how teen TV addresses its audience through "recourse to a sense of community based on generation."[2] Part of the difficulty lies in the fact that media culture, especially television, has significantly altered how generations are characterized and consolidated in popular consciousness, as well as how individual members of a given generation come to understand and experience the times in which they live. Thomas de Zengotita describes this phenomenon:

> Youth culture is representational through and through, and it has been moving in that direction since the 1950s, and so the whole cultural trajectory has been preserved and is continuously recycled. It is perpetual. Elvis lives.... My kids can distinguish instantly between 1970s movies and 1960s movies; they have a feel for the hairstyles, the outfits, the manners and settings, all the little conventions that marked those decades as they came and went. They can even feel nostalgia for the 1950s. *They can feel nostalgia for times they never lived through.* That's how much a part of the contemporary environment representations have become. And that's why it is possible to have a media memoir of the past few decades that is collective, that works in various ways for people of all ages, whether or not they lived through those decades physically. We've all lived through them virtually [34–5].

*Veronica Mars* takes full advantage of this phenomenon in order to heighten its intergenerational appeal. Fiction and reality are often blended when the series draws on historical events that younger viewers may have experienced virtually and that older viewers actually lived through. For example, the series depicts college life as an amalgamation of contemporary issues and historical memories. To illustrate, the spirit of fervent protest present on many college campuses during the Vietnam War is re-contextualized in *Veronica Mars* as the Lilith House students protest the serial rapes taking place at Hearst College.

This strategy comes to the fore on a couple of different occasions during Season Three. In the episode "Lord of the Pi's," (3.8), Patty Hearst makes a guest appearance in the semi-autobiographical role of Selma Hearst Rose.[3] Selma is the granddaughter of the founder of Hearst College, and her swing vote determines whether or not Hearst will abolish the Greek system of fraternities and sororities. (These organizations are believed to play a role in the serial rapes taking place on campus). When Selma disappears, Dean O'Dell (Ed Begley Jr.) hires Veronica to find her. This disappearance, of course, asks Boomer viewers to recall images of Patty Hearst being kidnapped by, and subsequently joining forces with, the Symbionese Liberation Army in 1974. Also in Season Three, "My Big Fat Greek Rush Week" (3.2) includes a subplot in which Logan and Wallace volunteer to take part in a psychological experiment designed by their professor. The experiment involves two groups of students, one group pretending to be prison guards and the other pretending to be inmates. Again, Boomers, or psychology students for that matter, will recognize the experiment as being very similar to the well-known Stanford Prison Experiment performed by Dr. Philip Zimbardo in 1971. Zimbardo's experiment, which was supposed to last two weeks, was ended after only six days, because the "guards" were becoming dangerously aggressive and the "inmates" were showing signs of depression and extreme stress. Zimbardo's shocking findings still inform much of what we know about the "groupthink" mentality that can lead to atrocities such as the violence committed by prison guards at Abu Ghraib (Zimbardo). By referencing this experiment, *Veronica Mars* addresses sensitive issues of importance to everyone, not just teenagers.

Perhaps, then, the biggest mistake we make when we talk about "teen television" is assuming that it is always intended solely for today's teenagers. As Jeremy Butler asserts, "network-era television contradicts itself frequently and haphazardly. It presents many heterogeneous meanings in any one night's viewing. This polysemy contributes to television's broad appeal" (10). Teen shows are no exception to this rule; they can and do contain messages that can be interpreted and appreciated by viewers outside of the target demographic. Moreover, teen television has traditionally been used as a means of placating adults worried about the dangers that "sex, drugs and rock 'n roll" pose for their children. One of the earliest programs directed at teenagers in America was ABC's *TV Teen Club* (1949–1954), best described as "a parade of young people playing accordions, singing vaudeville tunes, performing acrobatic stunts, competing for cash and prizes such as refrigerators — all presided over by a balding, rotund, middle-aged bandleader given to outdated slang interjections" (Martin 27). That band leader was series creator Paul Whiteman, and TV legend has it that the creation of *TV Teen Club* was "an almost mythological tale of one man's efforts to battle juvenile delinquency" assuming that "television had the power to create a 'virtual space' in which teenagers could congregate in small groups nationwide, under the watchful gaze of parents" (Martin 27). Although television viewing has undergone rapid transformation in recent years, both in programming and the technology used to view that programming, teen television is still somewhat obligated to provide a "safe space" through which teens can explore the troubling issues that affect their lives as they move from childhood to adulthood. Morality and social responsibility are still paramount, particularly when dealing with sex, drugs and violence. _Veronica Mars_, however, takes up these issues in a variety of different ways that render them startlingly relevant to adults. The strategies that the series uses to accomplish this task are both immensely entertaining and thought-provoking.

## _Teen Idols, Guest Stars and Intertextuality_

In the episode "Postgame Mortem" (3.13), a brooding Logan Echolls (Jason Dohring) answers his cell phone and has a conversation with his long-time pal, Dick Casablancas (Ryan Hansen). Dick spontaneously got married in Las Vegas, and we can only assume he wants to have the marriage annulled when he asks Logan (who has had many legal troubles of his own) if he knows a _good_ lawyer. Logan, after a pause, says "I know _a_ lawyer." The source of humor in this moment is twofold. Firstly, the lawyer to whom Logan is referring is Cliff McCormack (Daran Norris), the county-appointed attorney who often represents the less wealthy residents of Neptune, and he would not necessarily be described as a "good lawyer." Secondly, this line has been uttered before. Veronica said the same thing to Wallace (Percy Daggs III) when he was in need of a good lawyer after being wrongfully accused of a hit-and-run that killed a homeless man (2.13). Inside jokes such as this are examples of intratextuality, wherein episodes ask us to recall information from previous episodes (Wilcox 193). These references are evidence that _Veronica Mars_ is a series that rewards viewers for their loyalty and diligence. Rob Thomas states: "Sure, we don't do well in the ratings, but our fans are fervent, and they pay attention to detail" (7). Indeed, close attention is required not only to follow the show's complex narrative, but also to enjoy a variety of running gags (like the one described above), parodies and allusions.

> If texts and audiences are surrounded by multiple discourses of what a text or genre means, with genres operating across multiple cultural realms, for us to piece together an understanding of genre, and to work out contexts and groupings into which we as readers should place any given text, we rely on our intertextual competence [Gray 30].

_Veronica Mars_ is a series that demands a high degree of intertextual[4] and intratextual competence from its viewers. Though intertextual references sometimes require viewers to "dig deeper" and conduct their own research beyond the initial viewing experience in order to fully appreciate them, many of the references found in _Veronica Mars_ are simply in keeping with the ways in which contemporary youth culture is formed and disseminated. Intertextual references, as was pointed out by Davis and Dickinson, are a common feature of series that target a Gen Y audience. Intertextuality is often used as a form of cross-promotion, which is essential for any would-be teen idol desiring to capture the notoriously short attention span of Gen Y viewers.

It is for this reason that many of the intertextual references in *Veronica Mars* come in the form of guest stars; actors and other notorious public figures appear on the series, bringing with them any number of connotations based on appearances they have made in other pop culture venues. Jeff Bussolini uses the term "casting intertextuality" to describe this phenomenon ("Television Intertextuality"). In other words, no guest star comes without "textual baggage." For example, in "Versatile Toppings" (2.14), teen star Kristin Cavallari appears as Kylie, a popular Neptune High cheerleader who also happens to be a lesbian. Veronica comes to Kylie's aid when someone threatens to "out" her and all of Neptune High's other homosexual students. Cavallari's appearance would be unremarkable if not for the fact that she rose to fame on the MTV reality series *Laguna Beach: The Real Orange County* (2004).[5] This series chronicles the lives of wealthy teens, focusing primarily on their social lives and sexual exploits. Cavallari is particularly well-known for her flirtatious personality and supposed sexual promiscuity; her interactions with co-stars are known to produce much of the drama and tension that draws viewers into the series. Her presence on *Veronica Mars*, then, forms an ironic commentary on the nature of teen stardom, given that *Veronica Mars* is a series that aims to debunk much of the glamorous Orange County imagery found in popular teen programs like *Laguna Beach* and *The O.C.* (2003–2007). Paris Hilton's[6] appearance in "Credit Where Credit's Due" (1.2) produces a similar effect. In other words, commitment to one particular public image is not necessary to maintain one's status as a Gen Y teen idol; rather, reinventing one's image and appearing in a variety of different pop culture contexts are crucial for maintaining that status. Cavallari and Hilton are not particularly gifted thespians, but their acting abilities are irrelevant. Staying in the public eye and demonstrating an ability to ironically satirize one's own fame are now important prerequisites for the Gen Y teen idol.[7]

Though *Veronica Mars'* use of intertextuality is clearly influenced by the media sensibilities of its target audience, intertextuality is also used to broaden the series' appeal, adding adult viewers to the equation. During Season Three, Laura San Giacomo guest starred in three episodes as Harmony Chase,[8] a woman who hires Keith Mars (Enrico Colantoni), Veronica's father, to find out if her husband is being unfaithful. In "Charlie Don't Surf" (3.4), Harmony walks into Keith's office and politely says: "Hi, I don't have an appointment. Do you remember me, by any chance?" This moment is, of course, another inside joke for anyone paying attention. Keith may remember Harmony from

Judge Crawford's Christmas parties, but older viewers will remember that Laura San Giacomo and Enrico Colantoni acted together in the NBC sitcom *Just Shoot Me!* (1997–2003). San Giacomo's appearance on *Veronica Mars* reminds viewers that before he was Keith Mars, Veronica's loving and dutiful father, Enrico Colantoni played Elliot DiMauro, a womanizing photographer working for the fictional fashion magazine, *Blush*. Being a husband and father was never part of Elliot's plan (he spent much of his time bedding models), though he did enter a serious relationship with San Giacomo's character, Maya, for a short time. The reference to *Just Shoot Me!* is significant, because it was a show that attempted to capture the stereotypical Gen X attitude and outlook on life. The characters were often apathetic and cynical, and most of them eschewed marriage and family life in favor of careers and neurotic self-indulgence. Perhaps the endearing, if illicit, romance between Keith and Harmony is Thomas's (himself a member of Gen X) attempt to shed a more favorable light on a generation often defined as cynical slackers.

As an aside, it is important to note that Keith's quest for romance, in and of itself, adds an adult dimension to *Veronica Mars*. Though Veronica's tempestuous relationship with Logan often steals the show in the romance department, Keith's relationships throughout the series hold appeal for any adult who has built a family and then had to start all over again due to death or divorce. Throughout the series, Keith's attempt to balance his own personal fulfillment with the needs of his daughter is one of the most captivating aspects of his character. He often puts his own desires on hold for Veronica's sake (he ends his relationship with Rebecca James (Paula Marshall), the school guidance counselor, because Veronica is not ready for him to date), but he occasionally puts himself first (he for some time pursues Harmony even though Veronica disapproves of his dating a married woman). Ultimately, *Veronica Mars* acknowledges that teenagers and young adults are not the only people who find themselves on voyages of personal discovery. Adults too have times when they must think about who they are and what they want; that is something that *Veronica Mars* carefully represents and something that many adult viewers can appreciate.

## Logan Echolls: Timeless Bad Boy

Though the guest stars that frequently visit Neptune play a major role in forming the series' intertextual messages, they are not the only source of intertextuality. Sometimes series regulars draw our attention to other texts that influence how we read *Veronica Mars*. In a series filled with complex, highly developed characters, Logan Echolls (Jason Dohring) is perhaps the most complex one of all. Over the course of three seasons, Logan plays with our emotions and sympathies more than any other character. In early episodes, he appears to be, as Veronica describes him, a "psychotic jackass" (1.1); it is easy to dislike Logan when he is smashing Veronica's headlights and organizing "bum fights" (1.6). He is wealthy and attractive with a keen mind and a more than healthy sense of entitlement. In many ways, he is a textbook example of Gen Y youth. As the son of a movie star, he is certainly media savvy, and media imagery, especially celebrity culture, contributes greatly to his character.

Though we may despise Logan's self-indulgent witticisms, especially the snide remarks he makes at Veronica's expense, feelings of ambivalence inevitably creep into our consciousness when we find out that Logan's father, movie star Aaron Echolls (Harry Hamlin), is abusive and that his father's wealth, fame, and self-absorption have prevented any genuine bond from developing between father and son. Moreover, Logan is repeatedly depicted as a victim, not only of physical abuse, but also of his movie star father's fame. For Logan, the "textuality" of a postmodern, media-driven society is a constant bane. He is forced to relive his personal mistakes and his family's tragedies through a television program when his father is featured on *The Tinseltown Diaries*, a spoof of the real-life celebrity documentary series *E! True Hollywood Story* (1996). When the program airs in "The Quick and the Wed" (2.15), we see a number of different people watching it from different vantage points. Logan and Dick watch it from their hotel room; Logan is clearly irritated by the invasion of privacy, while Dick is amused. Logan's girlfriend Hannah (Jessy Schram) and her mother also see the broadcast; Hannah appears embarrassed, while her mother is concerned about her daughter dating someone with such a sordid reputation. Finally, we see Veronica watching the program from the coffeehouse where she works; her attention is focused on the part of the broadcast where Aaron asserts that he did not have an affair with Lilly Kane (Amanda Seyfried) and that Duncan Kane (Teddy Dunn) murdered his sister. We can only assume Veronica feels bitter and vengeful as she looks on. These scenes culminate in a powerful statement about the damaging aspects of media and technology, particularly their ability to turn private torments into public spectacle and manipulate the truth with disastrous results. This issue is a pressing one for Gen Y viewers raised with television and the Internet.

However, neither Logan's struggles nor his character appeal are limited to the Gen Y audience. Logan really is a bad boy for all ages, and his character is developed in such a way that he can be described as a composite of bad boy images culled from pop culture history. For the Boomer audience, Logan and his conflicts with the PCH biker gang are reminiscent of "rumbles" between "Greasers" and "Socs" (images popularized by S. E. Hinton's novel *The Outsiders* and the Broadway musical *West Side Story*). Indeed, during the pilot episode, when Weevil (Francis Capra) and his gang confront Logan and his friends for damaging Veronica's car, Wallace quips: "I suddenly feel like I'm in a scene from *The Outsiders*." Veronica responds without missing a beat: "Stay cool, Soda Pop." For the Gen X viewers, there are notable similarities between Logan and John Bender (Judd Nelson) from John Hughes' *The Breakfast Club* (1985). Roz Kaveney aptly describes Bender as "an antisocial cutup, who rebels against authority automatically and temperamentally rather than because of any ideological perspective" (14). Kaveney could just as easily be describing Logan Echolls. After all, both characters have abusive fathers with a penchant for putting cigarettes out on their sons.[9] Though Logan lives the media-saturated existence of Gen Y, he shrugs it off with the ironic detachment of Gen X and the rebellious spirit of the Boomers. He is the Swiss Army knife of bad boys.

## Revisiting Teen Angst

All of the abovementioned strategies that *Veronica Mars* uses to produce an intergenerational appeal are complex and require constant juggling and attention to detail on the part of the show's creative staff. Simultaneously wooing Boomers and Generations X and Y, three generations with differing experiences of the world and different sensibilities, is no easy task. Why go to all that trouble? What advantages are there to be had by drawing adults into what is, first and foremost, a teenage world? I would argue that re-introducing adults to many of the issues that are typically confined to the realm of adolescence creates unique opportunities to reflect on how those issues impact our postmodern society as a whole. We have long been short-sighted in our assumption that "teen issues" belong to teenagers alone. Kaveney states: "*Veronica Mars* is a show that often starts from the simple stock assumptions of the teen movie and renders them more complex" (179). There are a number of points in the show's narrative that adhere to this general rule. To clarify, *Veronica Mars* takes a holistic approach when it comes to diagnosing "teen problems." Drug use, violence, and sexuality are regular features, as they are in many teen films and television programs, but in *Veronica Mars* these problems are rarely depicted as symptoms of some mysterious teenage disease. Rather, these issues are repeatedly associated with adults and complex social relations that extend far beyond the high school environment. Drug use at Neptune High, for example, is routinely linked back to the community, particularly to Neptune's Irish crime family, the Fitzpatricks.[10] Rather than condemning teenagers for experimenting with illegal substances, *Veronica Mars* shifts some of the blame onto the people supplying those drugs and to the socioeconomic conditions that allow the drug trade to flourish in the first place. Neptune's poor, the Fitzpatricks and the PCH gang, profit by taking advantage of wealthy teens with too much money and too much time on their hands. Broadening its commentary on the drug trade even further, *Veronica Mars* uses its Southern California location to repeatedly comment on the relative ease with which wealthy people can procure illegal substances and services south of the border. Recall that Logan purchased the GHB that contributed to Veronica's rape during one of his many trips to Mexico.

The commentary on the drug trade is just one of the ways in which *Veronica Mars* broadens our view of "teen problems." In the wake of 1999's Columbine High Massacre, it is not surprising that *Veronica Mars* repeatedly takes up the issue of teen violence. The story of Cassidy "Beaver" Casablancas (Kyle Gallner) is perhaps one of the show's most chilling representations of teen violence. In true *Veronica Mars* fashion, Beaver's story is also extremely complicated. Beaver killed a bus load of his classmates, raped Veronica and possibly Mac (Tina Majorino) and committed fraud. His actions throughout Seasons One and Two rival the villainy of Aaron Echolls. Yet when he steps off the roof of the Neptune Grand in "Not Pictured" (2.22), we feel torn between relief and sadness. We do not feel the same sense of justice that we do when Clarence Wiedman (Christopher B. Duncan), head of security for Kane Software, puts a bullet in Aaron's head as he smugly watches one of his own movies. We are able to have sympathy for Beaver, because we know his violent actions stem from the fact that he was sexually abused by his little league coach, Woody Goodman (Steve Guttenberg), and repeatedly tormented by the macho antics of his father and brother.[11] Due to its narrative complexity, *Veronica Mars* is able to delve deeper into some of the social and psychological scenarios that lead to violence. Moreover, Beaver's story indicates that teen violence is not solely a teen problem brought on by typical teenage angst, but rather a symptom of much larger problems that affect our entire society, such as child abuse and overly strict codes governing sexuality and masculinity.

I am not suggesting that *Veronica Mars* asks viewers to wholeheartedly forgive murderers, rapists, and drug dealers simply because they are underprivileged or abused; things are never that simple in Neptune. The Fitzpatricks really are a despicable bunch; however, characters like Weevil and Beaver challenge our ability to make instantaneous, unbending moral judgments.

These characters also ask us to acknowledge that teenagers are a part of society and that their actions have real consequences for everyone in that society. Marcel Danesi argues that "teen problems" exist only because Western society has socially constructed "adolescence" in such a way that we expect teens to experience angst as a byproduct of the transition from childhood to adulthood:

> The largely uncontested view of adolescence as a stormy and stressful period of life constitutes, in effect, a case of a self-fulfilling prophecy. By making school obligatory during the pubescent years, by passing specific kinds of labour and family laws for the protection of adolescents, by targeting them as a market segment, by defining them as "half children, half adults," by pampering them, and by expecting them to defer the responsibilities of social adulthood until after the high school (and even college) years, we have brought about the social conditions that favour and sustain the peculiar (and often unwanted) behaviours that we associate with the modern adolescent period [10–11].

Film and television have long been complicit in this scheme by reinforcing and naturalizing the idea that adolescence is a "stormy period." *Veronica Mars*, however, strives to expose the flaws in our thinking. Though some may argue that the show's premise is farfetched (no teenager would ever get so intimately wrapped up in murder and intrigue), Veronica's involvement in the community of Neptune serves an important function. Her ability to move freely from the halls of Neptune High to the River Styx (the seedy bar that serves as headquarters for the Fitzpatricks) demonstrates that events taking place in the high school affect the larger community and vice versa. It may be unrealistic for a teenage girl to solve murder mysteries, but a world in which teenagers are completely protected and isolated from the rest of society, coping with issues that have no bearing on the adults, is equally unrealistic.

## Conclusion

The creators of *Veronica Mars* went to great lengths to produce a series that appeals to teens and adults alike. For three seasons, Thomas and others negotiated a delicate balance between tried and true conventions of teen television and quirky experiments with genre, narrative and character development that, ultimately, allowed them to tell a story that incorporates teen images familiar to more than one generation of youth. Though the series courts the attention of postmodern, media-savvy Gen Y viewers, there are many aspects of the show's narrative and aesthetics that have something to offer to members of Gen X and the Baby Boomer generation. All the tricks of postmodern intertextuality, fun and frivolous as they may be, help draw adult viewers into a world that desperately needs their attention. *Veronica Mars* demonstrates that it is possible to produce quality programming using content relevant to teens without patronizing young viewers or subjecting them to excessive moralizing. Furthermore, the series prompts us to rethink our understanding of the roles that teenagers play in modern society. That is to say, *Veronica Mars* does not portray the American high school as an insular world where preformed adults incubate until they are ready to enter the "real world." In Neptune, high school is the real world.

## Notes

1. For detailed discussion on this topic see Valerie Wee, "Selling Teen Culture: How American Multimedia Conglomeration Reshaped Teen Television in the 1990s" in *Teen TV: Genre, Consumption and Identity*, Glyn Davis and Kay Dickinson (eds).

2. On *Veronica Mars* marketing and the attempt to create community, see Gillan.

3. Patty Hearst is the granddaughter of publishing mogul William Randolph Hearst. In 1974 she was kidnapped by the Symbionese Liberation Army, a guerrilla group of self-proclaimed revolutionaries active within the United States. The group committed robbery, murder and other acts of violence ("Biography").

4. Intertextuality is a literary term coined by Julia Kristeva; its meanings are complex and varied. I use it here to describe the ways in which a "text" references other texts, "whether by its open or covert citations and allusions, or by its assimilation of the formal and substantive features of an earlier text or texts" (Abrams 285).

5. Cavallari currently stars in *The Hills* (2006), a similarly styled *Laguna Beach* spinoff. She took the "lead role" following Lauren Conrad's departure.

6. Paris Hilton is a socialite and heiress to the Hilton Hotel fortune. She gained notoriety in 2004 when a sex tape featuring her and then-boyfriend Rick Saloman leaked onto the Internet. Since then she has starred in her own reality series, appeared in a number of feature films, and dabbled, rather unsuccessfully, in the recording industry.

7. I am not suggesting that reinventing one's image and satirizing one's own fame are entirely new phenomena. Certainly, teen idols like The Beatles used these strategies to great effect. I am rather arguing that these strategies have gone from being employed by a select few who use them to their advantage, to being mandatory for anyone who wants to maintain any kind of lasting fame in the postmodern era.

8. Even the name, Harmony Chase, is an intertextual nod to Harmony Kendall (Mercedes McNab) and Cordelia Chase (Charisma Carpenter) of *Buffy* and *Angel*. Also, note that Charisma Carpenter's character in *Veronica Mars* is named Kendall Casablancas. Viewers familiar with all of these series could interpret the name, Harmony Chase, as foreshadowing a negative outcome for Keith and Harmony's relationship.

9. Yet another link between *Veronica Mars* and *The Breakfast Club* can be found in "The Girl Next Door" (1.7). This episode alludes to the premise of Hughes' film when Logan and Weevil bond and come to understand one another during a detention imposed by their English teacher.

10. Many students at Neptune High get their drugs from members of the PCH biker gang. Though Weevil forbids the gang from selling drugs, he is undermined by Thumper (James Molina), who gets drugs from the Fitzpatricks and distributes them at school.

11. The full extent of this abuse is not revealed until after his death. In "I Know What You'll Do Next Summer" (3.18), Dick reveals details from his childhood with Beaver; he admits that he and his father held contests to see who could make Beaver cry first. Dick also recounts the time he duct-taped Beaver's feet to the pedals of his tricycle and then returned hours later to find him still pedaling in circles.

## Works Cited

Abrams, M. H. *A Glossary of Literary Terms*. 6th ed. New York: Harcourt Brace, 1993. Print.

"Biography for Patricia Hearst." *The Internet Movie Database*. N.p. N.d. Web. 25 July 2009.

Bussolini, Jeff. "Television Intertextuality After *Buffy*." Slayage Conference on the Whedonverses, 3rd Biennial. Henderson State University, Arkadelphia, Arkansas. June 5–8, 2008.

Butler, Jeremy G. *Television: Critical Methods and Applications*. London: Lawrence Erlbaum, 2007. Print.

Danesi, Marcel. *Forever Young: The "Teen-Aging" of Modern Culture*. Toronto: University of Toronto Press, 2003. Print.

Davis, Glyn, and Kay Dickinson, eds. "Introduction." *Teen TV: Genre, Consumption and Identity*. London: BFI, 2004. 1–13. Print.

de Zengotita, Thomas. *Mediated: How the Media Shapes Your World and the Way You Live in It*. New York: Bloomsbury, 2005. Print.

Edwards, Lynne. "On the Down-Low: How a *Buffy* Fan Fell in Love with *Veronica Mars*." Thomas 73–80. Print.

Gillan, Jennifer. "Fashion Sleuths and Aerie Girls: *Veronica Mars*' Fan Forums and Network Strategies of Fan Address." *Teen Television: Essays on Programming and Fandom*. Eds. Sharon Marie Ross and Louisa Ellen Stein. Jefferson, NC: McFarland, 2008. 185–206. Print.

Gray, Jonathan. *Watching with* The Simpsons*: Television, Parody, and Intertextuality*. New York: Routledge, 2006. Print.

Kaveney, Roz. *Teen Dreams: Reading Teen Film and Television from* Heathers *to* Veronica Mars. London: I.B. Tauris, 2006. Print.

Martin, Jeff. "*TV Teen Club*: Teen TV as Safe Harbor." *Teen Television: Essays on Programming and Fandom*. Ed. Sharon Marie Ross and Louisa Ellen Stein. Jefferson, NC: McFarland, 2008. 27–42. Print.

McFadden, Kay. "Intriguing New Dramas Full of Possibilities." *The Seattle Times*. The Seattle Times Company, 22 Sept. 2004. Web. 9 November 2009.

Osgerby, Bill. "'So Who's Got Time for Adults!': Femininity, Consumption and the Development of Teen TV — from *Gidget* to *Buffy*." Davis and Dickinson 71–86. Print.

Thomas, Rob. "Introduction: Digressions on How *Veronica Mars* Saved My Career and, Less Importantly, My Soul." Thomas 1–7. Print.

_____, ed. *Neptune Noir: Unauthorized Investigations into* Veronica Mars. Dallas: BenBella Books, 2006. Print.

Wilcox, Rhonda. *Why Buffy Matters: The Art of* Buffy the Vampire Slayer. London: I.B. Tauris, 2005. Print.

Zimbardo, Philip G. "The Stanford Prison Experiment." N.p. N.d. Web. 25 July 2009.

# 9

## "We Used to Be Friends"
### *Breaking Up with America's Sweetheart*

SOPHIE MAYER

> Women's experience is a secret that is especially vital.... Even more
> deeply hidden has been the experience of the girl. It is the girl who
> is the most profound site of patriarchal investment, her unconstrained
> freedom representing the most fearsome threat to patriarchal control.
> Gateward and Pomerance 13

Hailed by *Buffy the Vampire Slayer* creator Joss Whedon as the only worthy inheritor of the Slayer's crown (Whedon, "Ace"), *Veronica Mars* offers a teen heroine with no fantastic superpowers, but with no fewer demons to fight. Veronica, the daughter of a private investigator, is committed to uncovering the doubled secret of, as Madonna asks, "what it feels like for a girl" that constrains girls to be no more than the sum of their feelings (of powerlessness). In each season, she confronts a secret — a murder, a bus crash, a series of rapes — that lead her to uncover the operations of patriarchal power as they affect young women, and particularly as they affect her. In this, Veronica is like Donna Haraway's relational feminist scientist, working in a model in which the object and subject of study intersect as "an actor and agent, not a screen or a ground or a resource, never finally ... a slave to the master that closes off the dialectic in his unique agency and authorship of 'objective' knowledge" (198).

*Veronica Mars* is thus part of an emergent cultural trend for texts that "represent a girlhood that truly serves girls: one that deserves and demands a respectful reaction from adults, and demands that girls themselves live as competent, self-determining subjects" who, Ilana Nash argues, are still absent from the mainstream (227). Yet the show is necessarily complicit in the consumerism that produces the figure Nash deems "American Sweetheart," the girl-woman who signifies unconsciously rather than reflexively. What she signifies, according to Nash, is an emptiness waiting to be filled — materially, by consumer goods; figuratively, by adult male desire. This conflation of consuming and consumption, layered with teenage girl's physical and intellectual "emptiness" or incompetence, is embodied in Shirley Temple, Lolita, and Gidget — and, argues Nash, in more recent model moppets such as the Disney Channel's Lizzie McGuire (the role that launched Hilary Duff's pop career), despite their surfactant of "girl power."

Looking at postmodern representations of such subjects on the margins of dominant power, Linda Hutcheon writes that "this is a strange kind of critique, one bound up, too, with its own *complicity* with power and domination, one that acknowledges that it cannot escape implication in that which it nevertheless still wants to analyze and maybe even undermine" (4). As Nash argues, the ground of representation of the teenage girl, as for the woman, in Western culture, is the body, and it is on Veronica's body (and its doubles) that this essay focuses, asking whether it can critique the semiotics of idealized teenage femininity, even as it is complicit in renewing such representations. Like Sarah Michelle Gellar (Buffy), performer Kristen Bell (Veronica) is white, blonde, slim, attractive, and able-bodied: the embodiment of mainstream culture's physical ideal. And like *Buffy*, *Veronica Mars* engages its audience in a curious avowal and disavowal of the central role of America's Sweetheart as the attractive lead character is necessary to the show's success.

As Patricia Pender discusses, "the rhetorics of transgression and containment that riddle both the academic and popular media response to *BtVS*" and similarly *Veronica Mars*, depend on "unspoken assumptions that ... work to circumscribe — to contain, in effect — the political and transgressive potential of the series" (36). Following Pender's insightful critique, this essay works to highlight the way in which *Veronica Mars* explicitly critiques structural power and foregrounds the marginalization of the teenage girl by showing Veronica's emergent reflexive awareness of her power/lessness, not despite, but because of, her normative embodiment.

Nash remarks (26) that "the key to successfully representing a girl's erotic appeal is to render her *un*conscious of it, or not in control of it — to 'hollow out' her subjectivity, her will, or her competence," and *Veronica Mars* explores tropes of unconsciousness in order to present Veronica, by contrast, as a heroine who is fully awake and alert, through her own lived experience, to social injustice. Veronica's consciousness comes via — and at the expense of— other teenage girls' unconsciousness. The show could be called "Veronica's Mirrors" as easily as *Veronica Mars*, as her doubles allow Veronica (and the viewer) to negotiate American girlhood by playing off recognizable tropes cited by the show.[1] (Veronica and) I investigate five contemporary cultural versions of America's Sweetheart, each addressing an aspect of Veronica's doubling: American Beauty; Girlfriend in a Coma; The Virgin Suicides; Girls Gone Wild; and finally, returning to Buffy's superpower, the Bionic Woman. These tropes are referenced knowingly, and yet such a postmodern gesture combines uneasily with their seemingly unconscious deployment. While apparently questioning the power attributed to America's Sweetheart, these references work to return power to Veronica (and no other character) through her investigation of what it means to be young, blonde, and female in America.

## American Beauty

> Poised between innocence and experience, her combination of a womanly body and a childlike mind offers male authorities the best of both worlds: a female both pure and ripe, young enough to leave unchallenged the dominance of mature men, but old enough to be "hot." This logic continues to operate today in such films as the Oscar-winning *American Beauty*.
>
> Nash 23

At first glance Veronica is a riposte to the persistent fantasy of the teenage *femme fatale*. In the pre-credits of the first episode, she spies on a tawdry extra-marital affair in a hotel; her gumshoe world-weariness appears to set her apart from the sexual intensities that rule the lives of her peers. As the episode reveals, her Chandler-esque pose results from a situation in which Veronica stood as Jane Burnham (Thora Birch) to the Angela Hayes (Mena Suvari) embodied and repeated by her best friend, Lilly Kane (Amanda Seyfried). Veronica's refusal to be "hot" is the flipside of Lilly's determination to be an American Beauty. It cumulates in "Happy Go Lucky" (2:21), where Veronica faces a doubly cumulative challenge: to win the Kane scholarship for which she has worked over the season, and — ending the arc of Season One — to provide testimony that will see Aaron Echolls (Harry Hamlin) jailed for the murder of Lilly, his sometime lover. In her determination to secure and witness the conviction, Veronica deliberately flunks the exam for the scholarship. But she is presented with a doubled failure, as the case is thrown out, in part due to her own apparently flawed testimony. Yet Veronica's statements in the witness box are no more impaired than her academic prowess:

just as a wealthy classmate's complicit family doctor is instrumental in eroding Veronica's lead in the scholarship contest ("I Am God" [2:18]), so the defense lawyer hired by the rich and famous Echolls destroys Veronica's credibility, despite (or in ironic contravention of) the fact that the name *Veronica* is popularly said to derive from the Greek *vera ikon*, "true image," after the Veronica who pressed her veil to Jesus' face. (See also Beeler, in this volume, on Veronica's name.) The lawyer casts Veronica as whore rather than saint, drawing the jury's attention to her seductive similarity to the murder victim. Teenage sexuality is cast as a double *agent provocatrice*. Yet this view, propounded by an expensive defense lawyer for a wealthy movie star accused of sexually-motivated murder, is not the view of *Veronica Mars* the series. The negative view's extreme form — and its success in sowing doubt in the jury's minds — makes explicit the way in which patriarchy sells girls down the river.

Lilly, whose double "l" makes you look again, and check your stereotype of the lily-white princess at the door, "loved guys," as former boyfriend Logan puts it ("Hot Dogs," 1.19). Unlike virginal Veronica, Lilly *uses* her cultural value as an attractive, wealthy teenage girl to secure consumable erotic pleasure for herself and to rebel against her parents — to the point where Veronica holds Lilly's father, Jake Kane, responsible for murdering his daughter. While her father is not the culprit, patriarchy is fingered, if not quite caught red-handed. The accused in the dock, Aaron Echolls, combines the sexual allure of the celebrity and the proximity of the pop (star)-next-door. The cynical lawyer peddles a series of rhetorical *double-entendres* that render Lilly, and Veronica by association, as the Lolita that her name echoes. Hinging his case is the circumstantial evidence produced by the show's paralleling of its male characters, in which Veronica first dated Lilly's brother Duncan (a suspect in the murder), then the policeman Leo (who sold the sex tapes Veronica claimed to have secured as evidence), and then Lilly's ex-boyfriend Logan, son of Aaron, and himself a former suspect, who bought and erased the tapes. Veronica is cast as the *femme fatale* masterminding a sting, using her sexual attractiveness as Lilly used hers, to secure the power of false accusations.

In flashbacks and dream sequences, Lilly and Veronica are frequently shown together, exchanging clothes, or posed in such a way as to suggest their doubling. Corinn Columpar, commenting on a similarly fantastic and fantasmic friendship in *Heavenly Creatures*, argues that this "relationship between the girls is ultimately a mutual one characterized by both identification and desire, confounding the heterosexual matrix that would separate them" (326). Veronica's Lilly-ness is marked most strongly in "Wrath of Con" (1.4), as the heteronormative ritual of the prom prompts Veronica's memories of the previous year's celebration with Lilly. These flashbacks are doubled by the video tapes of the remembered events that Veronica loans to Logan so he can create a fitting tribute to Lilly. This transition from immaterial memory to virtual reality is taken a step further when Veronica wears the prom dress that Lilly picked out for her the year before, repeating Lilly's prom night behavior by stripping off the dress to go skinny-dipping. In effect, Veronica goes to the prom both with, and as, Lilly, disrupting "the heterosexual matrix that would separate them." On Veronica's graduation day, Lilly appears to Veronica in a dream and reveals that she has been "experimenting" with lesbianism at college.

Lilly's death, however, marks the *difference* between the two in more ways than one: not only is Veronica still alive, but — because of Lilly's death — she has passed from being an unreflective member of Neptune High's socially powerful clique to a reflective and rueful member of the town's social underclass. Veronica's downward mobility is a result of her father's demotion from sheriff to private investigator (both economic demotion and social stigma), after accusing Lilly's father of his daughter's murder. The facts that Veronica uncovers about the lives of the super-rich as she assumes her father's investigative mantle lead to her greater awareness about the power that Lilly believed she had, as a thin, rich, white girl of the kind typified by Paris Hilton, who guest starred in "Credit Where Credit's Due" (1.2). Veronica comes to realize firstly that such power is invested in girls by dominant culture, and secondly that such disempowerment subjects girls to the exclusion practiced by capitalist patriarchy against those deemed unacceptable to the hierarchy — including the newly-excluded Veronica. Her investigations reveal her marginality, but also the powers of observation and resistance that the margins can offer.

Season One concludes powerfully with Veronica uncovering the identity of Lilly's murderer by first uncovering a mystery about herself, revolving around a flashbacked party that is linked to Lilly's death from the first few minutes of the pilot, when the scene of one crime (murder) cuts to the scene of another, parallel crime (Veronica's rape at the party). When another student's memory of being drugged at the same party — thrown by 09er Shelly Pomeroy — requires Veronica to investigate, visual parallels establish the connection between the crime/scenes: the flashbacks are introduced by an impressionistic shot of the Pomeroys' pool that is similar to the pool next to which Lilly died at the Kane house. Like Veronica/Lilly, the swimming pool represents an American ideal of both conspicuous consumption and physical purity, of teenage innocence and adult debauchery, a "liquid emanation of the American Dream" (Sprawson 222). It is a liminal space, and it is the space in which both girls are confronted by the double standard of the same American ideal: the contested space of female teen sexuality. Recovering, through investigation, the narrative of her experience at the party — consensual sex with Duncan while they were both inadvertently high on GHB — frees Veronica to enter into a sexual relationship with Logan, who had been a deliberately misleading suspect in both Lilly's murder and Veronica's rape.

Logan remains circumstantially complicit in Lilly's murder as his and Veronica's first erotic encounter leads her to discover video evidence that Lilly was having an affair with Aaron in the very bed in which she had been kissing his son. Lilly's fate is mapped onto Veronica as a potential or warning, as Veronica suspects first Logan and then (correctly) Aaron of Lilly's murder. Veronica's investigation reveals the ways in which the power of seduction identified by Nash is granted to girls only so long as it is used to pleasure men rather than to contest their authority, as Lilly does when she demands hush money from Aaron about their affair, and as Veronica does when she seeks evidence to convict Aaron. This not only echoes *American Beauty*, but also replays the narrative arc of David Lynch and Mark Frost's 1990–91 TV series *Twin Peaks*, a high school *noir* in which the answer to the central question "Who Killed Laura Palmer?" was refracted through Laura's highly sexualized behavior and her many older male lovers, and the ambiguity concerning Laura's "responsibility" for her own death. Veronica's investigation of Lilly's death begins at the same point as *Twin Peaks'* initial mystery ends, with the idea of a father murdering his daughter.

It ends closer to *American Beauty*, played (responsibly) as *noir* rather than black comedy. In its oscillation between these two cultural texts, it questions the difference between them. Jake Kane is seen as colluding in the structural power that allows Aaron Echolls to get away with murder, although he thinks he is defending his son Duncan. Murder is shown as the pastime of wealthy white men who use their wealth as political power. Jake Kane buys an innocent (terminally ill) man, Abel Koontz, to act as a patsy and confess. Yet Koontz is also revealed as the father of a teenage daughter, Amelia Delongpre. Rather than working effectively to obscure the tangled web Kane has created, Veronica uncovers the way in which this paralleling points back to the Law of the Father as responsible for Lilly's death. Not only do fathers make the law by hook (Keith Mars was sheriff) or, like Jake Kane, by crook, but the show separates the realm of the maternal semiotic, in which Veronica's dreams of happy families and her best friend provide key clues to her cases, and the paternal symbolic, in which everything real turns out to stand for something else. By construing the chains of associations (Veronica/Lilly/Amelia/Trina Echolls, Keith/Jake/Abel/Aaron, hinged by the son-brother-boyfriend tag team of Duncan and Logan), Veronica proves her case, almost dying at Aaron's hands in doing so, and the season (almost) ends with a peaceful dream in which Lilly and Veronica float on lilies in a turquoise swimming pool, and Lilly disappears, merging into Veronica.

## Girlfriend in a Coma

Veronica ends Season One startled from sleep, emerging shockingly from unconsciousness as she will throughout Season Two in order to confront and investigate the literal unconsciousness of another double: Meg, Veronica's replacement in Duncan Kane's affections. In the final moments of Season One, Veronica awakens to open her apartment door to an unknown figure (either Logan or Duncan?). Season Two reveals the shadowy figure at the door to be Logan, although Veronica swiftly returns her affections to Duncan, whose presence connects Veronica to two further doubles. Amelia, like Veronica (who is thought to possibly be Jake's child), is offered hush money from the Kane family to stay quiet about Jake Kane's guilt. Amelia is robbed and killed because of this money, while Veronica survives, and indeed finds Amelia's body in a Norman Bates–like motel. The *Psycho* reference recalls that it is Lila Crane (an echo of Lilly Kane), Marion's sister, who investigates her disappearance in the Hitchcock movie. The show knowingly suggests the lineage of the "dead blonde" that *Veronica Mars* is both exploiting and exploding. Veronica takes responsibility for Amelia at Abel Koontz' request from his hospital bed. After piecing together Amelia's death — yet another jealous boyfriend — Veronica goes to Neptune General to talk to Abel, and learns that he is days from death.

Later walking through the hospital with Abel's possessions, Veronica passes by the third girl with whom her investigations (and love life) are entangled: Meg, whose name triangulates her with the "M&Ms" of Neptune High — computer geek Mac, and Madison, with whom Mac was swapped at birth. 09er Meg and would-have-been 09er Mac are Veronica's only female friends. When Meg starts dating Duncan, however, she makes the transition from friend to double, and thus has to be dispatched like Lilly and Amelia. Veronica had facilitated Duncan and Meg's relationship in Season One, and also been the cause of their break-up. In the Season Two opener "Normal Is the Watchword," it is Veronica's desire to be friends with Meg — and Meg's refusal to accept her overtures — that means Meg not only takes the bus rather than the 09ers' limo back to Neptune, but deliberately keeps her silence when Veronica fails to return to the bus after a pit stop, allowing the driver to drive off, stranding Veronica on the freeway.

When the bus blows up shortly after, plunging over the cliff, with Meg the only (comatose) survivor, Veronica becomes obsessed with their doubled identity: she should have been in Meg's place, and Meg should have been in hers. She also believes that the bus accident was aimed at her, possibly by Aaron in retribution for his current jail time. Veronica's guilt is compounded by the knowledge that she also substituted for Meg in Duncan's affections, and complicated by the fact that Duncan still seems hooked on Meg. Comatose Meg appears to communicate with Veronica through dreams, just as Lilly did in Season One. These communiqués help Duncan discover that Meg was keeping a secret from her strict religious family, one that is revealed dramatically when Veronica passes her hospital room.

Entering the room illicitly, Veronica discovers that Meg is pregnant with Duncan's child. In an unscreened alternate episode ending, Meg is smothered by her mother as Veronica watches, trapped in the corner: an ending that took to the logical extreme the behavior of Meg's ultra–Christian parents, who locked her younger sister in the closet. It is Veronica who witnesses and decries that act, saving Grace, but in the hospital she falls silent. Veronica is marked deliberately as the connection between Amelia's death and Meg's — a noirish *femme fatale*, whose trail of dead female doubles does nothing for her love life. Meg's death concludes the deadly doubling spiraling out from Lilly's murder, although its tidy dispatch of Meg parallels with other cultural texts to suggest a surprisingly moralistic attitude to teen female sexuality.

Like Karen, the comatose protagonist of Douglas Coupland's 1999 novel *Girlfriend in a Coma*, Meg is delivered of a child while unconscious, and her unconsciousness itself seems to operate as a punishment. Karen falls into a coma as a teenager shortly after losing her virginity; Meg, more convolutedly, is comatose due to her anger at Veronica, which is a result of her own accidental pregnancy (and presumably the loss of her virginity) by Duncan, who will end up taking care of his and Meg's child, as Richard, the narrator of Coupland's novel, takes care of his and Karen's daughter. The fact that the child in the novel is named Megan seems more than coincidence, suggesting that the TV show is executing a deliberate pastiche or critique of the novel, which is itself is a cultural double: The Smiths' song "Girlfriend in a Coma." First the singer attests murderous thoughts toward his girlfriend revealing a culture of casual, violent misogyny that is both foregrounded and demonstrated by *Veronica Mars'* cavalier treatment of its young female characters and the frequency with which they are raped and murdered. The song continues with an ambivalent expression of concern for the well-being of the singer's girlfriend; Veronica constantly defies both the protective and aggressive attitudes of the boys and men around her: she survives (yet risks) Meg's death at the hands of the bus bomber Cassidy Casablancas, who will try to kill

Veronica when she unravels the crash and reveals his culpability. Veronica's survival appears to result from her refusal of the "coma" of America's Sweetheart.

## No More Virgin Suicides

Fade in on a close-up of a girl's hand removing a CD case from a stack, and inserting a silver disc into a stereo ("Donut Run," 2.11). Cue dreamy strains and a glimpse of the CD's title as the case lingers in the girl's hand: the soundtrack to *The Virgin Suicides*, Sofia Coppola's adaptation of Jeffrey Eugenides' 1993 cult novel about a family of five sisters who enchant and haunt a group of teenage boys living in their 1970s suburban neighborhood. The Lisbon sisters, like Meg and her sisters, are subject to the dictates of their strictly Christian parents, whose rules and regulations lead to tragedy when the four older Lisbon sisters follow their youngest sister into death by suicide. Veronica's choice of musical score to abet Duncan in hiding Meg's baby in the empty apartment next door is instructive. Meg's death is not suicide but it *is* caused by her parents' religious severity. The music suggests the haunting mystery that both Meg and Lilly exercise over Veronica's imagination, making her in turn like the boys who tried to save the Lisbon girls and — when they failed — collected every bit of memorabilia they could in an effort to understand them.

The music refers to the way that Veronica is doubled by Lilly and Meg as a victim. In the show's opening episode, Veronica's "morning after" scene following her rape visually resembles the scene in the film where Lux Lisbon (Kirsten Dunst), the wildest and blondest of the sisters, awakens on the school football field the night after the prom to discover that she has been deserted by her boyfriend after she broke her parents' strict curfew to stay out and lose her virginity to him. Veronica's solitary awakening on an expanse of white sheet and her dazed walk home, the color processed to faded pastels reminiscent of Coppola's film, are the prompt to both her commitment to investigation and the self-protectiveness that saves her from repeating her friends' fates.

That flashback scene repeats *The Virgin Suicides* aurally as well, with a melancholy, pulsing electro musical score that sounds suspiciously like Air's score, and is used frequently thereafter, particularly for the flashback of Veronica seeing Lilly's dead body. The show recognizes this quotation in the moment that Veronica takes down and plays the soundtrack. Supposedly mourning her break-up with Duncan, she sits on the floor cutting up photographs in a pose similar to the languid Lisbon sisters, when they are trapped in their bedroom playing records down the telephone to the adoring boys. It is only at the end of the episode that Veronica's ironic sonic communication with Duncan is revealed; her pose as a Lisbon sister is a sign that she is masquerading as a Lisbon sister: a consumer who fashions and expresses her interiority through music as a product and as a refusal of articulate speech, as a symbol of her inchoate emotional vulnerability. Although the CD represents a knowing pop culture quotation, it also signals Veronica's inability to express her emotions at Duncan's flight.

"This fantasy of what girls do in their rooms reifies girls as omnivorous consumers of popular culture and fashion, and implies the paradox that girls can best express their individuality through mimicry" (Nash 224). Harking back to Veronica's flashback of Spice Girls' karaoke with Lilly, this moment shows Veronica's ability to manipulate the signifiers of adolescent femininity to her own advantage. Her manipulation operates in a twofold manner: she uses the music to signal a (false) melancholy to ensure her privacy from her father, and to warn Duncan of the fate that potentially awaits Meg's daughter — whom Duncan slightly creepily names Lilly. This affords Lilly 2.0 the opportunity to grow up somewhere healthier than the Lisbon-like family home where Meg was raised. Or indeed in Neptune, where blonde hair and a XX chromosome continue to promise disaster.

## Girls Gone Wild

Season Two's closing revelation that Veronica *was* raped — and not only survived but confronted her attacker — is pivotal to the minor key doubling of Season Three. Veronica's new double is a stranger: a girl called Parker, from Colorado, Mac's roommate at Hearst College. Like Lilly, Parker is presented as sexually forward and adventurous, an attitude not condemned by the show although it differs from Veronica's serial monogamy, and Mac's claim that she is "dead from the waist down" after apparently being raped by Cassidy in the final episode of Season Two ("Not Pictured," 2.22). Nothing ever happens once in this show. Mac and Veronica's shared experience comes to include Parker, when she is raped by a campus rapist who drugs his victims and takes their hair as a trophy.

Veronica's doubling with Parker is underlined by a romantic quadrille (with Logan and Logan lookalike campus DJ Piz), whose casual incestuousness marks the transition to college, where girls can go wild and not die. Veronica is inadvertently responsible for Parker's rape, as she enters the dorm room while the attack is in progress, and — on hearing noises in the dark — makes a presumption of consensual sex based on Parker's rumored history. Parker's sense of betrayal only abates when Veronica makes it clear that she has also been "Roofied" and raped,[2] and that she will help Parker identify and stop her assailant. In a reversal that comes closest to the neat doubling of previous seasons, it is Parker who raises the alarm when Veronica is drugged and paralyzed by the rapist ("Spit and Eggs," 3.9).

Yet Parker's sunny-temperamented resilience without risk undermines Veronica's key character attribute, of constantly putting herself in the way of physical danger in order to help others. Her experience of rape and her loss of social status have given her a fearlessness, one that is often commented on by other characters, possibly because it is accompanied by a credibility-testing indestructibility. When Veronica is tasered by Cassidy, she is able to get up and taser Cassidy back — despite the fact that we have seen her taser grown men into unconscious submission ("Not Pictured," 2.22). This resistance to all attempts on her life is a quality she shares with teen heroines such as Buffy, suggesting that part of the mythology of the white, middle class, blonde teenage girl is that she is not just indestructible but impenetrable, thus healing all wounds, especially those of rape.

The show's repeated naming of the act of rape — and, concomitantly, of survival — in the context of a teen drama, its insistence on the absolute wrongness of non-consensual sex, and conversely its institutionalization as a morally acceptable act within dominant male culture, is both brave and topical in the year that the Duke lacrosse team were put on trial (see Whitney in this volume). In Season Three, the rapist initially seems to be a fraternity member as part of an organized campaign of sexual misdemeanors sanctioned by the idea of rush week. At the behest of newspaper editor Nish, Veronica investigates a sorority that seems to be complicit in the fraternity's abusive behavior towards women, but reveals that they are not — thus falling out with Nish, who is part of a campus militant feminist group dedicated to ousting the fraternities. Rob Thomas, the creator of the show, has defended his decision to make the fraternity "innocent" and to portray the feminist group as wrongheaded aggressors who — in the season's second mini-arc — are even regarded as potentially the Dean's murderers (Couch Baron).

While these reversals could be said to add ethical complexity to the Veronicaverse, it is worrying how frequently they fall in line with conservative politics. Kimberley Roberts, writing on "angry girl" films, quotes Lyn Mikel Brown's insight "if we take away girls' anger, then we take away the foundation for women's political resistance" (218) — a telling comment in light of Veronica's falling out with Nish's feminist group, and her repeated failure to align herself with a female role model at Hearst. The smart African American professor with whom Veronica juried a trial in "One Angry Veronica" (2.10), and who invited her to Hearst, seems to have disappeared, and taken with her the anger that caused Veronica to delay judgment in the trial until the jury had fully considered the politics of race and gender which were obscuring the facts. The show's experiment in female anger appeared to be sputtering out as Veronica revealed a number of angry girls as frauds. These angry girls are part of Nish's group the Liliths, whose name suggests the women's music festival Lilith Fair, but also — in their use of violent tactics — repeats the dominant cultural attitude that demonizes women who are (sexually) aggressive.

## Save the Cheerleader, Save the Show

Veronica not only lacks a female role model, but also — losing the show's original impetus — a female friend. She becomes increasingly feminine in her appearance, growing her hair long and curly, as if in nostalgia for the innocent long-haired Veronica seen in Season One flashbacks. In distancing Veronica from the Liliths, who are associated with lesbianism, from Veronica's Katy Perry–style action at the fraternity party ("My Big Fat Greek Rush Week," 3.2) to Hallie's seduction of Selma Rose Hearst ("Lord of the Pi's," 3.8), the show enforces what Farah Mendlesohn calls, with reference to the foreclosure of queering the Buffy/Willow friendship, "heterosociality" (49). Nash argues that "the real threats of youth's political unrest and social activism in the 1960s displaced the symbolic threat of the loss of a girl's virginity as culture's worst nightmare," and in curtailing the multivalence of Veronica's friendship-doubling with Lilly, Mac, and Meg (and displacing Veronica's anxiety about the loss of her own sexual integrity), Season Three cuts Veronica off from social activism while conservatively repositioning the teenage female body as the site of the "real threat" (217).

In the season closer, resonantly titled "The Bitch Is Back" (3.22), Veronica's disregard for her personal safety (and conversely her obsession with sexual secrecy) result in the loss of political and legal safety for Neptune, as her burglary of the new Kane mansion, and the resulting news stories, contribute to Keith's loss of votes in the election for sheriff. Her fearlessness in pursuing a secret society called The Castle is a result of sexual exposure reminiscent of Season One's high school jinks, particularly the cell phone video of a classmate giving a popsicle blow job that led Veronica to uncover the (first version of the) story of the 09er party where she was raped. By Season Three, there's an upgrade to a video of what is suggested to be full-blown sex between Veronica and her new boyfriend Piz ("There's a video of you and ... Piz having sex" ["The Bitch Is Back," 3.20]), circulated by email rather than held in reserve as blackmail. Veronica's initial investigations lead her back to Chip Diller, the head of the fraternity initially suspected for the Hearst rapes, and also to Nish, who helps Veronica bust The Castle.

The episode is full of such returns: it is a giant portrait of Lilly that tips Veronica off to the identity of the Castle's king: a neat reference to the portrait of the protagonist on which the gumshoe muses in 1944 proto-*noir Laura*, itself an intertext for *Twin Peaks*. In a salute to the cultural and political intelligence of the show's fans, Thomas and the show's creators return to the original girl-noir that marked the unique vision of/through the Eyes of Veronica Mars. The Laura of *The Eyes of Laura Mars*, unlike the ghostly almost-murdered Laura conjured forth by the portrait in the 1944 film and the dead, blue Laura of Frost and Lynch's television show, is a murder investigator rather than a victim. Unlike her almost-namesake Veronica, however, her investigative powers are inadvertent (premised on second sight) and she comes dangerously close to being killed. Condensing all the Lauras into the frame within the frame, the episode restores Veronica to her role as willed and willing investigator.

This final arc offers a slight return to the Veronica we first knew, the Harawayan observer investigating herself, something that that been lost in Season Three's multiple mini-arcs. It is highlighted by Veronica knowingly performing herself (although unknowingly performing for a diegetic camera). At the beginning of the Veronica/Piz sex tape — itself calling to mind Paris Hilton's cameo — Veronica offers to perform a cheer for Piz, evoking the innocent cheerleader type she had been before Lilly's death destroyed her social privilege. It was perhaps also a gesture towards the popularity of the newest indestructible femme on the block, Claire Bennett (Hayden Panettiere, *Heroes*), whose second season adversary, Elle, would be played by Kristen Bell (in a *reductio ad absurdum* of Veronica, Elle is a daddy's girl who can Taser people with her bare hands). Claire's appearance was followed by the swift announcement of a remake of *The Bionic Woman*, whose original version Veronica explicitly references when she risks her physical safety jumping over a wall, chiding her father's anxiety with a cute "Shananananana" ("Lord of the Pi's," 3.8). Its equally swift cancellation (as well as the cancellation of *Terminator: The Sarah Connor Chronicles*, and the final erasure of *Battlestar Galactica's* Starbuck [Katee Sackhoff, whose nemesis role brought a lesbian frisson to *The Bionic Woman* remake]) suggests that U.S. television has not yet worked out how to have its physically-invincible women *and* contain their threat.

This manifestation of her physical perfection is both inspiring in that it attributes physical and mental resistance to a class of individuals whose desirable perfection makes them vulnerable to harm (both by others and themselves), and disturbing in its resolute refusal of consequence and permeability. In this, *Veronica Mars* is in line with the dominant, Puritan exteriorization of goodness in a flawless body. "Bodily integrity is a *moral* as well as physical quality," writes sociologist Ann Oakley, "and all this circles round the epicentre of youth-ism" (25). So it is that Veronica's boldest assault on patriarchy, in the form of The Castle, must be packaged in a cheerleader's outfit.

The ironic bionic cheerleader was not enough to save the show, perhaps because it recalls what the show is missing, the first person with whom we associate the cheerleader's uniform: Lilly. Veronica is out of mirrors, compromised by her own visibility, on the sex tape and the security tape from the Castle. Caught with her hyper-vigilance down, Veronica experiences the same vexation as *Veronica Mars*: that complicitous critique is compromised by the insistent specularization of the (thin, white, able) teenage body. Her polyvalence is elided by what Tanya Cochran calls "'visual dilution,' a particular form of (in)visibility that can blur and, as a result, weaken the intended meaning or full potential of an image or portrayal" (51). Without her doubles, who raise the possibility/specter/potential of both lesbianism and feminist activism, Veronica is no longer the observer but the observed, no longer the reflective double, canceling out the show's premise: Veronica holding up the veil imprinted with her sacrificed double's face as evidence for the damage done by the myth of America's Sweetheart. When she strikes the cheerleader's pose, Veronica acknowledges her own doom.

## Notes

1. For a different perspective on doubling in the series, see Wilcox in this volume.
2. Though Veronica at first assumes she has been "roofied," the drug used on her is later identified as GHB. However, the word "roofied" could be considered to have general applicability to the act of drugging for the purpose of rape.

## Works Cited

AIR. The Virgin Suicides *OST*. Astralwerks, 2000. CD.
Cochran, Tanya R. "Complicating the Open Closet: The Visual Rhetoric of *Buffy the Vampire Slayer*'s Sapphic Lovers." *Televising Queer Women: A Reader*. Ed. Rebecca Beirne. London: Palgrave Macmillan, 2008. 49–63. Print.
Columpar, Corinn. "'Til Death Do Us Part: Identity and Friendship in *Heavenly Creatures*." Gateward and Pomerance 232–42. Print.

Coppola, Sofia, scr. and dir. *The Virgin Suicides.* By Jeffrey Eugenides. Perf. Kirsten Dunst. Paramount, 2000. Film.

Couch Baron. Interview with Rob Thomas. *Television Without Pity.* Television Without Pity, 18 Jan. 2007. Web. 29 Jan. 2007.

Coupland, Douglas. *Girlfriend in a Coma.* New York: Harper Perennial, 1999. Print.

Eick, David, creator. *Bionic Woman.* Perf. Katee Sackhoff. 1 season. NBC, 2007. Television.

_____ and Ronald D. Moore, creators. *Battlestar Galactica.* Perf. Katee Sackhoff. 4 seasons. Sci-Fi, 2004–09. Television.

Gateward, Frances, and Murray Pomerance, eds. *Sugar, Spice and Everything Nice: Cinemas of Girlhood.* Contemporary Film and Television Series. Gen. ed. Barry Keith Grant. Detroit: Wayne State University Press, 2002. Print.

Haraway, Donna. *Simians, Cyborgs and Women: The Reinvention of Nature.* London & New York: Routledge, 1991. Print.

Hitchcock, Alfred, dir. *Psycho.* 1960. Universal, 2005. DVD.

Hutcheon, Linda. *The Politics of Postmodernism.* 1992. 2d ed. New York: Routledge, 2002. Print.

Jackson, Peter, dir. & scr. *Heavenly Creatures.* Miramax, 1994. Film.

Kershner, Irving, dir. *The Eyes of Laura Mars.* Columbia, 1978. Film.

Kring, Tim, creator. *Heroes.* Perf. Kristen Bell, Hayden Panettiere. 3 seasons. NBC, 2006–09. Television.

Lynch, David, creator. *Twin Peaks.* 2 seasons. 1990–91. DVD. CIC Video/Paramount, 2001/2007. Television.

Mendes, Sam, dir. *American Beauty.* UIP, 1999. Film.

Mendlesohn, Farah. "Surpassing the Love of Vampires: Or, Why (and How) a Queer Reading of the Buffy/Willow Relationship Is Denied." Wilcox and Lavery 45–60. Print.

Nash, Ilana. *American Sweethearts: Teenage Girls in Twentieth-Century Popular Culture.* Bloomington: Indiana University Press, 2006. Print.

Oakley, Ann. *Fracture: Adventures of a Broken Body.* London: Policy, 2007. Print.

Pender, Patricia. "'I'm Buffy and You're ... History': The Postmodern Politics of *Buffy.*" Wilcox and Lavery 35–44. Print.

Preminger, Otto, dir. *Laura.* 1944. Fox, 2005. DVD.

Roberts, Kimberley. "Pleasures and Problems of the 'Angry Girl.'" Gateward and Pomerance 217–233. Print.

The Smiths (Johnny Marr and Morrissey), wr. and perf. "Girlfriend in a Coma." *Louder Than Bombs.* Warner Bros/WEA, 1987. CD.

Sprawson, Charles. *Haunts of the Black Masseur: The Swimmer as Hero.* London: Jonathan Cape, 1992. Print.

Whedon, Joss, creator. *Buffy the Vampire Slayer.* Perf. Sarah Michelle Gellar. 7 seasons. 1996–2003. DVD. Fox, 2004.

_____. "Ace of Case." *EW.com.* Entertainment Weekly, October 7, 2005. Web. 22 Apr. 2007.

Wilcox, Rhonda and David Lavery, eds. *Fighting the Forces: What's at Stake in* Buffy the Vampire Slayer. Lanham & Oxford: Rowman and Littlefield, 2002. Print.

# 10

# "No Longer That Girl"
## *Rape Narrative and Meaning in* Veronica Mars

### SARAH WHITNEY

"You want to know how I lost my virginity?" Veronica Mars asks the audience in the series' pilot episode. "So do I." With that extraordinary introduction, viewers learn of the most personal of the teen sleuth's many cases. By the end of the season this mystery seems to be solved, but the specter of rape returns in the second year (which features a startling re-writing of the original conclusion). The third season also features a rape storyline involving Veronica's investigation of serial assaults at Hearst College. Lynne Joyrich rightly observes that "if there is a dominant 'story'—or actually, set of stories—that has defined *Veronica Mars*, it is the ugly story of rape" (Part I, par. 3).

*Veronica Mars* makes an original and significant contribution to the representation of rape on television. Initially, it explores the impact of sexual violence upon the heroine, resisting traditional television portrayals of rape while thoughtfully exploring its heroine's search for justice. The textual re-scriptings of Veronica's rape (initially as consensual intercourse, and then subsequently as a forcible acquaintance rape committed *before* the original incident) explore the metaphorical power of rape, offer a dramatic tele-visual exploration of trauma, and leave open alternative readings of Veronica's experience. Finally, in its last season, *Veronica Mars* tackles the politicization of rape (a subject upon which it casts a jaundiced eye) via the third season's conflict between the heroine and a group of feminist activists on campus. For three years, *Veronica Mars* has embodied rape's real and ongoing trauma.

## Historicizing Representations of Rape

From Zeus tricking Danae, to Lovelace pursuing Samuel Richardson's *Clarissa*, from male assault in James Dickey's *Deliverance* to dead victims bearing posthumous witness in Alice Sebold's *The Lovely Bones*, rape has served as a prominent part of Western storytelling. A full analysis of rape narrative cannot be accomplished here, but understanding several prominent tropes that have historically represented rape and its victims can help us grasp how sexual violence operates in *Veronica Mars*.

Americans' modern understanding of rape is heavily influenced by the efforts of the 1970s women's movement. Feminist works including Susan Brownmiller's *Against Our Will* (1975) asserted that rape was rooted in hostility and violence (as opposed to mental disease or uncontrollable sexual urges). The redefinition of rape as a crime of violence against women also increased public understanding of victims' trauma. Support services such as counseling, emergency-room accompaniment, and legal advocacy evolved during this period, and rape victims finally emerged as serious subjects of sympathy in film and print. Alice Walker's novel *Meridian* (1976) frankly discussed myths about inter-racial rape, while Gloria Naylor's *The Women of Brewster Place* (1982) contained a story of a rape committed to "punish" a lesbian. Many works employed first-person narration to emphasize the victim's perspective.

On television, new ground was also broken. In 1974, the TV-movie *A Case of Rape*, which Maria Bevacqua describes as "the first victim-sympathetic fictionalized description of rape on television," debuted to record Nielsen ratings (126). The attempted rape of beloved *All in the Family* character Edith Bunker in 1977 was also a watershed television moment. Of course, rape has also been an easily exploitable subject on the small screen. The crime drama *Police Woman* (1974–1978), which featured many rape storylines, frequently engaged in blame-the-victim ideology. "Invariably, the rape victims in these episodes were young and single, and their occupational choices usually meant that they were 'asking for it,'" Susan Douglas writes. "For the purposes of viewer titillation, these women were humiliated in some way" (210).

The depiction of victims as "bad girls" is one version of what Wendy Hesford calls "rape scripts" (13). Other rape scripts include certain "stock" scenes that, through their repetition over time, come to represent rape in viewers' minds. For instance, we understand that "trauma" is being communicated onscreen when we watch a victim physically and emotionally cleanse herself with a long shower. Sometimes, rape dramas utilize earnest verbal exposition. When teenage melodrama *Felicity* (1998–2002) dealt with date rape, a series of professionals (an intake counselor, police officers, and more) engaged in heavy-handed lectures about rape reporting, medical options, and common aftershock patterns. For the most part *Veronica Mars* avoids these more familiar scripts, or it self-consciously comments upon them. For example, in the episode "A Trip to the Dentist" Veronica ritually cleanses her body and the Mars Investigations office, observing wryly that "the whole ritual cleaning thing is textbook for a reason. For a couple of minutes you're in control, and everything's the way it should be. At least on the surface" (1.21).

Viewers' first "detection" of rape in *Veronica Mars* comes in the pilot, when the heroine narrates her traumatic experience accompanied by visual flashbacks. At a party of wealthy elites called "09ers" (a group to which Veronica used to belong), she sipped a spiked drink, passed out, and awakened without her underwear in a strange bedroom. Veronica was at the party after experiencing several other traumas, including an inexplicable breakup with boyfriend Duncan Kane, the murder of her best friend Lilly Kane (Duncan's sister), and family problems that included her mother's abandonment and her father's job termination.

Veronica clearly suffered horror after horror, and the rape's placement in the pilot is the trigger that moved her from a place of extreme (perhaps saccharine) innocence to the "tough chick" she is now. In the first season, the show often used blue-drenched flashbacks to show an exceptionally innocent "old" Veronica. Judy Fitzwater notes that "Sixteen-year-old Veronica questioned very little.... She wore her hair in long, soft curls, chose modest, age-appropriate clothing, and wore lots of pastels" (196). That self survived up until Veronica's entrance to the fateful party; the smudgy black eyeliner that ringed her eyes the morning after, as she reported her rape to an unsympathetic Sheriff Lamb, was the first visual sign of the transformation into "tough" Veronica. Cutting off her hair was another. Such changes in appearance visually allude to rape trauma syndrome, in which a victim often significantly alters personal style as a self-protective measure ("Rape Trauma Syndrome").

"I'm no longer that girl," Veronica told viewers in the pilot, creating distance from her former self. While her original incarnation stressed virginity, purity, and conformity, the girl she is now possesses sarcasm, quick wits, and an ingrained sense of justice. The rape narrative has "given her a story," as uncomfortable as it might sound. Sarah Projansky writes of several such narratives in which raped heroines develop "a newfound post-rape persona" which is overtly independent and feminist (98). This is the pattern in *Veronica Mars*, where viewers witness the protagonist's evolution from the meek best friend of Lilly Kane to sardonic and outspoken avenger of the powerless. Projansky describes this kind of story as including "a sense of a latent feminism that is available in all women's subconscious, only needing the experience of or the threat of rape to bring it forward" (118). I want to turn now to exploring the show's development of this "sense of a latent feminism" as epitomized in narratives of rape-revenge.

## *I'm No Longer That Girl: Rape and the Detective*

Crime shows have been one of the primary vehicles for the depiction of rape on television. They have framed how we see female victims, how male detectives respond to rape, and much more. By presenting a competent female detective who is also a rape victim, *Veronica Mars* stakes an unusual space in the mystery genre. Though it does have its share of Jessica Fletchers,[1] TV's sleuthing world has historically featured male detectives and female victims. Additionally, while fictional detectives are frequently either threatened with or subjected to violence in the course of fighting crime, relatively few are themselves sexually victimized.[2] *Veronica Mars* takes some of its cues from the "hard-boiled" detective genre, which is usually traditionalist when it comes to depicting masculinity and femininity. Scott Christianson observes that "hard-boiled language or style is a generically distinctive combination of active verbs and fast-moving prose, of tough talk, wisecracks, and the often crude vernacular or colloquial idiom familiar to readers of the hard-boiled tradition" (129). Hard-boiled language itself might be gently parodied in *Veronica Mars*, yet the narrative *control* associated with the noir style is definitely present.[3] Christianson says of the hard-boiled narrator: "He or she talks tough, talks smart, and talks all the time to the reader in an attempt to assert personal autonomy, to make sense of experience, and to exercise language as power" (130). Voice-overs begin and end many of the series episodes, reminding viewers that the narratological point-of-view is Veronica's.

The heroine's narrative control is particularly important in light of television's tendency to center *male* detectives in rape narratives. Lisa Cuklanz has described the pervasive phenomenon of the "hegemonic male" detective who solves the crime, and in doing so becomes the real narrative focus. These detectives "are caring and sympathetic to rape victims and even demonstrate reformed or enlightened views about rape as compared with other characters, but they still establish their masculinity in part by ... routinely resorting to violence to solve problems and avenge the victims of rape" (18). The hegemonic male detective reproduces violence, and turns the narrative into *his* story.

Cuklanz's paradigm is alive and well today in American crime procedurals like *Law & Order: Special Victims Unit* (1999– ). On this program, detective Elliott Stabler exudes sympathy for victims, but also unleashes torrents of violent rage as he pummels rapists and molesters in the station house. Stabler's anger and personal dramas, rather than the victim's narrative, often become the focus of the program.[4] It is true that *Veronica Mars* does have a volatile male character, Logan Echolls, who erupts with violence whenever Veronica is mauled ("Spit and Eggs," 3.9) or humiliated ("The Bitch Is Back," 3.20). However, the narrative control and authority associated with the detective — restorer of law and order — remains with Veronica as she solves her most personal mystery.

The crime genre is also concerned with redressing injustice and righting the balance of the moral universe. "In the crime story the knowledge that is sought is about the nature of a crime and closure is achieved at the level of the social through some form of retributive justice," writes Sue Turnbull (75). Within the noir genre to which *Veronica Mars* is indebted, this process is complicated. Justice often fails, and even successful revenge narratives can be bereft of happy endings. In real life, the prosecution of sexual crimes is itself frequently noir-ish. A woman seeking redress against her assailant is often left feeling angry with and abandoned by the legal system. Perhaps this helps to explain the ongoing appeal of the wish-fulfillment "rape-revenge" subgenre. Jacinda Read's compilation of rape-revenge narratives includes Westerns (*Hannie Caulder*, 1971), slashers (*I Spit on Your Grave*, 1978), legal thrillers (*The Accused*, 1988), melodrama (*An Eye for an Eye*, 1996), and more (24–25). Thematically, these works share an interest in a victimized woman seeking violent revenge against her assailant.[5]

*Veronica Mars* has many plotlines that involve Veronica seeking justice on behalf of women and girls who, like her, have been sexually violated and humiliated. For example, Veronica comes to the rescue of her neighbor Sarah, who was raped and impregnated by her stepfather, in "The Girl Next Door" (1.7). In "Like a Virgin," Veronica assists Meg, who endures verbal and e-mail harassment when a sexual "purity test" makes her the butt of school jokes (1.8). Veronica also aids overachieving senior Sabrina after she is pilloried in a phone sex ad and subsequently harassed ("Kanes and Abel's," 1.17). Finally, shy student Carmen is aided by Veronica when Carmen's boyfriend blackmails her with provocative pictures taken while she was unknowingly drugged ("M.A.D," 1.20.) Alaine Martaus points out that if we are to consider episodes that "reference sex as it relates to power, especially abuse of power," then "nearly every episode of the show's three seasons fits the profile" (75).

In these storylines, Veronica often voices her most personal and emphatic desires for justice and revenge. "Here's what you do. You get tough. You get even," she tells Meg (1.8). Veronica even suggests sexually humiliating Carmen's boyfriend in revenge for his own ill behavior, but Carmen demurs. Kristen Kidder writes that the show condemns Veronica's vengeful ethos during this exchange. Carmen, she asserts, "privileged the traditionally feminine traits of forgiveness and understanding over the masculine dominance associated with vengeance ... [the] audience was clearly left with the impression that Carmen's character was taking the high road" (131). Yet despite Carmen's reluctance to exact revenge, she remains indebted to Veronica for the latter's passionate work on her behalf. Martaus observes of Veronica that "her rape, her detective skills, and the treatment of women she sees within her high school and as part of her work reinforce her understanding of the world as gender unbalanced" (79). While Veronica's thirst for justice for her own rape may not always be dealt with onscreen, it is consistently embodied through the plethora of rape-revenge stories woven through the series.

## Rape and Re-scripting: Memory and Trauma

Rape itself is also textually unstable throughout the first two seasons of *Veronica Mars*. As viewers know, Veronica's rape is first re-written as "seduction" when it is learned that Veronica and Duncan, both drugged with GHB, slept together under voluntary although troubling circumstances. (I say "re-written" because throughout the entire season, viewers and Veronica herself have been led to believe that she was forcibly raped).

The politics of the transformation of rape into not-rape at the conclusion of season one's "A Trip to the Dentist" are troubling. Lynn Higgins reminds us that rape "can be discursively transformed into another kind of story" (307). It can be rewritten "into 'persuasion,' 'seduction,' or even 'romance'" (307). One of the reasons this ending has always been problematic for me as a viewer is that it is a *too*-familiar script. Women are frequently told (or tell themselves) that they have "misinterpreted" sexual situations by missing cues ("leading men on") or by being "unclear" about their lack of consent. Furthermore, the episode leaves us bereft of a villain that can be nailed to the wall for forcible rape.

Yet the narrative style of "A Trip to the Dentist," in which Veronica's fate unfolds through flashbacks focalized through her various peers, establishes in fact the opposite — that *everyone* bears guilt for the season-long exploitation of the heroine. Meg describes a drunk Veronica receiving body shots (a process by which alcohol is served off the erogenous zones of someone's body) from various classmates. Sean narrates a particular vile vignette in which Dick

Casablancas drags an unconscious Veronica into the guest bedroom and invites his younger brother Beaver to rape her. The list of abuses goes on: Madison spit in Veronica's drink and defaced her car, Logan mocked her and supervised the body shots, and a group of classmates encouraged Veronica to engage in risqué acts with another woman for their own amusement. In effect, while "no one" raped Veronica, everyone bears responsibility for an evening in which she was repeatedly violated. Had the sympathetic Meg, the affable Casey, or even the odious Sean handled any portion of their interaction with her differently, she would not have been so abused. In its exploration of the bystander's responsibility, *Veronica Mars* joins films such as *The Accused* (1988), *Bad Girls* (1994), and others which interrogate what happens when people fail to intervene in violent scenarios.[6]

What happens to Veronica, then, can be read as the indictment of an elite social group who acts by turns viciously and carelessly towards a disgraced former member. It is a metaphor of class warfare in a town that is depicted as being "without a middle class" (1.1). My reading is different than that of Samantha Bornemann, who writes that "Veronica's rape was revealed as a cosmic joke brought on by circumstance and foolish pride.... She wasn't chosen or targeted; she was unlucky" (190). But though I think the flashback narrations of "A Trip to the Dentist" clearly establish Veronica's humiliations as "rape" by a predatory social class of elites, I also see the danger in leaving the analysis here in the realm of metaphor. Sabine Sielke writes that rape has become a politically powerful "master metaphor" and a "strong trope" in feminist and popular discourse, but she reminds us that it is the *materiality* of the experience of rape that needs attention (370).

This materiality re-emerges at the end of *Veronica Mars'* second season, when it is revealed that she was forcibly assaulted by Beaver Casablancas on the night of Shelly Pomeroy's party ("Not Pictured," 2.22). If we subsequently re-view the previous version of that night as laid out in "A Trip to the Dentist," there are some interesting revelations about the Casablancas brothers, particularly the not-so-subtly named elder brother Dick. The quintessential villain in "A Trip to the Dentist," Dick is a potential rapist who spiked Madison's soda (a drink which ultimately ended up in Veronica's hands). According to Sean, Dick also offered up the now-unconscious Veronica for rape by his younger brother Beaver. Dick carried the white-gowned Veronica upstairs to the guest room while humming "Here Comes the Bride" (an ominous reference to the "devirginization" of wedding-night mythology).

During this scene, Dick delivers an effectively thorough speech that expresses his unenlightened views of women and insults Veronica on several levels. "She's actually kind of hot when she's quiet. Perfectly cute piece of ass.

Ready and willing," he chuckles. When Beaver remarks that Veronica is not willing, but rather unconscious, Dick responds callously: "That's probably the best you're going to do, bro." As he heads out the door, Dick tosses Beaver a condom, ostensibly for protection from the sullied or infectious Veronica. "You don't know where she's been," Dick sneers (1.21).[7]

The show's inclusion of an overtly objectionable male suspect like Dick works to minimize Duncan's questionable actions in sleeping with a drugged woman (and one whom he erroneously believed to be his half-sister). In Dick's speech, several key tenets of feminist rape ideology are fulfilled. Susan Brownmiller wrote that "a woman is perceived by the rapist both as hated person and desired property," and the "used" and "dirty" Veronica fulfills this role for Dick (185). The Casablancas brothers' scene is an unusually raw and unflinching portrayal of male privilege and misogyny. The rape narrative backs off from it, however, in favor of a different ending. The first season's official resolution of the rape narrative denies a traditional "whodunit" ending. Instead, it creates a strong rhetorical statement (Veronica was rhetorically "raped" by an unfeeling class of people) while failing to indict one particular assailant.

But although Veronica's rape is turned into an act of mutually incapacitated seduction, there remains space for alternate endings, and the foreshadowing of sexual violence in the words and actions of Dick Casablancas. This violence returns in the form of Dick's younger brother Beaver in the second-season finale "Not Pictured." As she dramatically unmasks Beaver as the bus crash killer, Veronica also accuses him of raping her the year before at Shelly's party. Beaver assents, and suddenly the rape narrative is destabilized again.

Of course, not everything connected to the re-writing of this story has to do with the politics of rape. Making Veronica the victim of Beaver Casablancas ties her to his other victims in the bus crash, thus personalizing a season-long mystery that had not packed the emotional wallop of the earlier rape mystery or Lilly Kane's murder. However, we can also interpret this re-writing in psychological terms. Describing the effect of narrative re-visitation and clarification in soap opera (a process she calls The Return), Martha Nochimson writes that as television programs revisit prior closures, "the viewer retains the original magic of the original closure, but in addition also experiences a distancing effect that revivifies alternative, hitherto unexpressed possibilities within the original situation" (28). There had always been such a possibility vis-à-vis Beaver's actions towards Veronica in the guest bedroom. His claim that no rape occurred was supported only by his word.

Because that word is now proven insufficient, the re-scripting throws similar doubt on other testimonials. Duncan's reading of consensual sex between himself and Veronica is again open for revisitation and scrutiny. One effect of this re-scripting is to destabilize the role of memory altogether, and suggest that testimony is either debased or worth little — a cynical attitude appropriate for the *noir* genre. Viewers might recall that the denouement of the bus-crash and rape storylines nearly coincide with Aaron Echolls' trial for Lilly Kane's murder ("Happy Go Lucky," 2.21). Veronica's courtroom testimony features the humiliating revelation of her chlamydia (in what seems like a veiled reference to the Rape Shield Law protecting accusers' past sexual histories). Ultimately, Veronica's heartfelt testimony is discarded, and Aaron is set free.[8]

Official memory, then, can be discarded by the law (as is Veronica's testimony), or may be proven false (as is Beaver's version of events). This narrative thread recalls legal rape discourse, which is preoccupied by ideas of intention, consent, and memory. We can also read "The Return" of season two against a particular strain of rape text which became popular in the 1990s. This narrative, called "trauma writing," foregrounds "complicated narration, fragmentation, temporal discontinuities, and often, a lack of tidy resolution" (Field 173). Well-known examples of such disjointed, fragmented rape narratives include Toni Morrison's *Beloved* (1987) and Sapphire's *Push* (1996). Stories like these are characterized by chronological gaps and fissures (much as there is a year-long space between the revelations of "A Trip to the Dentist" and "Not Pictured") because they are trying to capture the hazy and broken nature of traumatic memories. Veronica processes such an uncomfortable memory "flash" when Keith informs her that Woody Goodman had chlamydia (2.22). Though it violates our traditional narrative expectations about closure, the re-scripting of Veronica's rape is consistent with theory of trauma and the imprecise nature of memory. We can read the show's re-embodiment of rape through the figure of Beaver Casablancas as evidence that the original story ending was ultimately insufficient. Through the use of traumatic narrative, rape moves from being "Not Pictured" to ever-present.

## *The Personal, Not the Political: Season Three*

In the noir world of Neptune, California, violence follows Veronica from the halls of high school to the sun-splashed campus of Hearst College. The first portion of the show's third season tracks a sadistic serial rapist who knocks coeds unconscious, rapes them, shaves their heads, and keeps their hair as a trophy. Veronica's new friend Parker becomes an early victim. Ultimately, Veronica unmasks college radio host Mercer and his accomplice Moe as the villains, but not before being physically assaulted and sexually threatened herself.

Despite Veronica's connection to Parker, and despite the violence she faces as she works the case, this particular rape narrative is less "personal" for the heroine. While Veronica's rape narrative and its personal trauma are fundamental to the construction of her character's toughness, the Hearst storyline criticizes the *politicization* of rape. This criticism is expressed through the ongoing conflict between Veronica, the "objective detective," and a group of feminist women who inhabit the "Lilith House" dorm. Veronica wages a crusade of justice to find a particular perpetrator, while the Lilith House denizens are portrayed as suspicious of all men. A series of confrontations between Veronica and the Liliths suggests that Veronica pursues the morally right and productive path, while the actions of the Liliths (including a faked rape) actually impede the investigation and imperil other women.

Within the Hearst rapist storyline, there are multiple discourses of sexual violence circulating. On one hand, female students are terrorized by an unknown assailant — the "stranger-in-the bushes" figure of nightmare. On the other hand, the show gives ongoing attention to the sexist fraternity culture at Hearst and its capacity for sexual violence. This culture of entitlement was prefigured in season two's "The Rapes of Graff," when Veronica discovered a fraternity's "scoreboard" (2.16). Sexual relations were treated as a sports competition amongst the men, with points awarded for conquest comeliness and number of women involved. In the third season, the show zeroes in on Greek culture and male sexual privilege again in "Lord of the Pi's," which tells of a sorority pledge whose sisters sexually humiliated her by stripping her and "critiquing" her body with permanent marker (3.8). This activity was designed for the benefit of the Pi Sigma men, who had been watching in a secret room designed for voyeurism and perhaps other, darker things.

Veronica condemns this treatment of women and expresses sympathy for Patrice, the pledge who was victimized. But ultimately we are "faked out" again. Pi Sigma is seemingly guilty of little more than sexist and archaic attitudes; the men are exonerated from the rapes through Veronica's detection. This is the point of distinction that separates Veronica's feminism from the organized anti-rape activism of the Lilith House women. The latter view the Greek organizations on campus as pure evil, and are convinced that they are responsible for the serial rapes. To this end, they aggressively investigate the inner workings of the houses. Nish (one of the leaders of the Lilith House) crows vindictively "one down, nine to go!" when Veronica's sleuthing inadvertently closes a Greek house ("My Big Fat Greek Rush Week," 3.2). Their activities also include several unconscionable acts, including faking a rape at a fraternity party, and anally penetrating a fraternity president.

The unlikable portrayal of the Lilith House women drew fire from some critics. Rachel Fudge described the housemates as "dour, shrill, unreasonable, judgmental, and vindictive — in other words, as feminazis: humorless haters of men, of women who wear makeup, and of any intimation of fun in general" (15). A real-life model influenced the portrayal of these characters. "I will say that the portrayal of those women ... it was affected by the coverage of the Duke lacrosse scandal," Rob Thomas said in an interview.[9] "There was certainly some notion of putting the strident people who I reacted to in the Duke lacrosse thing into the show" (Couch Baron). The Lilith House women are "strident" in their belief that the fraternity system is bankrupt and must be shut down; they are not willing to consider any shades of moral indeterminacy.

Sally Robinson discusses a very similar group of outspoken feminists — the "Ellen Jamesians" — who inhabit John Irving's *The World According to Garp*. Ellen James is a young woman who suffered rape and mutilation when her assailant cut out her tongue in order to ensure her silence. Ellen's trauma attracts a cult following of sorts; her feminist supporters mutilate their own tongues and declare themselves to be "Ellen Jamesians." In similar fashion, some Lilith House residents fake their own rapes (e.g., Claire) and wear a hairstyle that recalls the victims' shaved heads (e.g., Nish) in solidarity. "The difference between Ellen James and the Ellen Jamesians is coded in familiar terms," Robinson writes. "Ellen's trauma is authentic because personal; the Ellen Jamesians' trauma is false because political" (105). Irving expands on the political import of the Ellen Jamesians by noting that some of these women "felt as if their tongues were gone. In a world of men, they felt as if they had been shut up forever" (quoted in Robinson 105). In other words, they appropriate Ellen's private anguish as a general complaint of "feeling silenced" in a patriarchal culture.

I see a similar tug-of-war over rape appropriation in *Veronica Mars*. As the "objective" detective, Veronica views Parker's rape as a tragedy which can be alleviated by the capture of her assailant. She is genuinely concerned about potential victims, and works diligently to solve the crime, but she doesn't connect the serial rapes to the political notion of "a rape culture" in the same way that the Lilith students do. Most crucially, Veronica is positioned as "anti-anti-male." She undertakes the exoneration of several male suspects (Troy Vandergraff in "The Rapes of Graff," 2.16, and the Pi Sigma fraternity in "Charlie Don't Surf," 3.4), and these actions earn her the Lilith House's ire. As Veronica is embraced by a shirtless Dick on the porch steps of the fraternity, she is greeted by cold glares of women demonstrating for "no more rapes at Hearst." "When did the Greek chorus of feminist shame arrive?" Veronica wonders (3.4; see Beeler in this volume). The comment rhetorically sets Veronica apart from the feminist "chorus," and onscreen she is visually positioned opposite the crowd. Of course, her work in solving the crime in order to protect women's safety is indeed feminist. So this moment onscreen separates Veronica from one unsympathetic *kind* of organized feminism which has already pre-judged the fraternity's guilt. We are encouraged to identify, I think, with Veronica's individualist and objective approach. When Parker tries to make her feel guilty for assisting Pi Sigma, Veronica asks: "You want to nail someone to the wall just to have someone nailed there, or do you want the person responsible to pay?" ("Charlie Don't Surf," 3.4). The question has an obvious moral answer.

Veronica's methods pay off when she apprehends the real rapist, who is not a fraternity brother. The narrative switches back from exploring Greek privilege issues to unmasking a psychotic perpetrator. True villains in *Veronica Mars* tend to speechify at length — think of Aaron Echolls, or of Beaver Casablancas' soliloquy before suicide. Mercer is no different; as he holds a chilling "conversation" with his unconscious future victim, he expresses contempt for the woman's room décor, and for the bother of having to acquire consent for sex at all. "If I'd met you in a bar or, uh, at a party, I would have had you back here and on your back in an hour," he tells the still form on the bed with biting anger. "But that's an hour of my life I would have never had back..." ("Spit and Eggs," 3.9).

While the punishment of such an over-the-top misogynist is fulfilling, the shift away from Hearst's Greek subculture puts an end to some interesting discussions about substance use, sexual coercion, and the "rape culture." These issues are murkier, and don't provide the clearest villains and victims, although the show has tackled such gray areas in the first season's rape narrative. With the apprehension of the serial rapist, the Lilith House women too faded away, to my disappointment. *Veronica Mars* sharply critiqued the Lilith women's tendency to be "Ellen Jamesians" — to appropriate and politicize rape, and to presume men's dastardly guilt by association with fraternities. Yet when their tongues were also silenced at the conclusion of the narrative arc, an intriguing storyline was lost.

In three short years, *Veronica Mars* provided valuable contributions to the representation of rape on television. Its depiction of a victimized sleuth who works diligently to solve her own crime, and its melding of the "rape-revenge" narrative with criminal investigation mark striking developments in the detective genre. The re-scripting of the first season's rape is both maddening and thought-provoking, raising questions about materiality and metaphor, as well as the fragile nature of memory. Its third-season story arc

dealt with contemporary college issues surrounding sexual assault and fraternity culture, while also resisting the politicization of rape through the Lilith
storyline. In life, the agony of rape results in many questions — "why?" or
"what if...?" — that ultimately cannot be answered. It may seem odd that a
detective story would return to this narrative again and again. But for one
teenaged girl in a town full of secrets, the issue proves too important not to
try.

## Notes

1. The renowned Angela Lansbury portrayed Jessica Fletcher, a mystery writer/
detective, in the *Murder, She Wrote* television series (1984–96).

2. There are a few notable exceptions. See Cuklanz, *Rape on Prime Time* on female
detectives (usually minor characters) victimized or used as rapist "bait" in 1970s–
1980s procedurals (111–117).

3. For example, in "Return of the Kane," Veronica calls Keith "Philip Marlowe,"
and Keith utters a faux-noir monologue about his encounter with a "dame" with great
"getaway sticks" (1.6). *Veronica Mars'* gendered re-writing of the hard-boiled genre is
elegantly explored by Alaine Martaus in "'You Get Tough. You Get Even': Rape,
Anger, Cynicism, and the Vigilante Girl Detective in *Veronica Mars*." Placing the show
within the hard-boiled literary tradition, Martaus demonstrates how the influence of
the contemporary female-empowerment movement (particularly as it relates to Veronica's rape and her subsequent evolution as a detective) re-shapes the noir canon.

4. This phenomenon is not limited to crime procedurals. In teen melodrama *Felicity*, main character Julie is date-raped, but the arc largely revolves around her friend
Ben. Ben confronts and beats the assailant, lectures him about consent, lectures Julie
about her depression, and reveals his own traumatic experience with a deadbeat father.
Ben is enlightened and supportive, but his problems take up an inordinate amount
of space and minimize Julie's struggles.

5. I use "woman" in the victim position because this is usually the case both
onscreen and in real life. *Deliverance* (1972) remains the only major motion picture
to explore male victimization. On TV, male rape has begun to be represented on programs like *Cagney & Lacey* (1982–1988), the prison series *Oz* (1997–2003) and the
*Law & Order* franchises.

6. For more on the bystander in rape narrative, see Sarah Projansky's *Watching
Rape* (2001).

7. After she loses her high-status relationship with Duncan Kane, Veronica is sexually slandered by her classmates. Weevil makes crude references about her "reputation"
in the pilot, and in later flashbacks, we see Madison Sinclair spray-paint the epithet
"slut" on Veronica's car.

8. In an uneasy conflation of the Kane murder story and the rape narrative, Veronica
is trapped in a hotel elevator with Aaron Echolls on her way to her terrifying confrontation of Beaver Casablancas.

9. The "Duke lacrosse scandal" is a well-publicized 2006 case in which an African
American woman hired as a stripper for a Duke University lacrosse team party accused

three white players of raping her. The incident provoked national conversations about race, false rape claims, and "town and gown" issues. Charges against the men were withdrawn in April 2007 after DNA evidence failed to connect them to the crime, and amidst reports that the accuser had changed her story.

## *Works Cited*

Bevacqua, Maria. *Rape on the Public Agenda.* Boston: Northeastern University Press, 2000. Print.

Bornemann, Samantha. "Innocence Lost." Thomas 184–193. Print.

Brownmiller, Susan. *Against Our Will: Men, Women and Rape.* New York: Simon & Schuster, 1975. Print.

Christianson, Scott. "Talkin' Trash and Kickin' Butt: Sue Grafton's Hard-boiled Feminism." *Feminism in Women's Detective Fiction.* Ed. Glenwood Irons. Toronto: University of Toronto Press, 1995. 127–147. Print.

Couch Baron. Interview with Rob Thomas. *TelevisionwithoutPity.* 18 Jan. 2007. Web. 29 Jan. 2007.

Cuklanz, Lisa M. *Rape on Prime Time.* Philadelphia: University of Pennsylvania Press, 2000. Print.

Douglas, Susan J. *Where the Girls Are: Growing Up Female with the Mass Media.* New York: Times Books/Random House, 1994. Print.

"Drawing the Line, Parts I and II." *Felicity.* The WB. 1998. Television.

Field, Robin E. "Writing the Victim." Diss. University of Virginia, 2006. Print.

Fitzwater, Judy. "From Golden Girl to Rich-Dude Kryptonite." Thomas 194–203. Print.

Fudge, Rachel, and Juliana Tringali. "Point/Counterpoint: *Veronica Mars* and Its Feminist Stereotypes." *Bitch: Feminist Response to Pop Culture.* 35 (Spring 2007): 15. Print.

Hesford, Wendy. "Rape Stories: Material Rhetoric and the Trauma of Representaton." *Haunting Violations: Feminist Criticism and the Crisis of the "Real."* Ed. Wendy Hesford and Wendy Kozol. Urbana: University of Illinois Press, 2001. 13–46. Print.

Higgins, Lynn A. "Screen/Memory: Last Year at Marienbad." *Rape and Representation.* Ed. Lynn A. Higgins and Brenda R. Silver. New York: Columbia University Press, 1991. 303–321. Print.

Joyrich, Lynne. "Women Are from Mars?" (Part 1). *Flow* 5.8 (23 Feb. 2007). n. pag. Web. 15 Aug. 2009.

_____. "Women Are from Mars?" (Part 2). *Flow* 5.9 (9 Mar. 2007). n. pag. Web. 15 Aug. 2009.

Kidder, Kristen. "The New Normal: Breaking the Boundaries of Vigilantism in *Veronica Mars.*" Thomas 125–133. Print.

Martaus, Alaine. "'You Get Tough. You Get Even': Rape, Anger, Cynicism, and the Vigilante Girl Detective in *Veronica Mars.*" *Clues: A Journal of Detection* 27.1 (Spring 2009): 74–86. Print.

Nochimson, Martha. "Amnesia 'R' Us: The Retold Melodrama, Soap Opera, and the Representation of Reality." *Film Quarterly* 50:3 (Spring 1997): 27–38. Print.

Projansky, Sarah. *Watching Rape.* New York: New York University, 2001. Print.

"Rape Trauma Syndrome." RAINN (Rape, Abuse & Incest National Network), n.d. Web. 15 Aug. 2009.

Read, Jacinda. *The New Avengers: Feminism, Femininity and the Rape-Revenge Cycle.* Manchester: Manchester University Press, 2001. Print.

Robinson, Sally. *Marked Men: White Masculinity in Crisis.* New York: Columbia University Press, 2000. Print.

Sielke, Sabine. "The Politics of the Strong Trope: Rape and the Feminist Debate in the United States." *Amerikastudien* 49.3 (2004): 367–384. Print.

Thomas, Rob, ed. *Neptune Noir: Unauthorized Investigations into* Veronica Mars. Dallas: BenBella, 2006. Print.

Turnbull, Sue. "'Nice Dress, Take It Off': Crime, Romance and the Pleasure of the Text." *International Journal of Cultural Studies* 5.1 (2002): 67–82. Print.

# 11

# Neptune (Non-)Consensual
## *The Risky Business of Television Fandom, Falling in Love, and Playing the Victim*
### Tanya R. Cochran

"I'm never getting married. You want an absolute? There it is. Veronica Mars: spinster. I mean, what's the point? ... Sooner or later, the people you love let you down."
— Veronica Mars, Pilot

"You wanna know how I lost my virginity? So do I."
— Veronica Mars, Pilot

"[Leading up to today's cancellation of the series,] I have had months of speculation and rumour, hopes lifted and dashed, during which time my mind was made up for me...."
— sjoanzors, *Veronica Mars* fan

Like many other television viewers, I am always looking for a long-term relationship when I sit down in front of the flat screen or turn on my laptop and click "Hulu" on my list of bookmarked web pages. I am not as interested in one-night trysts, though I enjoy a good, stand-alone film now and then. I am searching for a committed partner, a series that will last, that will satisfy my desire for rich storytelling, complex characters, and narrative arcs. Of course, television series are not lovers; a consensual, mutual, reciprocal relationship I will never find. No audience member will. The industry that creates the series that any of us might fall in love with can neither be trusted nor expected to put the well-being of its audience, its fans, before the well-being of its financial fecundity. Because the industry is just that: an industry, a business. As Veronica herself might sardonically say, "Love is an investment. [Ratings] are insurance" (Pilot). As a result, relationships between a television series and its fans, though not without emotion, are much more akin to business transactions than life partnerships.

We all know that television series, one way or another, "let you down." For one, all shows eventually "die." In fact, the death of any series is inevitable, so devout fans in particular ultimately have to say their literal and symbolic goodbyes.[1] And most of the time, they *do* bid their favorite shows farewell.[2] But when death comes prematurely, when the audience members find themselves pleading for more time —*Firefly* (2002), *Farscape* (1999–2003), *Wonderfalls* (2004), *Jericho* (2006–2008), *Pushing Daisies* (2007–2009), etc.— rather than exhaling a sigh of collective resolution or relief when a series finally passes on, fascinating things can happen. Though *Veronica Mars* enjoyed a three-season run, its fans were not prepared to let it go, bemoaning its cancellation as untimely. Sometimes comparing the ending of the sleuthy teen series to the much swifter demise of Joss Whedon's *Firefly*, fans immediately exhibited and continue to exhibit a range of emotions, from disappointment to anger. Initially, they also threatened to display or actually displayed a variety of (re)actions, from mourning to boycotting. In considering the language that some online *Veronica Mars* fans have used to articulate the stages of their grief, a striking metaphor presents itself, a metaphor that, consciously or unconsciously employed, suggests that some fans sympathize so deeply with Veronica that they borrow the language of her victimization.

As viewers discover in the very first episode of the series, Veronica has endured a string of traumatic events in the previous year: the murder of her best friend, the abandonment of her mother, the reassignment of her and her father's social and economic status, and the loss of her virginity. Of the pilot, critic Robert Bianco suggests, "In its attempts to show the dangers Veronica already has overcome, the show may load too many traumas on its young heroine, including one that is brushed off without significant enough psychological repercussions" (4D). Presumably, the "one" to which Bianco refers is the trauma of rape. The evidence comes from Veronica herself, in her unaffected voiceover that recounts the night of Shelly Pomeroy's party, an event viewers witness in flashback. Though the audience hears cynical matter-of-factness in her voice when she tells them she was drugged and raped at that high school party, any viewer can identify — some more closely than others — with the fear Veronica conveys when she awakens the next morning between someone else's sheets, her virginal white panties crumpled on the floor next to the bed. Tears stream down her cheeks as she infers what has happened. After collecting herself, the audience watches as she walks away from the scene, dazed and barefoot, clutching only one white, open-toed slingback in her left hand, a purse in her right. Most horrifying, she has no memory of what has happened: "You wanna know how I lost my virginity? So do I" ("Pilot," 1.1).[3] In other words, Veronica's mind was made up for her, an experience holding emotional and metaphorical resonance for fans. This non-consensual encounter — Veronica's victimization — becomes three years later the metaphor through which some fans express their own loss. In order to ascertain the significance of that metaphor, though, one must first understand how *Veronica Mars* enthusiasts come to define what they perceive to be the CW network's betrayal of their relationship with the series, specifically the betrayal of President of Entertainment Dawn Ostroff. In part, that understanding comes by accounting for the gamut of investments, some deeply personal, that most if not all fans make.

## *Love Is...: Investing in* Veronica Mars

Upon first glance, *Veronica Mars* fans are no different than any other devoted followers of genre television, film, or sports. As Scott Thorne and Gordon C. Bruner observe, fans — from soccer lovers to science fiction buffs — share four characteristics: they care deeply and personally about the object of their passion, relish getting outside of merely internal thoughts and feelings, tend to accumulate material artifacts and experiences related to their fandom, and seek the company of other enthusiasts (53–55). Of course, in a culture steeped in technology and thus ease of communication, many of these fan markers converge in online settings. In fact, Sharon Marie Ross notes that particularly the Internet encourages "tele-participation" or completely novel ways for both audiences and authors of popular series to watch and create televisual texts (4). Arguably, the Internet also creates many ways for viewers to construct meaning(s). Because virtual spaces make this meaning-making easy to locate and examine, much of the data presented here comes from the Internet.

Thorne and Bruner portray fans as intensely and intimately invested in their favorite texts or pastimes. In fact, fans devote a lot of time and spend considerable amounts of money on their fandoms (53). As an act of personal commitment, aesthetic admiration, or even with the intent to "convert" others into fans, a *Veronica Mars* devotee, for example, might host a viewing party. The event may be a regular one that includes friends who also enjoy the show, or it might be a special, one-time occasion that includes themed snacks, games, and/or costumes (see also Reeves, Rodgers, and Epstein 26). Schnappycat shares that she hosted a *Veronica Mars* viewing party that featured many of the foods present or mentioned in the series and decorations in colors that represent the show. Though her statement cannot be confirmed, Schnappycat claims that "extra fun" came from a special phone call: "An actor/friend from the show also called us during the [episode]." Such a party could coincide with the real-time broadcast of the show or, with the aid of the latest technologies, could be recorded and saved for a later date or even watched later online using the official website of the broadcast company or sites such as Hulu or Fancast. In an online post titled "Conversion Week Day 3: Planning a Viewing Party," Masarath details what one must do in preparation for an evangelistic-style gathering: first, the host should select the number of episodes that can be viewed in the allotted party time; second, the host has to choose which episodes to screen; third, the host might plan a menu. As Masarath notes, deciding which episodes to show is by far the "hardest part," so this poster offers several strategies:

- *Show the episodes in order.* [I] recommend showing as many episodes in order as possible in order to layout the storylines and characters for your guests. Some episodes can be skipped without too much confusion. It might be a good idea to skip "The Girl Next Door" [(1.7)] and "Drinking the Kool Aid" [(1.9)] in order to make room for "Like a Virgin" [(1.8)] and "An Echolls Family Christmas" [(1.10)].
- *Show the most important episodes.* Another approach is to show the episodes that layout who killed Lilly. While almost all episodes have clues regarding Lilly's murder, some episodes have key plot points that shouldn't be skipped. Skipping episodes may leave new viewers confused about some plot points, but it's a good way to hook people who may be [skeptical] about whether or not the mysteries are ever solved.
- *Show the fan favorites.* This last approach involves showing your guests episodes you know they will *love*. The ones we consider classics. "An Echolls Family Christmas" [(1.10)] is almost guaranteed to hook viewers, as is "Clash of the Tritons" [(1.12)]. "Ruskie Business" [(1.15)] is another good one to show, especially if your guests LOVE the 80s. If you know of any episodes you think will appeal to your guests in particular, feel free to add it to the mix.

While refreshments are not a requirement, says Masarath, they are a fun addition to the event. Suggestions include the following:

- Marshmallows, because Veronica is one, at least according to Wallace (Pilot).

- Waffles and Ice Cream. It is after all, Veronica's favorite dessert ("You Think You Know Somebody," [1.5]).
- Lopsided Cake, because all of Veronica's cakes turn out lopsided ("You Think You Know Somebody," [1.5]).
- Ice Cream Sundaes, complete with maraschino cherries to satisfy your requirement of fruits ("Return of the Kane," [1.6]).
- Snickerdoodles, because they're Wallace's favorite cookies ("Betty and Veronica," [1.16]).

For a *Veronica Mars* viewing party, the time, money, and especially caloric commitments can be significant! Marasath's three strategies for selecting episodes demonstrate both the critical thinking and rhetorical savvy required for making those choices: which method will produce the desired outcome ("conversion") from the particular audience ("non-believers")? Also, the level of concern for detail Masarath shows in the list of potential menu items (e.g., citing episodes) showcases highly specific familiarity with the series.

Obviously, a viewing party, among other types of gatherings, becomes the venue for observing and understanding two other characteristics typical of all fans: getting outside of merely internal musings and feelings and seeking the company of other enthusiasts. Although Thorne and Bruner discuss these two markers separately, they often coincide. The Internet makes externalizing thoughts and emotion quite easy, and once those thoughts and emotions are public, online fans quickly gather. A question as simple as "Why do you love *Veronica Mars?*" posted to a fan forum can draw immediate responses and create a sense of community, even if temporarily. At the prompting of beautifulgarbage, allied fans contributed to a growing list of "100 Reasons Why We Love Veronica Mars" — the series and the character: "excitement and mystery" (lindab123); "snappy dialogue, great casting choices, continuing story arc, the show doesn't take itself too seriously, but takes its viewers very seriously" (StarrChild); "the Papa Mars and daughter Mars relationship" (thuggie8); "great music choices" (amys21); "strong female lead" (Miss_Mars). This sampling of reasons, as varied as they are, brings enthusiasts into conversation and, sometimes, relationship with each other. At the same time, being the object of critique or even attack remains a risk of getting outside of one's own head, so it would be deceptive not to underscore that fan communities experience internal as well as external conflict. Also, purposely or not, fandoms maintain hierarchies. On the Fan Forum website where the above conversation takes place, fans are demarcated with stars and titles according to how many posts they have made: from no stars, which earns the title "New Fan," to six stars or "Addicted Fan"; from seven stars or "Obsessed Fan" to thirteen stars, the mark of an "Elite Fan." Still, these risks do not seem to deter. "New Fan" VMars_fan ventures out for the first time to explain that she loves the show because Veronica herself "makes us watchers ... feel how she feels and makes us suffer with her and love her for being such a strong person." Moving beyond musings and feelings, emotional resonance might even lead to practice: "She makes me wonder why [I'm not] doing anything to improve my life ... she also inspires me to start planning my future." Why does VMars_fan feel this way? He or she cannot explain, yet is sure that someone on the forum thread might understand "how it feels."

In the case of television series, like *Veronica Mars*, that become threatened by low ratings — the "writing on the wall" for cancellation — these virtual gatherings can and do result in corporeal gatherings, many of which bring about direct action.[4] For example, the Watch Veronica Mars website chronicles every save-the-show effort made by Cloud Watchers, "fans of *Veronica Mars* who want network executives and advertisers to see that they are committed to the show, not just as viewers, but as promoters" ("Cloud Watchers are..."). Weeks before the end of the second season, the Cloud Watchers arranged for a small airplane to fly from Los Angeles to Burbank on the day the finale was set to air. Trailing behind the plane, a banner shouted in all caps "RENEW VERONICA MARS! CW 2006!" ("About Cloud Watchers"; Turnbull 320). This tactic stemmed from fans' fear that the series might get lost in the shuffle of the merger between UPN, the original home of *Veronica Mars*, and The WB, a union between CBS and Warner Brothers that resulted in today's CW network. And the fans wanted to do something out of the ordinary. As a co-founder of the Cloud Watcher community, Anna Smith explains to *Media Life* that fans usually opt for traditional but ineffective strategies such as sending flowers, postcards, or letters, none of which can be tracked to judge whether or not fan efforts are noticeable to "the powers that be." Assuming that most of the disregarded bouquets and unopened bushels of mail quickly find their way to trash receptacles and recycling bins, Smith notes that she and cohorts instead planned to "come together as a united front and do something that would require the executives to take notice" (qtd. in Vasquez, "Taking to the Air"). Cloud Watchers wanted executives to "Look to the Skies" for answers about renewing the show. Even media outlets such as *The Washington Post* carried the story: "[Dawn] Ostroff was the target of a heavy lobbying campaign by fans who wanted to see their series survive, including some who rented an airplane to fly a sign over CW headquarters" (Bauder). Of course, having a banner made and hiring a pilot required funding, so the Cloud Watchers rallied their friends through cyberspace; within a few days of creating a PayPal account and putting a "Donate" button on their website, the community of devotees had raised close to $7000. But only a portion of donations paid for the plane and banner. The rest supported an array of strategic efforts. On May 8, 2006, the day before the second season finale, the Cloud Watchers delivered to future CW executives, other decision makers, and some media staff "care packages containing *Veronica Mars*–inspired gifts, information about the plane's flight plan, and binoculars — to aid decision makers when they looked to the skies.... We explained to them that on May 9th 'CW' would stand for something entirely different: *Cloud Watchers*" ("About Cloud Watchers"; Turnbull 320).

The Cloud Watchers knew that renting a plane, flying a banner, and assembling a few care packages would not necessarily change anyone's mind; they had additional plans. To ensure that not only executives but also potential viewers — therefore, potential fans and supporters — learned of *Veronica Mars*, the Cloud Watchers focused on a DVD drive, not only purchasing them but also strategically placing them. In an astutely rhetorical and novel move, devotees all over the United States bought DVD sets of the first season and donated them to local libraries. By the time the banner was streaking through southern California's skies, DVD sets had been placed in libraries in all ten of Nielsen's top markets. Just four months later, in September of 2006, fans had donated and public libraries had shelved 500 sets of *Veronica Mars*, Season One. The Cloud Watchers reached every U.S. state and every Nielsen market in the top 100. When the second season was released, that DVD set also went to over one hundred libraries ("About Cloud Watchers"). As the website records, the DVD Campaign for Libraries ultimately did not prevent *Veronica Mars* from being cancelled, but the effort nonetheless unified fans and solidified their support for the series. The drive remains a piece of activism fans are "very proud of" and demonstrates the depth of devotion and, more importantly, foresight some enthusiasts have. In many ways, the library campaign represents a selfless, dare I say *loving*, act because all over America "new viewers are discovering the series every day in their local libraries." The Cloud Watchers continue to live up to their self-description as viewers as well as promoters of the series. Their LiVEJOURNAL community remains active years after Veronica walked into a Neptune rain shower.[5]

Of course, viewing parties, online communing, and the footwork required for street (or sky) campaigning are only a few examples of the kinds of investments made by *Veronica Mars* admirers. Other examples include fans creating websites, making music videos (a.k.a. vidding), writing fan fiction, tracking actors' careers, following characters' fashion trends,[6] drawing or painting original art, reviewing or analyzing episodes, and fundraising for nonprofit organizations.[7] All of these activities, many of which are engaged in by the same individual fan, confirm such intimate and strong attachment that they may cause concern among family and friends who might see these activities as abnormal, unhealthy, or obsessive. Though fandom for many of us constitutes everyday life (Sandvoss 3), followers of genre television, unlike sports enthusiasts, can still experience askance looks and teasing or derogatory comments for investing so much of their *selves* in "fantasy." But as Thorne and Bruner report, the strength of fan devotion generally diffuses any threat of discomfort, shame, or guilt created by non-fans. In other words, very few fans care if others think they are "crazy" for doing what they do. This I-don't-care attitude derives partly from the mutual support fans provide for each other and the satisfaction they get from participating in their chosen fantastic universe. In sum, fans seek comfort, companionship, and camaraderie in relationship — with the series (and by extension, with its creator; see Ross 230–231) and with each other.

Such a relationship may exact costs — some of them tangible, some intangible. Most obviously, commitment to a series can be expensive. Without doubt, fans are a niche market. They want to connect with other fans as well as their favored texts and actors, and they have or find money to spend on meeting friends face-to-face and acquiring both material items and experiences related to their passion. Ideal venues for meeting this desire for association and consumption include conventions such as the industry-run Comic-Con or the fan-run Dragon*Con. A *Star Wars* and *Veronica Mars* fan, Andy Fenlock posted a series of blog entries chronicling his and his friends' week in Los Angeles in 2007, during which time he attended two days of Celebration IV (C4 or CIV), a convention primarily designed to celebrate the *Stars Wars* franchise. That year, other guests included the writers and director of *Fanboys* (2008), a film starring Kristen Bell. Fenlock effuses, "So Saturday was probably the most exciting day for me.... Yes, that's right. That's me and Kristen Bell [in the picture] a.k.a. Veronica Mars herself." He goes on to explain in detail how the meeting serendipitously came about and what happened during the encounter. Having a minute or so to chat after Bell agreed to a photo, Fenlock confessed his fandom and then took the opportunity to express his concern and curiosity: "I told her ... I was totally bummed when they cancelled it. I asked her if there was any news on the pilot they shot where they take Veronica after college going into the FBI. She said that they won't find anything out till June 15th." After wishing her luck in her career, the two parted ways. Fenlock summarizes, "She was so friendly and nice.... So meeting her set me on cloud 9 the rest of the day." In addition to meeting Bell and many other celebrities, the enthusiast collected autographs and met a friend he had previously only known through LiVEJOURNAL. One picture suggests he also went home with other fan paraphernalia: t-shirts, action figures, and more. For many fans, though, a week-long trip to Los Angeles may be out of reach financially. However, if a summer trip to San Diego for Comic-Con or a Labor Day weekend in Atlanta for Dragon*Con is too costly, *Veronica Mars* enthusiasts can log on to their computers and easily purchase *Veronica Mars*, Mars Investigations, Neptune High, 09ers, Java the Hut, Hearst College, PCHers, and Backup (Veronica's faithful pooch) t-shirts, coffee mugs, totes, hoodies, buttons, magnets, stickers, teddy bears, journals, throw pillows, beer steins, ball caps, Christmas tree ornaments, messenger bags, greeting cards, kitchen aprons, bumper stickers, mouse pads, or underwear — to name a few items. Even years after its cancellation, the series inspires close to ten thousand products on Café Press alone.

Considering how deeply and personally fans cared and still care for *Veronica Mars*, how much time and how many concrete and abstract resources they have invested in the series, and how actively they participate in continuing the storylines or lobbying for the series' resurrection, the metaphor of an intimate relationship seems obvious. And there are some aspects of reciprocity to this relationship between the storylines, characters, and fans; both give and take, so to speak. As Roger C. Aden explains, we seek popular stories such as *Veronica Mars* because those narratives offer us "alternative visions" and allow us "an opportunity to use our imaginations to see new promised lands" (8). If the relationship were not somewhat mutual, the metaphor of victimization would be far more peculiar and much less powerful. As one admirer declares about the final episode of the series, "The [network] has destroyed all that is good and wholesome in my life" (Devoted Veronica Fan). Such a statement would be ridiculous unless a relationship were assumed. Yet the living out of the victim metaphor, the way in which that metaphor shapes fans' everyday experiences, must be examined, closely scrutinized in the context of fans' emotional resonance with Veronica herself.

## *She's a Marshmallow, I'm a Marsaholic: Sympathizing with Veronica*

By fans, critics, and scholars alike, she has been called the female Philip Marlowe, the next Buffy the Vampire Slayer, and the contemporary Nancy Drew. Yet she is none of these. As critic Terry Kelleher argues, the Nancy Drew stories do not begin with Nancy staking out "a hot-sheets motel" and later sharing with her audience "a lurid recollection of the night she lost her virginity" (42). Fans and commentators have consistently credited Veronica's rape as the catalyst for the changes she experiences and makes — from the seemingly simple alterations of hairstyle and clothing choices to the more substantive transformation of personality and demeanor, from the "good girl" to the jaded noir detective with thick, nearly impenetrable emotional armor. In other words, much of the series' audience specifically attributes Veronica's strength — her resolve to solve Lilly's murder, to find and bring home her mother, to discover and punish the person who raped her, and even to fight for justice for others — to the loss of her sexual innocence. As Alaine Martaus summarizes, "Veronica's rape makes her the detective that she is" (76).[8] Evelyn Vaughn suggests that the particular line "You wanna know how I lost my virginity?" turns a decent episode into a extraordinary one because the line conveys "tough guy" with just a touch of "young, feminine vulnerability" (42). Vaughn goes on to insist that Veronica would not pass as a tough character if she had not suffered something worth getting tough about. Veronica is taken advantage of, the act itself blocked from her memory by the drug GHB or Liquid X ("M.A.D.," 1.20). When she attempts to report what she thinks has happened to her, Sheriff Lamb adds insult to horror by dismissing her. But, as Vaughn puts it, "in being able to forge on after this treatment ... Veronica proves herself tough indeed" (42). She is the character many of us want to be: strong and determined, smart and savvy enough to pursue justice for herself and others along the way.

Yet Martaus finds it ironic that a series hailed, rightfully so, for its strong female lead "maintains strong ties to sexual abuse, sexual misconduct, and rape, the last of which is in many ways the ultimate form of female *dis*empowerment" (75; see also Harris 154–155). Taking into account a variety of subplots that run through the three seasons of *Veronica Mars*, Martaus persuasively argues that in some way the whole series holds fast to the topic of sexual assault (see also Braithwaite 142–146; Purtek; Rebecca; Turnbull 317; and Whitney in this volume). Possibly this choice of subplots, which together make loss of innocence a central theme of the series, was intentional on the part of Rob Thomas and his team of writers. After all, insists Martaus, if Veronica's own experience fuels her detective work, that personal experience also explains why she becomes so invested in the lives of others: "Veronica's status as rape victim directly influences how she reacts to these cases, making her more likely to become emotionally involved in the detection process, personally invested in the case's solution" (75). As invested as she might be in justice for others, Veronica also seeks it for herself; she does not rest until every twist and turn — and there are many — of her own story is resolved.

It is not surprising, then, that some of those avid viewers who have a strong emotional and psychological affinity for the series' storylines and characters would borrow the language, the metaphor of victimization. Fan discourse echoing characters' experiences occurs often, actually. In a close look at *Firefly* fandom, for example, one finds that "the metaphors of war, resistance, and insurgency govern the symbolic paradigm" of devout fans who refer to themselves as Browncoats, the same name of the resistance fighters in the series itself (Cochran 243). This representative comment demonstrates what I mean: "Browncoats. It's not just a cute name because that's what they called people on the show. That's who we are. We're the people who lost, and we're the people who were brothers in arms when the cancellation came down" (Luke Piotrowski, qtd. in *Done the Impossible*). Others claim that "we Browncoats resemble more than a little the disenfranchised crew of the show. And not unlike Mal and Zoe, we have refused to lay down in defeat and accept the choices that the 'Alliance' has left us" ("What Is a Browncoat?"). Much like Browncoats, Marsaholics speak in metaphors that align them with the characters they love. While I have not found any online *Veronica Mars* fans who directly state feeling "raped" (the word *screwed* has been used, though) as a result of their investment in a series cancelled too soon, their talk nonetheless metaphorically ties them to Veronica's experience, particularly her experience as a victim.

When Veronica wakes up at the Pomeroy mansion, she swings her legs over the edge of the bed and begins to take in her surroundings. The clues seemingly point to one conclusion: she has been raped. Yet her memory escapes her, leaving her all the more violated. Both her virginity and her recollection have been taken without consent. The person relating these events to the audience is Veronica herself, the present, hardboiled Veronica: "The only thing that remains of 'that [innocent] girl' ... is her personal strength, augmented in the aftermath of the rape by anger and cynicism" (Martaus 76). Some fans adopt that anger and cynicism; they discursively implicate Dawn Ostroff as the perpetrator in the aftermath of the series' cancellation, with the CW as the dismissive sheriff, and themselves as the victims. A point of particular upset continues to be the advertising of the third season's final episode as a *season* rather than *series* finale. Occurring during the first few days after the last episode aired (May 22–24, 2007), the following exchange between fans in their comments to the Give Me My Remote article "Veronica Mars Series Finale Recap & Spoilers" exhibits how the metaphor of victimization infuses their conversation:

> THURSDAY MORNING. Ok, according to [*Entertainment Weekly*'s Michael] Ausiello and [*E!*'s] Kristin [Dos Santos], the reason why it said season finale was because [the CW] technically have until June 15th to make the decision to whether or not pick [*Veronica Mars*] up as a mid-season starter. Even though it's highly unlikely, *7th Heaven* did get another season at the 11th hour.

I cried. Literally cried last night. So much that Rob couldn't do ... LoVe [the relationship between Logan and Veronica] wasn't resolved, looks like Veronica's involvement with the Kane family cost [her father] his sheriff's job, AGAIN (oh the irony), didn't even get to see what ends up with Mac, Wallace, Weevil (and that dang machine!), and Piz.
I seriously felt empty last night when the credits rolled....

There were some hit or miss moments, but at this point in my grief, I couldn't begin to list them off.

KILWIGGLE7. When the credits began to roll, I was in shock ... I didn't know what to say or do. I admire Rob Thomas's vision to make it difficult for [*Veronica Mars*] to be canceled, but given everything that happened last night, I just wish we had a little more closure.

Is there anything we can do, short of a huge miracle, to get a few more episodes? A half-season pick up would even be ideal.

THURSDAY MORNING. Well, *7th Heaven* got that miracle last year ... maybe the response Dawn [Ostroff] is receiving now will influence her. But if you read Kristin's article today, she hears it's done done. And apparently the reason why Dawn is taking her time with the announcement is to [head] off angry fans. Like we are going to forget between now and June 15th?!?

At first I thought Dawn was cool. Now, I dislike her very much. Please, give *Beauty and the Geek* another chance (and apparently there is a date a farmer show? huh?), but get rid of the highest quality written show you have. The only one that had wide critical acclaim. The only show that doesn't make you look like a bunch of losers who cater only to the younger crowd. Please, give [*One Tree Hill*] another chance. It seems shows like [*Veronica Mars*] and *Everwood*, GREAT shows, aren't your forte.

KILWIGGLE7. May 22nd is a day that will go down in the books as a day of grieving for me.... Every year, I'm going to remember the sadness I felt.

MANNIE. Unless [*Veronica Mars*] pulls the numbers the *7th Heaven* "Series" finale pulled in that year, it will not be picked up by CW, and since they didn't call it the series finale, I doubt it will. I'd rather know this is definitely the last episode (like I did for [*Gilmore Girls*]) than not know. That makes me even angrier, so I don't know what that idiot in charge of The Cancellation Waiting network thinks she's doing not making fans angry.

JENINTX. Hmm, I have very mixed emotions about last night's episode. I enjoyed it while I watched, but the minute it was over I felt sad and kinda depressed. Freakin' CW, not letting me know what happens to [Veronica], Keith, Logan, Wallace, Mac, Piz, hell even Dick and Parker. It worked wonderfully as a season finale, but really crappy as a series finale. Don't think I'll ever have faith in the CW to watch another of their shows even if it's quality (heck, especially if it's quality) for fear of exactly this sort of crap happening. Finales are supposed to leave you happy ... or on edge ... but this is just ... so ... sad.

KILWIGGLE7. It is tsk, tsk CW — not [*Veronica Mars*] or [*Gilmore Girls*] writers or cast, etc. ... the loose endings are because the CW doesn't cater to the shows it has on now. It screws over the viewers, plain and simple.

Months later, in September 2007, another viewer realizes what others have known for months but still must satisfy the need to speak and be heard:

HARPRIT. WHY???? It's September and I'm sitting here all excited and waiting for the new season of *Veronica Mars* ... only to learn that it ended for all time last season! How did this happen?? I love this show more than ANY other and they go and cancel it??? I don't understand it, I really don't. All I can ask is why? WHY?

In the morning light after the last episode, some fans felt betrayed (figuratively, raped) by the false advertising of the *season* finale and uninformed (symbolically, GHBed) about the decisions being made at the network. In fact, some fans still live in willful denial. When I asked friend and fan Ben Yancer which Veronica beau he rooted for — Duncan, Logan, or Piz — he replied, "Piz? There is no Piz. I reject Season Three!" Once some enthusiasts weathered the initial shock and denial, they got angry. On several online boards and forums, fans spent substantial amounts of time plotting revenge, usually in the form of boycotting the CW (e.g., see the comments in response to Malen).

Others bargained: Cloud Watchers, again, took to the streets. Mounting another grassroots effort to do the one thing they knew could actually save the series — garner more viewers and thus raise ratings — Cloud Watchers created a flier they distributed across the United States at malls and college campuses, sites frequented by the series' target-age audience. Asked how helpful such campaigns are for achieving a show's renewal, the Clouds Watchers optimistically reply, "If [*Veronica Mars*] gets a ratings increase from this campaign, and we prove that it is possible for the show to attract new viewers, even three seasons in, then we believe the network will take notice" (qtd. in Vazquez, "The Campaign"). And those who felt beyond bargaining, expressed a sense of depression. On the Pajiba website, Jenintx, cited in the above fan conversation, notes, "I'm trying to keep [how short British series can be] in mind when my anger and desire to throttle Dawn Ostroff overtakes me. I am very grateful to have had [*Veronica Mars*] for as long as we have, but damn, shit still hurts, especially since the last episode left me feeling lost and depressed."[9] In fact, all over the Internet the victim metaphor surfaces again and again. "Oh CW, why must you hurt me so," exclaims jhuck. Speaking directly to the network, cubiclequeen admonishes, "CW, you have taken all that is good to me away."

I find Martaus's argument about Veronica especially apropos when considering fans' use of the victim metaphor: "The actuality of the rape is less important ... than Veronica's belief in her rape, because it is from her belief in the rape that her anger and cynicism emerge" (76). At one point in her search for her own rapist, Veronica discovers that she and Duncan, both under the influence of GHB as well as mutual love and attraction, had sex the night of the Pomeroy party. Though eventually Veronica learns that Cassidy Casablancas did, in fact, rape her the same night, for a while Veronica relinquishes her anger and cynicism. Some fans mirror this emotion and attitude. Though they "consent" to a relationship with *Veronica Mars* when they turn on the television, their perceived victimization and actual grief emerge from their belief that they have been taken advantage of by the network. Unlike Veronica, however, they do not necessarily give up on their search for revenge.

Whether in the stage of denial, anger, bargaining, or depression, many fans looked for someone (Dawn Ostroff and occasionally reality television spectators) rather than something (low ratings) to blame. Some discussion boarders devoted entire threads to discussing their shared hatred for Dawn Ostroff. *Smallville* fans, who fault Ostroff directly for not effectively and sufficiently promoting their favorite series, started a similar thread in the fall of 2008, heading the thread with a poll that asks whether the executive should be "fired, tarred and feathered, lynched, promoted," or given a "good old stoning in [the] public square." Of the 91 people who voted, the majority believed she should be fired, followed closely by those who opted for a public stoning. In a January 2010 discussion of Ostroff and a possible 10th season for *Smallville* on the website TV by the Numbers, one commenter exclaims, "I'll always hate her. Long live Veronica Mars!" (Jay). Several others echo Jay's sentiments, specifically attributing their disgust for Ostroff to the cancellation of *Veronica Mars*. Clearly, for some audience members the anger and blame have lingered for years. And for still others, the only solace for their anger would be more of the canon story.[10]

While my focus here does not allow me to explore it in as much detail as it might merit, the movement to bring about a *Veronica Mars* film deserves mention. This strong desire to see the dangling, series finale storylines resolved seems rooted in an overwhelming and almost debilitating lack of closure. Just as Veronica's initial not-knowing drives her to solve and avenge her own rape, so fans appear driven to seek the light a film could shed on the darkness they perceive to be imposed on them by Dawn Ostroff and the CW. Arguably, the success of other fans also spurs the campaigners. When avid followers of series such as the cut-short *Farscape* and the short-lived *Firefly* lobbied for films, they were successful. Whether or not fans had a direct influence on the decisions to move forward with filmmaking remains debatable. Yet these tales of victory continue to be an integral part of each fandom's mythology. These few triumphs give other fans, including *Veronica Mars* devotees, the hope they need to remain relentless in their pursuit.[11]

## "*Oh* Felix Culpa*!*": *Moving into Acceptance*

According to George Lakoff and Mark Johnson, traditional views of metaphor do not allow that metaphor relates to how we think and how we reason because those views suggest that metaphors represent the simple act of naming, "of attaching words to concepts they ordinarily wouldn't go with" (73). On the contrary, Lakoff and Johnson argue that metaphors shape how we think and reason, and they do so because they are conceptual in nature. In fact, they are the very fabric of our thoughts. As a result, carefully considering the metaphors we use everyday continues to be an enterprise not only for scholars but also for every one of us; metaphors presume, accompany, and predict the form and substance of our lives.

In a discussion of Kate Roiphe's work on rape, university campuses, and Rape Crisis Feminism, therapist Marty Klein points out Roiphe's observation that "increasingly broad definitions of sexual trauma," definitions that include simply being made to feel uncomfortable around a man, undermine the activist work feminists attempt to do (147). If discomfort and intimidation are equated with assault — emotional or metaphorical rape — women are, in turn, equated with victimization; they are perpetual victims (see also Burr 103–105). As victims, women's sense of autonomy wanes (Burr 105). At its worst, insists Klein, the Rape Crisis Model "implies ... all emotional risk can be removed from sexual interactions" and limits any kind of consensual creativity partners may bring to their intimate relationships (148). The same can be said of the victim metaphor and mentality that manifests itself in *Veronica Mars* fan discourse. In fact, many people, including some fellow fans, argue that *Veronica Mars* enthusiasts who cannot move into acceptance represent irrationality and immaturity. But as Lakoff and Johnson would argue, simply assigning these adjectives to particular fans misses the point. The point is to observe and consider not whether fans are rational by the standards of formal logic but how fans *actually* reason. And that reasoning is grounded in metaphor.

When I was ten years old, my grandmother, who had been living in our home for six years, died of cancer. One of the most distinct memories I have of the day of her funeral places me at her graveside. In the eyes of the remaining adults in my life, I had been a brave little girl all day because I had not cried. But in the cemetery, I could not be brave by that standard any longer. The tears came quickly, forcefully. My mother approached me as I stood on the hillside watching the workers shovel dirt into the manmade mouth in the earth. "Would Grammy want you to cry?" my mother queried, rubbing my back. Even then, I knew her question was inauthentic, a statement clothed in a question. And I thought I knew the correct answer: no, Grammy would not want me to cry. Now I think otherwise. Of course Grammy would have wanted me to cry because tears release pain, allowing the denial and anger and bargaining and depression to escape and one day evaporate. Many, many days, weeks, and months later, I came to acceptance, a mental space in which I could enjoy tangibly good memories and the sense of resolution only acceptance affords. I think Veronica would want the same for her admirers. Eventually, beyond solving mysteries and crimes, Veronica accepts that Lilly will never come back, that her mother will never be a mom, and that she will never again be a virgin. Though she never consents to experiencing loss, she does consent to living life. And life goes on — for Veronica and for all those who love(d) her.

Many fans *have* "moved on" in that they have come to realize and acknowledge that the series is truly over, even if the third *season* finale turned out to be the *series* finale. Though the bitterness over their thwarted expectations for a fourth season lingers for some devotees, others express gratitude for the seasons with which they were blessed. In many ways, McDermott's words describe fans just as much as they describe Veronica: "Beneath the tough façade remains a little girl grieving because she has been abandoned by everyone she loves except her father. Though she eschews her peers, she pursues the truth as though it might repair those relationships. It never does.... What is more, in a sense it does not need to. On 'Mars,' with suffering comes empathy and new, unexpected possibilities" (27). Unintentionally yet fittingly echoing McDermott, Marla Harris insists that *Veronica Mars* not only challenges the notion of happily-ever-after but also refuses "closure as convenience; endings or conclusions are tentative, subject to revision" (161). Rather than giving the audience a pat ending and faultless character, Rob Thomas offered an inconvenient, deftly flawed story and character, a Veronica who neither regrets the past — though she sometimes relives it — nor regrets the present — though she sometimes re-imagines it. By way of her experiences, Veronica suggests that life can be new and surprisingly wonderful after a storm, even if that future never appears on screen.

Finally, the question of significance must be answered. Fans invest in Veronica and her world and the various metaphors they use to describe their sense of loss when that world stopped turning. So what? Noting television's recent trend toward eschatology by way of natural disaster, alien invasion, or spiritual depravity, McDermott, drawing on *The Truce of God* by Anglican Archbishop of Canterbury Rowan Williams, cautions his readers that "catastrophe fantasies" allow us to blame circumstances or other beings for our crises rather than take personal responsibility (27). *Veronica Mars*, he posits, embraces the very opposite notion:

We are not powerless, Veronica Mars tells us. Our society is built upon the choices we make. The catastrophe is the world that we have created, a reality in which some people's wants overwhelm everyone's needs, and life is marred by infidelity and rejection. Friendships are possible, and family can survive, but callousness and indifferences prevail.

Filled with unkind but also fragile adolescents longing for connection with their parents, many of them emotionally battered and alone, [*Veronica Mars*] cries out like the prophets of old that our American dreams and escapist fantasies come at far too high a price. We must change our ways. And for our troubles, we have only ourselves to blame [27].

When fans invoke the victim metaphor, they are in danger of disenfranchising themselves even more than they may already be disenfranchised. Playing the victim reinforces the belief that the television industry is omnipotent when fans hold a power that cannot be scripted or filmed or produced or broadcast by that industry. They have the power of choice. They can choose what to watch and what not to watch. And they can choose how they conduct themselves when too few people watch with them. When low-rated series are canceled, fans can refuse the victim role and simply grieve — and maybe get a bit of their revenge on — until they find acceptance.

There is no such thing as a non-consensual relationship between a story, a fan, and a network. For the story, power manifests in the eye(s) of the beholder(s). For the fan, power resides in the remote. And for the network, power comes from the advertising revenue generated by those behind the remotes. It is a risky endeavor, falling in love with television. Freelance writer and English teacher Simron Khurana comforts her readers with wise words because, she argues, they "can heal wounds and help us reflect on the tragedy." The love and loss of *Veronica Mars* are real; the passion and grief are genuine. And any one of the quotes Khurana lists could express the sorrow fans experience, especially when a series ends as life often does: abruptly and without tidy resolution. However, a quote by G. K. Chesterton stands out: "The way to love anything is to realize that it might be lost." The stakes are high when any one of us turns on the television, yet we do just that: turn on the television. We consent, even in the face of potential loss, to falling in love all over again. And for *Veronica Mars* fans, what a fortunate falling it was and always will be.

## Notes

1. Of course, a notable exception is *Star Trek*, which for years has experienced multiple reincarnations across multiple mediums. The same might be argued for the *Stargate* universe.

2. See Matt Hills for a discussion of cyclical fandom, "wherein the fan-consumer moves from one fan object to another, experiencing intense affective relationships to a variety of texts" (801). Hills notes the differences between what he calls cyclical fandom and other notions of fans' emotional attachments: enduring fandom and phasal fandom (803).

3. According to Marla Harris, Veronica and her contemporary sister sleuths do not always have control over how their bodies are viewed or used by others. Using the character's rape as an example, Harris argues that Veronica "feels detached from what her body has experienced, as if she is watching a film of someone else's life" (156–157). Such a detached feeling explains the unaffected tone of voice with which Veronica recounts the event to the audience.

4. Of course, actors often help campaigns along by recognizing their loyal fans' efforts as well as by suggesting their solidarity with their admirers. As Michele Greppi reports, Kristen Bell "refuses to let the low ratings beat her.... 'You just have to let it go and know that you can only do so much.... You just hope that because our fans are so cool and committed to the show — just look at our fan mail — that they will continue to tell all their friends about it'" (qtd. in Greppi).

5. Fans kicked off yet another campaign — "Bars for Mars"— after the series was officially cancelled in 2007. For more detail on the candy crusade, see Turnbull 320 as well as Strong.

6. For an extended treatment of *Veronica Mars* fans and fashion trends, see Gillan 185–206.

7. In "I Know What You'll Do Next Summer" (3.18), Veronica helps a client prove that Apollo, a Hearst student from Africa, is the son he lost years ago to the Ugandan rebel army. Following the airing of the episode, actors Kristen Bell, Jason Dohring, and Ryan Hansen informed viewers of the ongoing war in Uganda. Bell sent viewers to the website of youth-begun organization Invisible Children, a non-profit that determines to interrupt and eventually end the Ugandan conflict and the rebel army's use of child soldiers. Fans responded immediately by raising donations for the cause. Currently, the PSA for the effort can be viewed on YouTube and the Watch *Veronica Mars* website under the Invisible Children tab.

8. Martaus addresses the comparisons often made between Veronica Mars and Buffy Summers. Specifically, she posits that for Veronica being raped thematically corresponds to Buffy inheriting the Slayer's extraordinary abilities since "Veronica's detective skills often resemble superpowers" (76). Yet there are significant differences between Veronica and Buffy. Increased power marks Buffy's transition to Slayer while diminished power — loss of "innocence, virginity, and reputation"— characterizes Veronica's transition to teen detective. Martaus also argues that the young women differ in that before they experience their unique turning points, Buffy is popular and has a stable family life while Veronica is excluded from her usual circle of friends and has a family that crumples under pressure. As Martaus herself establishes, though, Veronica discovers renewed power through her sleuthing skills; like Buffy, she does not choose to play the victim (see also Harris 158–159). Martaus's brief discussion of Buffy and Veronica, however, remains somewhat inaccurate. Though Buffy gains supernatural power when she becomes the Slayer, she arguably experiences significant loss as well: like Veronica's, Buffy's family and social life quickly disintegrate. Both face social marginalization and must piece together a chosen family (see Battis). The young women are much more alike than Martaus allows.

9. I am not suggesting here that Jenintx experienced clinical depression, only that

the certainty of the cancellation was becoming real. Also, Jenintx shares much company; the word *depressed* is used over and over again by fans on a variety of message boards and discussion forums. Of course, there is no good way to confirm that the depression devotees attest to meets Elisabeth Kübler-Ross's definition.

10. Like most if not all devotees, *Veronica Mars* adherents have created their own form of resolution through fan fiction in which they answer who wins the election for Neptune's next sheriff and which beau Veronica ultimately chooses: Logan or Piz. Still, for many fans only canonized closure will suffice; they want to know Rob Thomas's answers to their questions.

11. See especially the nearly 12,000-member-strong Facebook page "I will go see Veronica Mars: THE MOVIE." Under the Discussions tab, the thread "Photo Campaign!!" includes links to pictures of fans holding up signs that declare to Joel Silver, whose company would produce the film, that they would definitely see the film if he will make it happen. Emma, who started the campaign, asks fans to send the pictures directly to Silver and provides a mailing address. And if that sounds too difficult, Emma says she will send them herself if only fans will post the pictures online. In April 2010, just a month before I completed this essay, campaigners were still posting pictures to the thread.

## Works Cited

Aden, Roger C. *Popular Stories and Promised Lands: Fan Cultures and Symbolic Pilgrimages*. Tuscaloosa: Universioty of Alabama Press, 1999. Print.

"About Cloud Watchers." *Watchveronicamars.net*. Watch Veronica Mars, 2006-2007. Web. 20 May 2010.

Ausiello, Michael. "'Veronica Mars' Creator Insists Movie Is 'Not Dead.'" *EW.com*. Entertainment Weekly, 7 Apr. 2010. Web. 11 May 2010.

Bauder, David. "New CW Network Revives '7th Heaven.'" *Washingtonpost.com*. The Washington Post, 18 May 2006. Web. 25 May 2010.

Bianco, Robert. "'Veronica Mars': Intelligent Life." *USA Today* 22 Sept. 2004, Life sec.: 4D. Print.

Braithwaite, Andrea. "'That girl of yours — she's pretty hardboiled, huh?': Detecting Feminism in Veronica Mars." *Teen Television: Essays on Programming and Fandom*. Ed. Sharon Marie Ross and Louisa Ellen Stein. Jefferson, NC: McFarland, 2008. 132–149. Print.

Burr, Jennifer. "Women Have It. Men Want It. What Is It?: Constructions of Sexuality in Rape Discourse." *Psychology, Education & Gender* 3.1 (Apr. 2001): 103–105. Print.

"Cloud Watchers are...." *Livejournal.com*. Cloud Watchers on LiVEJOURNAL, n.d. Web. 20 May 2010.

Cochran, Tanya R. "The Browncoats Are Coming!: *Firefly, Serenity*, and Fan Activism." *Investigating* Firefly *and* Serenity: *Science Fiction on the Frontier*. Ed. Rhonda V. Wilcox and Tanya R. Cochran. New York: Tauris, 2008. 239–249. Print.

cubiclequeen. Online post. *Buzzsugar.com*. Buzzsugar, 22 May 2007. Web. 30 May 2010.

Devoted Veronica Fan. Online post. *Givememyremote.com*. Give Me My Remote, 23 May 2007. Web. 15 Mar. 2010. 23 May 2007.

*Done the Impossible: The Fans' Tale of* Firefly *&* Serenity. Dir. and prod. Brian Wiser et al. Rivetal, 2006. DVD.

Fenlock, Andy. "LA. Day 5. Veronica Mars Edition." *Slurpeekingdom.com.* Slurpeekingdom, 27 May 2007. Web. 22 May 2010.

Gillan, Jennifer. "Fashion Sleuths and Aerie Girls: *Veronica Mars'* Fan Forums and Network Strategies of Fan Address." *Teen Television: Essays on Programming and Fandom.* Eds. Sharon Marie Ross and Louisa Ellen Stein. Jefferson, NC: McFarland, 2008. 185–206. Print.

Greppi, Michele. "Kristen Bell." *Television Week* 18 July 2005: 12–15. *EBSCOhost.* Web. 15 Feb. 2010.

Harprit. Online post. *Givememyremote.com.* Give Me My Remote, 30 Sept. 2007. Web. 12 Mar. 2010.

Harris, Marla. "Not Nancy Drew but Not Clueless: Embodying the Teen Girl Sleuth in the Twenty-first Century." *Nancy Drew and Her Sister Sleuths: Essays on the Fiction of Girl Detectives.* Eds. Michael G. Cornelius and Melanie E. Gregg. Jefferson, NC: McFarland, 2008. 152–163. Print.

Hills, Matt. "Patterns of Surprise: The 'Aleatory Object' in Psychoanalytic Ethnography and Cyclical Fandom." *American Behavioral Scientist,* 48.7 (2005): 801–821. Print.

Jay. Online post. *Tvbythenumbers.com.* TV by the Numbers, 9 Jan. 2010. Web. 30 May 2010.

jhuck. Online post. *Buzzsugar.com.* Buzzsugar, 22 May 2007. WEb. 30 May 2010.

Jenintx. Online post. *Givememyremote.com.* Give Me My Remote, 23 May 2007. Web. 12 Mar. 2010.

_____. Online post. *Pajiba.com.* Pajiba, 23 May 2007. Web. 31 May 2010.

Kelleher, Terry. Review of *Veronica Mars. People* 27 Sept. 2004: 42. Print.

Khurana, Simran. "Top 10 Lost Love Quotes." *About.com.* About.com, 2010. WEb. 21 May 2010.

Kilwiggle7. Online post. *Givememyremote.com.* Give Me My Remote, 23 May 2007. Web. 12 Mar. 2010.

Klein, Marty. "A 'Progressive' Movement Holding Sexuality Hostage." *Journal of Sex Research* 31.2 (June 1994): 146–148. Print.

Lakoff, George, and Mark Johnson. "The Metaphorical Logic of Rape." *Metaphor and Symbolic Activity* 2.1 (1987): 73–79. Print.

lindab123. Online post. *Givememyremote.com.* Give Me My Remote, 23 May 2007. Web. 15 Mar. 2010.

Malen, Daniel. "*Veronica Mars* Officially Cancelled." *Thetvaddict.com.* The TV Addict, 17 May 2007. Web. 12 Apr. 2010.

Mannie. Online post. *Givememyremote.com.* Give Me My Remote, 23 May 2007. Web. 12 Mar. 2010.

Martaus, Alaine. "'You Get Tough. You Get Even': Rape, Anger, Cynicism, and the Vigilante Girl Detective in *Veronica Mars.*" *Clues: A Journal of Detection* 27.1 (Spring 2009): 74–86. Print.

Masarath. "Conversion Week Day 3: Planning a Viewing Party." *Livejournal.com.* LiVEJOURNAL, 19 Dec. 2005. Web. 20 May 2010.

McDermott, Jim. "Life on 'Mars': The Price of Dreams and Fantasies." *America* 7 Nov. 2005: 26–27. Print.

Miss_Mars. Online post. *Givememyremote.com.* Give Me My Remote, 23 May 2007. Web. 15 Mar. 2010.

Purtek. "Rape in Veronica Mars: Part 1." *Thehathorlegacy.com.* The Hathor Legacy, 26 Jan. 2007. Web. 12 Apr. 2010.

_____. "Rape in Veronica Mars: Part 2." *Thehathorlegacy.com.* The Hathor Legacy, 26 Jan. 2007. Web. 12 Apr. 2010.

_____. "Rape in Veronica Mars: Third (and final)." *Thehathorlegacy.com.* The Hathor Legacy, 2 Feb. 2007. Web. 12 Apr. 2010.

Rebecca. "An Unfortunate Oxymoron." *Allreb.blogspot.com.* A Nerd at Peace, 30 Nov. 2006. Web. 12 Apr. 2010.

Reeves, Jimmie L., Mark C. Rodgers, and Michael Epstein. "Rewriting Popularity: The Cult *Files.*" *"Deny All Knowledge": Reading* The X-Files. Ed. David Lavery, Angela Hague, and Marla Cartwright. Syracuse: Syracuse University Press, 1996. 22–35. Print.

Ross, Sharon Marie. *Beyond the Box: Television and the Internet.* Malden, MA: Blackwell, 2008. Print.

Schnappycat. Online post. *Buzzsugar.com.* Buzzsugar, 18 Aug. 2009. Web. 20 May 2010.

sjoanzors. Online post. *Givememyremote.com.* Give Me My Remote, 23 May 2007. Web. 15 Mar. 2010.

StarrChild. Online post. *Givememyremote.com.* Give Me My Remote, 23 May 2007. Web. 15 Mar. 2010.

Strong, H. T. (a.k.a. Hercules). "Help Flows in to Save *Veronica Mars.*" *Aintitcool.com.* Ain't It Cool News, 7 June 2007. Web. 15 June 2010.

Thorne, Scott, and Gordon C. Bruner. "An Exploratory Investigation of the Characteristics of Consumer Fanaticism." *Qualitative Market Research: An International Journal* 9.1 (2006): 51–72. Print.

thuggie8. Online post. *Givememyremote.com.* Give Me My Remote, 23 May 2007. Web. 15 Mar. 2010.

Thursday Morning. Online post. *Givememyremote.com.* Give Me My Remote, 23 May 2007. Web. 12 Mar. 2010.

Turnbull, Sue. *"Veronica Mars." The Essential Cult TV Reader.* Ed. David Lavery. Lexington: University of Kentucky Press, 2010. 314–321. Print.

Vasquez, Diego. "The Campaign to Save 'Veronica Mars.'" *Medialifemagazine.com.* Media Life, 9 May 2006. Web. 25 May 2010.

_____. "Taking to the Air Over 'Veronica Mars.'" *Medialifemagazine.com.* Media Life, 9 May 2006. Web. 25 May 2010.

VMars_fan. Online post. *Givememyremote.com,* Give Me My Remote, 23 May 2007. Web. 15 Mar. 2010.

Vaughn, Evelyn. "Veronica Mars: Girl. Detective." *Neptune Noir: Unauthorized Investigations into* Veronica Mars. Ed. Rob Thomas with Leah Wilson. Dallas: BenBella, 2006. 34–45. Print.

"What Is a Browncoat?" *Browncoats.com.* Browncoats, 2005. Web. 30 May 2010.

# Episode Credits

*Episode / Airdate / Title / Writer / Director*

## Season One

1.1 / 9.22.04 / Pilot / Rob Thomas / Mark Piznarski

1.2 / 9.28.04 / Credit Where Credit's Due /Rob Thomas / Mark Piznarski

1.3 / 10.12.04 / Meet John Smith / Jed Seidel / Harry Winer

1.4 / 10.19.04 / The Wrath of Con / Diane Ruggiero / Michael Fields

1.5 / 10.26.04 / You Think You Know Somebody / Dayna Lynne North / Nick Gomez

1.6 / 11.02.04 / Return of the Kane / Teleplay: Phil Klemmer; Story: Rob Thomas / Sarah Pia Anderson

1.7 / 11.09.04 / The Girl Next Door / Teleplay: Jed Seidel and Diane Ruggiero; Story: Jed Seidel / Nick Marck

1.8 / 11.23.04 / Like a Virgin / Aury Wellington / Guy Norman Bee

1.9 / 11.30.04 / Drinking the Kool-Aid / Teleplay: Russell Smith; Story: Rob Thomas / Marcos Siega

1.10 / 12.14.04 / An Echolls Family Christmas / Diane Ruggiero / Nick Marck

1.11 / 1.04.05 / Silence of the Lamb / Jed Seidel and Dayna Lynne North / John T. Kretchmer

1.12 / 1.11.05 / Clash of the Tritons / Philip Klemmer and Aury Wellington / David Barrett

1.13 / 2.08.05 / Lord of the Bling / John Enbom / Steve Gomer

1.14 / 2.15.05 / Mars vs. Mars / Teleplay: Jed Seidel and Diane Ruggiero; Story: Rob Thomas / Marcos Siega

1.15/ 2.22.05 / Ruskie Business / Phil Klemmer and John Enbom / Guy Norman Bee

1.16 / 3.29.05 / Betty and Veronica / Diane Ruggiero / Michael Fields

1.17 / 4.05.05 / Kanes and Abel's / Carolyn Murray / Nick Marck

1.18 / 4.12.05 / Weapons of Class Destruction / Jed Seidel / John T. Kretchmer

1.19 / 4.19.05 / Hot Dogs / Dayna Lynne North / Nick Marck

1.20 / 4.26.05 / M.A.D. / Phil Klemmer and John Enbom / John T. Kretchmer

1.21 / 5.03.05 / A Trip to the Dentist / Diane Ruggiero / Marcos Siega

1.22 / 5.10.05 / Leave It to Beaver / Teleplay: Rob Thomas and Diane Ruggiero; Story: Rob Thomas / Michael Fields

## Season Two

2.1 / 9.28.05 / Normal Is the Watchword / Rob Thomas / John Kretchmer

2.2 / 10.05.05 / Driver Ed / Diane Ruggiero / Nick Marck

2.3 / 10.12.05 / Cheatty Cheatty Bang Bang / Phil Klemmer and John Enbom / John Kretchmer

2.4 / 10.19.05 / Green-Eyed Monster / Dayna Lynne North / Jason Bloom

2.5 / 10.26.05/ Blast from the Past / Phil Klemmer and Cathy Belben / Harry Winer

2.6 / 11.09.05 / Rat Saw God / John Enbom and Phil Klemmer / Kevin Bray

2.7 / 11.16.05 / Nobody Puts Baby in a Corner / Diane Ruggiero / Nick Marck

2.8 / 11.23.05 / Ahoy, Mateys! / John Enbom and Cathy Belben / Steve Gomer

2.9 / 11.30.05 / My Mother, the Fiend / Phil Klemmer and Dayna Lynne North / Nick Marck

2.10 / 12.07.05 / One Angry Veronica / Russell Smith / John Kretchmer

2.11 / 1.25.06 / Donut Run / Rob Thomas / Rob Thomas

2.12 / 2.01.06 / Rashard and Wallace Go to White Castle / John Enbom / John Kretchmer

2.13 / 2.08.06 / Ain't No Magic Mountain High Enough / Diane Ruggiero / Guy Norman Bee

2.14 / 3.15.06 / Versatile Toppings / Phil Klemmer / Sarah Pia Anderson

2.15 / 3.22.06 / The Quick and the Wed / John Serge / Rick Rosenthal

2.16 / 3.29.06 / The Rapes of Graff / John Enbom / Michael Fields

2.17 / 4.05.06 / Plan B / Dayna Lynne North / John Kretchmer

2.18 / 4.11.06 / I Am God / Diane Ruggiero and Cathy Belben / Martha Mitchell

2.19 / 4.18.06 / Nevermind the Buttocks / Phil Klemmer / Jason Bloom

2.20 / 4.25.06 / Look Who's Stalking / John Enbom / Michael Fields

2.21 / 5.02.06 / Happy Go Lucky / Diane Ruggiero / Steve Gomer

2.22 / 5.09.06 / Not Pictured / Teleplay: Rob Thomas and John Enbom; Story: Rob Thomas / John Kretchmer

## Season Three

3.1 / 10.03.06 / Welcome Wagon / Rob Thomas / John T. Kretchmer

3.2 / 10.10.06 / My Big Fat Greek Rush Week / Diane Ruggiero / John T. Kretchmer

3.3 / 10.17.06 / Wichita Linebacker / Phil Klemmer and John Enbom / Harry Winer

3.4 / 10.24.06 / Charlie Don't Surf / Diane Ruggiero and Jason Elen / Jason Bloom

3.5 / 10.31.06 / President Evil / Jonathan Moskin and David Mulei / Nick Marck

3.6 / 11.07.06 / Hi, Infidelity / John Enbom / Michael Fields

3.7 / 11.14.06 / Of Vice and Men / Phil Klemmer / Harry Winer

3.8 / 11.21.06 / Lord of the Pi's / Diane Ruggiero / Steve Gomer

3.9 / 11.28.06 / Spit and Eggs / Rob Thomas / Rob Thomas

3.10 / 1.23.07 / Show Me the Monkey / Teleplay: John Enbom and Martin Hull; Story: John Enbom / Nick Marck

3.11 / 1.30.07 / Poughkeepsie, Tramps and Thieves / Diane Ruggiero / John T. Kretchmer

3.12 / 2.06.07 / There's Got to Be a Morning After Pill / Teleplay: Jonathan Moskin and Phil Klemmer and John Enbom / Story: Jonathan Moskin and David Mulei / Tricia Brock

3.13 / 2.13.07 / Postgame Mortem / Joe Voci / John T. Kretchmer

3.14 / 2.20.07 / Mars, Bars / Teleplay: Phil Klemmer and John Enbom; Story: Joe Voci and Phil Klemmer and John Enbom / Harry Winer

3.15 / 2.27.07 / Papa's Cabin / John Enbom / Michael Fields

3.16 / 5.01.07 / Un-American Graffiti / Robert Hull / John T. Kretchmer

3.17 / 5.08.07 / Debasement Tapes / John Enbom / Dan Etheridge

3.18 / 5.15.07 / I Know What You'll Do Next Summer / Jonathan Moskin and David Mulei / Nick Marck

3.19 / 5.22.07 / Weevils Wobble / Phil Klemmer / Jason Bloom

3.20 / 5.22.07 / The Bitch Is Back / Rob Thomas and Diane Ruggiero / Michael Fields

# Cast Credits

## Season One

Veronica Mars: Kristen Bell
Keith Mars: Enrico Colantoni
Logan Echolls: Jason Dohring
Wallace Fennel: Percy Daggs III
Eli "Weevil" Navarro: Francis Capra
Duncan Kane: Teddy Dunn
Jake Kane: Kyle Secor
Celeste Kane: Lisa Thornhill
Cindy "Mac" Mackenzie: Tina Majorino
Sheriff Don Lamb: Michael Muhney
Aaron Echolls: Harry Hamlin
Lynn Echolls: Lisa Rinna
Trina Echolls: Alyson Hannigan
Lianne Mars: Corinne Bohrer
Lilly Kane: Amanda Seyfried
Deputy Leo D'Amato: Max Greenfield
Dick Casablancas: Ryan Hansen
Cassidy "Beaver" Casablancas: Kyle Gallner
Cliff McCormack: Daran Norris
Meg Manning: Alona Tal
Vice Principal Clemmons: Duane Daniels
Ms. Dent: Sydney Tamiia Poitier

## Season Two New Cast

Jackie Cook: Tessa Thompson
Woody Goodman: Steve Guttenberg

## Season Three New Cast

Stosh "Piz" Piznarski: Chris Lowell
Parker Lee: Julie Gonzalo
Harmony Chase: Laura San Giacomo
Dean Cyrus O'Dell: Ed Begley, Jr.

# Contributors

**Stan Beeler** teaches in the English department at the University of Northern British Columbia, Canada. His areas of interest include film and television studies, popular culture, and comparative literature. His publications include *Reading* Stargate SG-1 (I.B. Tauris), *Investigating* Charmed: *The Magic Power of TV* (I.B. Tauris), and *Dance, Drugs and Escape: The Club Scene in Literature Film and Television Since the Late 1980s* (McFarland).

**Tamy Burnett** holds a Ph.D. in English with a specialization in women's and gender studies from the University of Nebraska–Lincoln, where she is currently a lecturer in English and women's and gender studies. She is the co-editor of a collection of essays exploring literary influences in Joss Whedon's *Angel* from McFarland. Her research frequently focuses on representations of gender in popular culture, especially television.

**Tanya R. Cochran,** Ph.D., is an associate professor of English and communication at Union College in Lincoln, Nebraska, where she teaches first-year writing and rhetoric and coordinates the Studio for Writing and Speaking. Her essays on *Buffy the Vampire Slayer* appear in *Televising Queer Women* (Palgrave, 2007) and *Sith, Slayers, Stargates + Cyborgs* (Lang, 2008). With Rhonda V. Wilcox, she coedited *Investigating* Firefly *and* Serenity: *Science Fiction on the Frontier* (I.B. Tauris, 2008). Past chair of the Science Fiction and Fantasy Area of the Popular/American Culture Association, she holds editorial board positions for the online journals *Slayage* and *Watcher Junior*.

**Lisa Emmerton** is a Ph.D. candidate in the cultural studies program at Trent University. Lisa completed her M.A. in English at the University of Northern British Columbia and graduated with the Governor-General's Gold Medal. Her thesis dealt with the satirical strategies used to develop countercultural messages in the popular animated TV sitcoms *The Simpsons* and *King of the Hill*. She studies popular media with a particular focus on intersections between literary, televisual, and online methods of storytelling.

**David Lavery** is a professor of English and popular culture at Middle Tennessee State University and the author/editor/co-editor of numerous essays and books, including *Joss: A Creative Portrait of the Maker of the Whedonverses* (I.B. Tauris, 2011) and

*The Essential Cult TV Reader* (University Press of Kentucky, 2009), and volumes on such television series as *Twin Peaks, The X-Files, Buffy the Vampire Slayer, The Sopranos, Lost, Deadwood, Seinfeld, My So Called Life, Heroes,* and *Battlestar Galactica.* He co-edits the e-journal *Slayage* and is one of the founding editors of *Critical Studies in Television: Scholarly Studies of Small Screen Fictions.*

**Lewis A. Leavitt** is a professor of pediatrics at the University of Wisconsin School of Medicine. His publications include work on infant speech perception, children's language play, language development in children with Down Syndrome, and the role of parental expectations in determining parent-child interaction. His publications include *Psychological Effects of War and Violence on Children, Improving Communication in Children with Down Syndrome* and *The Role of Early Experience in Development.*

**Sarah A. Leavitt** is a curator at the National Building Museum in Washington, D.C., where her most recent exhibition, "House of Cars: Innovation and the Parking Garage," opened in 2009. She previously held the position of associate historian and curator at the Office of NIH History at the National Institutes of Health in Bethesda, Maryland. She wrote *From Catharine Beecher to Martha Stewart: A Cultural History of Domestic Advice* (University of North Carolina Press, 2002). Leavitt graduated from Wesleyan University and holds a Ph.D. in American studies from Brown University.

**Sophie Mayer** bridges visual media, literature and feminist theory in her teaching, activism and critical and creative writing. She is a regular contributor to *Sight & Sound* and *Little White Lies,* and is *DIVA*'s books editor. She has published critical essays in, among others, *reconstruction, Screen* and *SubStance.* In 2009, she published a collection of film poetry, *Her Various Scalpels* (Shearsman); a critical study, *The Cinema of Sally Potter: A Politics of Love* (Wallflower, 2009); and as co-editor with Corinn Columpar, a new anthology of feminist film theory, *There She Goes: Feminist Filmmaking and Beyond* (Wayne State University Press).

**Melissa Townsend** is a graduate student at the University of Nebraska–Lincoln, working in the fields of political science, public administration, and women's and gender studies. She is also a full-time staff member at the university, working as a project associate at the Center on Children, Families, and the Law.

**Sue Turnbull**, Ph.D., is the chair of Communication and Media Studies at the University of Wollongong in Australia. She has published broadly in the fields of media education, audience and television studies, and is a co-editor of *Participations, the Journal of Audience and Reception Studies,* and editor of the Australian journal *Media International Australia.* Her recent collaborative research projects involve a study of Australian screen comedy and a history of Australian television from the perspective of the audience.

**Sarah Whitney** is a member of the English department at Penn State Behrend in Erie, Pennsylvania. At Behrend, she directs the women's studies minor and teaches courses in women's studies, British and American women writers, and disciplinary-based writing. She received her Ph.D. in English from the University of Virginia. She is writing a book investigating the post-feminist Gothic novel as rendered by Alice Sebold, Jodi Picoult, and other contemporary American authors.

**Rhonda V. Wilcox,** Ph.D., is a professor of English at Gordon College, Barnesville, Georgia. She is the editor of *Studies in Popular Culture,* the coeditor of *Slayage: The Journal of the Whedon Studies Association,* and a founding editor of *Critical Studies in Television.* She is the author of *Why Buffy Matters: The Art of* Buffy the Vampire Slayer (I.B. Tauris, 2005) and the coeditor (with David Lavery) of *Fighting the Forces: What's at Stake in* Buffy the Vampire Slayer (Rowman & Littlefield, 2002) and (with Tanya R. Cochran) *Investigating* Firefly *and* Serenity: *Science Fiction on the Frontier* (I.B. Tauris, 2008).

**Paul Zinder** is an associate professor of film and digital media at the American University of Rome. He is also an internationally recognized film and video-maker whose documentary *Uno degli Ultimi (One of the Last),* screened at 35 international film festivals from 2008 through 2010, won five awards. His previous writing was published in the cult-television anthology *Investigating* Alias: *Secrets and Spies* in 2007.

# Index